CHILI MADNESS

CHILI MADNESS

A Passionate Cookbook by Jane Butel

Illustrations by Carolyn Vibbert

Workman Publishing · New York

For my mother and father,
who first taught me to like chili hot;
and for my friends,
who have helped me to understand those who don't.

Published simultaneously in Canada by Thomas Allen & Son Limited.

Library of Congress Cataloging-in-Publication Data is available.

ISBN 978-0-7611-4761-9

Cover design by Robb Allen after an original design by Milton Glaser
Book design by Francesca Messina
Illustrations © by Carolyn Vibbert
Chile illustrations by John Passineau

Workman books are available at special discounts when purchased in bulk for premiums and sales promotions as well as for fund-raising or educational use. Special editions or book excerpts can also be created to specification. For details, contact the Special Sales Director at the address below.

Workman Publishing Company, Inc.
225 Varick Street
New York, NY 10014-4381
www.workman.com

Printed in the United States of America

First printing October 2008
10 9 8 7 6 5 4 3 2 1

Contents

Chapter 6
Sweet Endings

Chapter 7
Good Libations

Chili in the 21st Century

In the nearly three decades since I wrote the original *Chili Madness*, enthusiasm for these bowls of blessedness has grown enormously. In the early 1980s, a group of us started petitioning our congressional representatives to make chili America's national food. We might not have been able to make it official back then, but a look around today proves that chili is one of the most beloved, argued over, and fiercely defended foods in this country. There are thousands of groups, contests, stores, and websites devoted to discussing, debating, and eating endless configurations of meat, beans, vegetables, and—of course—the all-important chile pepper.

While chili notoriously lacks one overarching definition, it's the chile pepper that really makes it what it is, whether it's a soup, a stew, or a regional variation (I've had Louisiana natives try to convince me that gumbo counts, and folks up north in Maine insist that spicy lobster chowder is as much a chili as anything else is). As far as I'm concerned, the more the merrier! The wondrous qualities of the chile pepper can be applied to a huge range of delicious concoctions, and I'm always thrilled when I hear about more and more people learning how exciting and inspiring it can be to make up a big batch of chili—of any kind.

This revised and expanded edition of *Chili Madness* contains the original recipes that made it a hugely popular bestseller when it came out in 1980, along with a wide assortment of recipes I've come across in the years since the book was first published. It also features a full range of festive new recipes that round out any chilicentric menu: delectable appetizers, sides, breads, desserts, drinks—even dishes to use up the leftovers. From overlooked old classics and "nouveau chilies" that stretch the boundaries of the dish to fiery salsas and palate-cooling quaffs, these recipes are the stuff of celebrations, contests, heated arguments, and warm meals.

Have fun!

Chili, the Irresistible Passion

Origins of the Bowl of Blessedness

Whenever I meet someone who doesn't consider chili a favorite dish, odds are that it's only because they've never actually tasted *good* chili. It's rare to find a food that inspires such a passionate following as this dish has: Chili has societies dedicated to its appreciation; newspapers devoted to the food and nothing but; cookoffs, contests, and exhibitions. And at every gathering where chili is served, there's an inevitable quarrel to be had about what constitutes a "perfect" preparation.

There's something about the personality of this bowl of fire that's given birth to a movement. Chili-lovers come from every walk of life: the dish attracts truck drivers, celebrities, doctors, lawyers, and schoolteachers. When the topic of conversation turns to chili, rich and poor alike undergo a Jekyll-and-Hyde transformation, formerly mild-mannered pillars of the community showing no mercy in defending their preferred preparation.

While each chili-lover has his or her own chosen ingredients and methods, they all have one thing in common: their love for the boiling pot. This band of passionate chili-eaters has come together in an organized network with rites and rituals and factions enough to rival a political machine.

Chili Fever

Although the first chili organization—the famed Chili Appreciation Society International (CASI)—was founded in the 1950s and membership and attention grew consistently, especially in the Southwest, the rumble was merely portending the storm.

The tempest hit in 1966, when Frank X. Tolbert, chili-lover, cook, and historian extraordinaire, published the

book *A Bowl of Red.* The next year, seeking to promote the book, Tolbert and his friends organized the first championship chili cookoff in Terlingua, Texas.

Untold numbers of chili-lovers came out of the woodwork to travel to this unearthly, forsaken patch of desert near the big bend of the Rio Grande to witness the event. The main attraction was the pitting of Wick Fowler, chief cook of CASI, against H. Allen Smith, a New York–based writer and humorist who had written an article called "Nobody Knows More About Chili Than I Do," published in *Holiday* magazine in August 1967. In his article, Smith lambasted Texas chili, raising the hackles of every true-blooded Texas chili cook. He was the perfect challenger for Fowler, and he was hardly likely to turn down a challenge to his claim.

Sparked by this event (which ended

in a tie), the infatuation with the bowl of red spilled over. The Chili Appreciation Society International grew, and rival organizations were formed. Today CASI is still going strong, and it's joined by innumerable local, regional, national, and international societies dedicated to the love of chili. Chili contests of every size and stripe are held in all corners of the land, and aficionados and novitiates travel hundreds of miles to be a part of cookoffs and seminars. There's even a newspaper dedicated to "chiliheads

Chile or Chili?

Even the spelling of the name for a bowl of red is controversial. "Chili," as used in "chili con carne," is often spelled with an "i" ending. As far as I can determine, "chili" is an Eastern and Midwestern spelling that might be derived from the way the British used to commonly spell the dish: "chilley." The other popular spelling, "chile," is based on the Mexican or Spanish spelling for the pod and is generally used to describe "chile" dishes in Mexican cooking. In this book, which is written for all serious chili-lovers— "chiliheads" as they are known in the West—we are using the "chili" spelling for the dish, the "chile" spelling for the peppers, and "chili powder" for the commercial premixed blends.

and their ilk," *The Goat Gap Gazette,* founded in 1974 and still to this day putting out issues to its devoted crowd of readers.

Secrets abound, with some famous chili chefs swearing that their favorite recipes will die with them. Others, such as C. V. Wood, one of the founders of the International Chili Society (ICS), another chili organization, have gladly shared their techniques. Wood claimed his secret was in the spices. He said, "I always soak my spices in a can of beer. That natural carbonation releases flavors that don't come out any other way." He advised simmering the spices and then cooling them in a refrigerator overnight before preparing the chili the next day. His chili was good enough to earn him the top prize in two world championships: 1969 and 1971.

Carroll Shelby, legendary race-car driver and a cofounder of the ICS, has a different view. He's very liberal about what comprises the basis of the brew, and says that chili is a matter of taste and inclination: "It's what you want when you make it. You can put in anything you feel like at the time. You make it one way one time, another time, a little different. Make it up to suit your mood."

Shelby's prowess surfaced way back in 1967 at the original cookoff, where he whipped up batches of chili and just gave them away. The stuff was so good that he developed a business out of selling his brown-paper-bagged chili fixings—still for sale today, still in a brown paper bag.

Frank X. Tolbert never thought it was quite right that Shelby and Wood founded the International Chili Society, which competes with his Chili Appreciation Society International. But then again Tolbert's book was so popular that he opened his own chili parlor in Dallas, Tolbert's Restaurant, where he satisfied thousands of chili lovers. He advocated using only beef, onions, garlic, chile, and cumin.

So the controversy rages—you might say boils—on, with questions of ingredients, secrecy, spelling. Unresolved is the debate over whether or not to add beans—and if you do, should they be red, kidney, or pinto? Also unresolved is the consistency question: thick or thin? Should masa harina (limestone-treated corn flour) be added for additional substance? Should other meats—pork, chicken, duck, or wild game—accompany the ubiquitous beef? Lots of vegetables or almost none? Do out-of-the-ordinary ingredients like tequila, wine, or raisins assist in building flavor or sully an otherwise pristine brew?

While there is no end in sight for this delicious debate, one thing is certain: chili seems to only grow in popularity.

As Legend Has It

There is probably as much controversy surrounding the origin of the "bowl of blessedness," as

Will Rogers called chili, as there is surrounding its ingredients. Only one thing seems to bear up under all scrutiny: chili did *not* originate in Mexico. While most of the stories about chili's genesis say that it is a product of gringos and tenderfeet, one rather fanciful tale (as detailed in *Bull Cook and Authentic Historical Recipes and Practices,* by George Herter) states that the first recipe for chili con carne was put on paper in the 17th century by a beautiful nun, Sister Mary of Agreda, mysteriously known to the Indians of the southwestern United States as the "lady in blue."

Legend has it that in 1618, at the age of sixteen, she entered a convent at Agreda in Castile, Spain. There Sister Mary began to go into trances, with her body lifeless for days. When she awoke from these spells she said her spirit had been to a faraway land where she preached Christianity to savages and counseled them to seek out Spanish missionaries.

A Long, Slow Simmer: Chili Then, and Now

Sister Mary of Agreda, Spain, writes the first recipe for chili, which she sampled during one of her out-of-body "visits" with the natives of the American Southwest.

Cattle drivers, gold prospectors, and chain gangs throughout Texas enjoy steaming bowls of long-simmered beef, chiles, and spices.

Wild West outlaw Jesse James mercifully decides not to rob a bank—because it's in the same town as his favorite chili parlor.

Chili queens spice up the San Antonio night, selling the fragrant brews from colorful booths set up in the Military Plaza. By some accounts, the queens fed the nighttime crowds for more than 100 years.

circa 1620

mid to late 1800s

late 1860s to late 1870s

late 1800s to 1943

It is certain that Sister Mary never physically left Spain: yet Spanish missionaries and King Philip IV of Spain believed that she was the ghostly "La Dama de Azul" of legend. For there were many witnesses (including members of native tribes and a missionary, Father Alonso de Benarifes) who claimed to have seen a holy woman who wore blue and worked among the Indians. When the Indians were shown a picture of Sister Mary, they said that she was indeed their lady in blue, but that when she came to them she was younger and more beautiful.

When Father Alonso returned to Spain, he visited this nun with the visions. She vividly relayed to him scenes and people of the Southwest—things she could never have known unless she had been there, in some form.

Herter claims that Sister Mary wrote down the recipe for chili con carne on one of her "visits." It called for venison

Chasen's Restaurant in Hollywood serves up a popular bowl of red that's beloved by chauffeurs and stars alike. According to legend, Elizabeth Taylor had quarts of the stuff shipped to her on the set of Cleopatra.

The Chili Appreciation Society International (CASI) holds the first chili cookoff in Terlingua, Texas. Wick Fowler and H. Allen Smith both vie for the top prize, but the judges can't decide, and the contest ends in a draw.

The Texas legislature proclaims chili con carne the state dish.

More than 1 million people attend festive chili cookoffs around the world.

1936 to 2000   **1967**   **1977**   **today**

or antelope meat, onions, tomatoes, and chile peppers. But if the Native Americans of the Southwest were indeed eating chili at the time of Sister Mary's "visit" during the Spanish occupation, no explorer recorded it—so who knows?

Down-to-Earth Birth

Another notion, and one that seems based on fact rather than myth, is that the first chili mix was concocted around 1850 by Texan adventurers as a staple for hard times when traveling to and in the California gold fields. They supposedly pounded dried beef, fat, pepper, salt, and chile peppers together, all to be boiled later on the trail. E. DeGolyer, the knowledgeable chili scholar who first documented this version of the origin of chili, called it the "pemmican of the Southwest."

Maury Maverick Jr. and Charles Ramsdell, two San Antonio writers, swear that chili con carne originated there among the poor (this poor-people's food is a continuing theme in many origin-of-chili tales). In an effort to stretch their slender budgets, folks bought meat of lesser quality, chopped it to the consistency of hash to make it tender, and added lots of chile pepper to give it flavor.

There are also some pretty tough customers who laid claim to the creation of chili: the residents of Texas prisons in the mid to late 1800s. The Texas version of bread and water—in other words, prison fare—was a stew of the cheapest available ingredients: gristly beef, hacked fine, then combined with chiles and spices and all boiled in water to an edible consistency. This "prisoner's plight" became a status symbol of the Texas prisons. Chain-gang chili is said to be among the best. Ex-cons who couldn't get a good bowl on the outside have allegedly broken parole so as to be recommitted—homesick for good chili!

And lastly there is the very popular old standby: the belief that chili originated in Texas with the cowboys who were "winning the West." Needing

. . . And Columbus Called Them Peppers

Why are chiles, members of the *Capsicum* genus, called "peppers"? When Spanish explorers arrived in the Caribbean, they sampled the unusual red pods the native population used to spice up their food. The Spaniards thought the pods' pungency was similar to that of the valuable black peppercorns they received from the Far East. In the mistaken belief that they had found a different version of the same spice, the Spanish called the pod "pepper." We know now that there is no botanical relationship between the pepper and the peppercorn, but the name has stuck.

hot, fill-up-the-stomach grub, the trail cooks came up with a sort of stew. Since chile peppers grew wild and there was plenty of beef around, it was a logical, hearty, and nutritious combination.

Certainly by the late 1800s chili had arrived, with San Antonio the chili center of the day. In the evening townspeople would stroll down to one of the city's plazas and partake of a bowl served up by one of the many outdoor vendors. In fact, it seems a night was not complete without a visit to one of these "chili queens"—the women who served their brews from bubbling cauldrons behind gaudy booths. The smells permeated the air, inviting passers-by to taste.

The chili queens spiced up the night in San Antonio until 1943, when they were put out of business due to their inability to conform to the sanitary standards enforced in the town's restaurants. Of course, by that time chili had already taken hold across Texas and the rest of the U.S. and was well on its way to becoming one of the country's best-loved dishes.

Chili Makings

The pulsating, pleasurable, passion-producing pot of paradise known as chili has its beginnings with the chile pepper. Chiles are part of the pod-bearing *Capsicum* genus, which encompasses more than forty species and more than 7,000 plant varieties. They range from the peppers that produce the mild-mannered ground paprika to those fiery, eye-watering varieties that really make you sit up and take notice. Pure chile peppers, whether you grind them fresh yourself or use those that are preground and securely packaged, give your "bowl of blessedness" the wonderful flavors that only come from the finest ingredients.

Chiles are very distinguishable from one another, although getting acquainted can be a bit mystifying at first. The first thing you need to know is that chile peppers are eaten both in their unripe green and their ripe red stages. Just like fruit (which chiles really

Chile Chart

Ancho: A popular Mexican chile that is used in both its green and red forms (when it's green, it's called a *poblano*), the ancho resembles a small bell pepper, but it is much spicier. Anchos are 3 to 4 inches in diameter and roughly 5 inches long, with waxy skins. They dry to a deep red, almost black, color. In southern Mexico, these chiles are referred to as *passillas*, whether they are red or green.

Arbol: These narrow, curved chiles start green and mature to bright red. Typically measuring 3 inches long and 3/8 inch wide, and punching in at 15,000–30,000 Scoville Heat Units (see page xix), they are most popular in western Mexico. Because of their vivid red color, these chiles are often used in decorative holiday wreaths.

Caribe: The historic caribe chile was developed by the Carib Indians, who left their ancestral home in the South American rain forests and settled in the Caribbean islands. In the early 16th century, the Caribs shared their chiles with the Spanish conquistadores, who later brought them to New Mexico. The conquistadores settled north of Santa Fe and colonized the village of Chimayo; sometimes the chiles go by that name. The chiles are small and yellow when fresh; in this book we use the crushed dried red variety, which has a sweet, moderate heat in the 15,000 Scoville range.

Cayenne: Originating in Central and South America, these pungent red chiles provide the heat for many spicy dishes and play an important role in Cajun cuisine. They are typically 1/2 inch in diameter and 2 to 6 inches long, though some are as long as 12 inches. Cayenne chiles are available fresh, but are usually sold dried and ground, or incorporated into commercial hot sauces.

Anaheim/New Mexico: Despite their name differences, Anaheims and New Mexicos are the same. The most popular chiles in the U.S., they originated in New Mexico and were brought to Anaheim in the late 19th century by the Ortega family (of the eponymous Mexican food brand), who hoped that the warmer California climate would yield more crops. The move was a success, and now the chiles are grown in both states. Sold both when red and when green, these chiles are long, about 5 inches or more, and 2 to 3 inches in diameter. Their heat usually ranges between 5,000 and 10,000 Scovilles.

Scotch Bonnet and Habañero: The short and chubby, slightly fruity chiles are quite popular in Caribbean and southern Mexican cooking, respectively, as they are the best-growing chiles in those regions. Because these chiles are so hot—some have been clocked at over 325,000 Scovilles—they must be dealt with carefully: wear gloves when handling, and always blend with lots of tomato or lime juice to help cut the heat.

Jalapeño: The most popular chile in America, these small-to-medium-size fiery monsters are dark green, firm, and round, about 2½ inches long and about 1 inch in diameter. They are available at most supermarkets, both fresh and canned, and are popular as a topping for chili and nachos. (Canned jalapeños are often pickled and thus have a slightly milder, vinegar-tinged flavor.) When ripe (red) jalapeños are smoked and dried, they are called chipotles.

Pequin: A chile that grows wild along the Mexico–U.S. border, pequins are itty-bitty—and fiercely hot! It's rare to find them fresh. The dried form is available in specialty stores; when crushed, it is called *pequin quebrado*.

Serrano: Tiny-skinny and usually only 1 to 1½ inches long, these little devils can make you cry or cough just by cutting one open! They have a crisp, slightly citrusy flavor.

are), the green unripe chile has a tarter, crisper flavor than the mature red one. The ripening process converts the starch in the green chile to a sugar, producing a sweeter, more robust flavor. The nutrition changes as well: green chiles have far more vitamin C, while red chiles are higher in vitamin A.

How a Chile Works

Uniquely among fruits, chiles contain a substance known as *capsaicin,* an oil-borne acid. Like all acids, capsaicin causes a burning sensation when it comes into contact with living tissue. When this happens in our mouths, we call it "spiciness" or heat. The capsaicin is found mainly in the chile's placental tissue, a cotton-like ball located directly under the stem, and is distributed through the pepper by four veins that travel the length of the chile, from the stem end down, where it enters the seeds that grow on the veins.

Measuring the heat of a chile is most popularly done in accordance with a system developed in 1912 by an American chemist named Wilbur Scoville. The Scoville scale measures Scoville Heat Units (SHUs), which range from zero (common bell peppers) to over a million for the very hottest chiles (to qualify as a chile, a pepper must have a Scoville rating of at least 5,000—anything milder and it's a paprika). A chile's Scoville rating is determined by the proportion of sugar water that is

necessary to dilute the pepper before its "heat" is undetectable, and is decided by committee. Despite the subjectivity of the scale, Scoville's system has prevailed: hot-sauce producers brag about their Scoville ratings on their labels, and there are even Scoville clubs where members dare each other to endure the hottest of the hot chiles.

The Heart of Chili

Many people are unaware that chiles have actual flavor hiding underneath their heat. The prepackaged powder that's the basis for all too many pots of chili masks the peppers' subtle flavors, thanks to the liberal addition of oregano, cumin, salt, garlic, and any number of additives and preservatives. The poor dried chiles don't stand a chance: not only is prepared chili powder often sold in transparent packaging that allows oxidation (good packaging is opaque, which prevents oxidation), but salt is a desiccant that dries out all it touches. Both these factors lead to evaporation of the flavor of the chile, leaving behind only the pepper's acidic heat. No wonder store-bought chili powder is no match for the real thing!

It is also important to remember that when you use commercial spice blends, the range of flavor possibilities is much narrower—you're forced to accept the manufacturer's idea of how chili should taste, rather than your own. If you don't want to buy humdrum flavoring mixes, blend your own, always using pure ground chiles and the freshest additional spices possible.

Choosing Chiles

Although they originated in the Americas, red and green chiles of all kinds play major roles in the cuisines of dozens of cultures around the globe. Dried chiles—whole, crushed, or powdered—are available year-round at virtually every supermarket, as well as from a large number of online retailers.

Fresh chiles, once limited to tropical regions, are increasingly available throughout the United States. In season, during the summer and fall months, they can be bought in bulk and frozen for enjoyment throughout the year, and can be found in prefrozen quantities. Chiles are also available canned, both diced and whole, plain or pickled; the canning process does affect the flavor, however.

Besides ground dried peppers, many chili recipes call for fresh or dried chiles in other forms. The most abundant, most popular, and most used chiles nationwide are the domestic hybrids developed in California and New Mexico and still largely grown there. These hybrids include the Anaheim/New Mexico varieties, which are broad-shouldered, on the average 2 to 3 inches in diameter at the stem end and 5 to 7 inches long, with a pointed or blunter tip, depending on the variety.

In selecting chiles, a rule of thumb is that the darker the color, the more pointed the tip, and the narrower the shoulders, the hotter the pepper will be. Similarly, the larger the pepper—particularly across the shoulders—the milder it is. A blunter tip is also a good indicator of mildness. While these are good guidelines, they're not foolproof: since chiles freely cross-pollinate, hotness is inconsistent within species, within varieties, and even within chiles coming from the same plant! Just watch out for those tiny, slope-shouldered little devils: undiluted, they can produce pure pain in even the asbestos-mouthed. Fresh chiles can be tamed by marinating them overnight in fresh lime juice.

Other Essential Ingredients

As important as chiles are to a good pot of chili, there are other necessary ingredients. These include appropriate seasonings, such as the classics: cumin (usually ground, and the fresher the better), fresh pungent garlic (never powder or granulated dried), and crushed or ground dried Mexican oregano (milder and mintier than its Greek or Italian cousins).

The backbone of traditional chili is beef, to which the chiles and spices lend their wonderful flavors. For the best flavor and consistency, the beef should be 80 percent lean or chuck roast. Don't shy away from fat! The fat marbling becomes the transportation system for

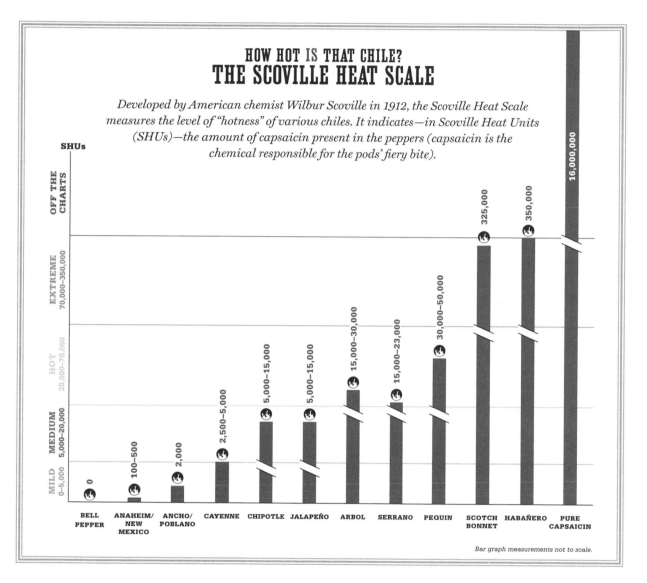

HOW HOT IS THAT CHILE?
THE SCOVILLE HEAT SCALE

Developed by American chemist Wilbur Scoville in 1912, the Scoville Heat Scale measures the level of "hotness" of various chiles. It indicates—in Scoville Heat Units (SHUs)—the amount of capsaicin present in the peppers (capsaicin is the chemical responsible for the pods' fiery bite).

SHUs

OFF THE CHARTS

EXTREME 70,000–350,000

HOT 20,000–70,000

MEDIUM 5,000–20,000

MILD 0–5,000

BELL PEPPER	ANAHEIM/ NEW MEXICO	ANCHO/ POBLANO	CAYENNE	CHIPOTLE	JALAPEÑO	ARBOL	SERRANO	PEQUIN	SCOTCH BONNET	HABAÑERO	PURE CAPSAICIN
0	100–500	2,000	2,500–5,000	5,000–15,000	5,000–15,000	15,000–30,000	15,000–23,000	30,000–50,000	325,000	350,000	16,000,000

Bar graph measurements not to scale.

flavoring of the chili. The beef should be hand-cut into ½-inch cubes, or it should be coarsely chopped, a preparation often referred to as "chili grind." Outside the Southwest, chili is often made with ground beef (the same kind used for hamburger patties), which does not yield the same texture and quality as hand-chopped chuck, but works just fine in a pinch.

It has become popular to improvise with meats other than beef. Pork is used in a variety of chili recipes and is delicious both on its own and used together with beef in the same pot. And there are some people who cook up their favorite brew using chicken. These days it's not uncommon to experiment with ingredients: many modern chilis feature turkey, wild game, even seafood.

Onions of most any type help make excellent chili; the stronger the onion, the better. In fact, some say that the more you cry when peeling and chopping the onion, the better the chili will be. Seriously, though, white or yellow ordinary round or Spanish-type onions are generally preferred. Sweet salad types such as Bermuda, Vidalia, and Maui onions are usually not as flavorful.

The Great Chili Controversy

While onions might seem to be essential to most chili-lovers, they—along with a host of other vegetable add-ins—are fodder for one of the most enduring debates in the history of chili. "True, honest-to-God chili" means a lot of things to a lot of people. To Texans, chili cookoff contestants, and other aficionados, the real thing contains no vegetables other than chiles, onions, and maybe garlic. In defiance of those traditionalists, some feel that tomatoes in one form or another are an absolute must—other folks, myself included, disagree.

Given all the controversy surrounding this great American dish, and in the interest of goodwill and understanding, I dedicate this book to individualism. I have included recipes from chili contest winners and from other formidable chili chefs. Some recipes are made with beef, others with pork, yet others with chicken or lobster; some contain tomatoes, beans, celery, and spices that traditionalists would question, and others are pure as can be. They are all the cream of the chili crop. Try them all—they are delicious.

1

Beginnings with Bite

Although most chiliheads would agree that chili is an entire meal in itself, sometimes the pot's not ready when you are. Times like those, I always find that a first course sets the tone for the meal. Whether it's elegant, casual, festive, or just a hearty smorgasbord of dishes, folks always love to have something to nibble on.

It's unlikely that you'll show up at an ICS-sanctioned chili cook-off and find yourself faced with a passed platter of hors d'oeuvres— the chili cooks and chili-eaters involved don't tend to stand too much on that particular type of formality. But any one of them would be hard-pressed to turn down a bite or two of one of the recipes in this chapter.

When the main dish is chili, I like to start out with appetizers that incorporate the flavors—and the spirit—of that delicious dish we'll be feasting on later. To maximize their impact, be sure to use the freshest ingredients for the brightest, cleanest, deepest flavors. When it comes to starters, every bite counts.

In this chapter...

Salsas & Dips
Spicy salsas, perfect guacamole, creamy spreads, layered dips, and the homemade chips to go with them.

Fabulous Nachos
A hearty, tempting platter of cheesy, chile'd chips, an elegant take on the same, and a surprising variation on the theme— made with fresh fruit!

Crowd Pleasers
Pigs-in-blankets, jalapeño poppers, and other finger foods that dare you to eat just one . . .

Elegant Openers
Sophisticated and unexpected, a handful of delicious appetizers to impress even the most discerning guests.

Some appetizer choices are obvious: When you're making a classic bowl of red, Southwestern- and Mexican-inflected flavors tend to be the natural selection. Try setting out bowls of Chile and Garlic Roasted Peanuts for nibbling, or offer a selection of salsas—I like to put out a trio of Salsa Roja, Black Bean and Corn Salsa, and Creamy Mango Salsa—plus a huge helping of tortilla chips: it's the perfect palate primer!

But don't feel restricted to Southwestern standards. The starters here found their inspiration in the novelty and diversity of chilies today. Some of them take their sizzle from putting a chilihead twist on appetizer classics: just try to eat only one Double-Chile Deviled Egg, or to resist the throwback charm of Hot Little Devils—pigs-in-blankets plus a little kick—or the single-serving bites of Nachos Elegantes. Others are undeniably modern: there's no ignoring the unexpectedly delicious combination of salty, spicy, and sweet in Fruity Nachos—sure to raise eyebrows,

---

SOME LIKE IT HOT . . .
These icons show how fiery each dish is.

🔥
MILD

🔥 🔥
A BIT OF BITE

🔥 🔥 🔥
HOT

🔥 🔥 🔥 🔥
HOT ENOUGH TO MAKE YOU . . .

---

and to have your guests (and you!) going back for seconds and thirds.

The selection of starters here should serve you well in virtually every context, for any type of party, at any time of year—from the simple no-cook refreshment of Watermelon Salsa to the showstopping combination of ingredients in the Roasted Duck and Portabello Quesadilla. You can serve them on their own (see page 30 for my suggestions for an all-appetizer meal) or let them pave the way for the rest of the meal—just make sure you leave room for the main event!

Tortilla Chips

🔥

Makes 4 dozen chips

It's surprisingly easy to make your own tortilla chips, and they yield terrific results: slightly warm, crunchy, with a deep corn flavor and a tinge of salt. If you like, boost the flavor by adding seasonings, such as lime zest or hot ground chile.

Vegetable oil, for frying (optional)
12 corn tortillas (6 inches each),
    cut into quarters
½ teaspoon salt
1 teaspoon fresh lime zest, ½ teaspoon
    ground cumin, and/or 1 teaspoon pure
    ground hot red chile, for seasoning
    (optional)

For fried chips: Place a Dutch oven or deep skillet over medium-high heat and add vegetable oil to a depth of 2 inches. When the oil registers 375°F on an instant-read deep-frying thermometer, place a layer of tortilla pieces in a fry basket and submerge in the hot oil. Fry until the rapid bubbling subsides, about 20 seconds. Transfer the chips to a paper-towel-lined plate. Let the oil come back up to temperature, and repeat with the remaining tortilla pieces, working in batches.

For baked chips: Working in batches, place the tortilla pieces in a single layer on large baking sheets, then place a smaller baking sheet on top of them (this keeps them flat as they bake). Place the tortillas in the oven and bake for 5 minutes. Then remove the smaller baking sheet and continue to bake the tortillas until they are crisp, 5 to 8 minutes more. Repeat with the remaining tortilla pieces.

Season the chips with salt, then sprinkle with the lime zest, cumin, and/or ground chile if desired. Serve warm or at room temperature.

Chipotle Verde Salsa, Sonora Style

😋 😋 😋 😋
Makes about 3 cups

Tomatillos, distant cousins of the tomato, add a sweet, somewhat tart flavor to this lively green salsa. Tomatillos can be eaten raw or cooked, but I always prefer them cooked. And while traditionally this salsa is prepared with boiled tomatillos, I think pan-roasting them complements the rich, smoky flavor of the chipotles and makes this dipping salsa much more elegant.

I like to use dried chipotle pods (the brown *meco* variety, not the red/black *moritas*), which have the very best smoky flavor and are available by mail order if you can't find them at your grocery store (see Sources). Chipotle powder is the next best thing and is widely available. As a last resort, you can use canned chipotles in adobo, but I think they impart a metallic, tomato-like flavor that is not desirable.

Try this wonderful salsa with tortilla chips, or served over fish, seafood, poultry, or vegetables.

**3 dried chipotle chiles, stemmed,
    or 1½ teaspoons chipotle powder
½ teaspoon cider vinegar
2 pounds fresh tomatillos,
    papery husks removed
1 large onion, coarsely chopped
⅓ cup fresh cilantro or Italian (flat-leaf)
    parsley leaves
Salt (optional)
Tortilla Chips (facing page), for serving
    (optional)**

1. If using dried chipotles, place them in a quart-size microwave-safe liquid measuring cup, and add water to cover. Add the vinegar, cover the measuring cup with plastic wrap, and microwave on full power until the skin slips off the chiles easily when touched with a fork, about 5 minutes. (Alternatively, place the chiles in a small saucepan, add water to cover and the vinegar, and simmer, covered, over low heat until the skins loosen, about 30 minutes.) Remove the chiles from the cooking liquid (reserve the liquid), and slip off and discard the skins. Set the chiles aside.

2. Slice the tomatillos in half and place them, cut side down, in a large, heavy, well-seasoned skillet over medium-high heat. (If you don't have a seasoned skillet, use a nonstick one instead.) When the tomatillos in the center of the skillet have browned on the first side, about 5 minutes, turn them over and rotate them to the outer edges of the skillet. When most of the tomatillos are browned and have been turned over, remove the skillet from the heat and cover it. Let the tomatillos steam in the covered skillet until they are very soft, about 5 minutes.

HOT STUFF

Eating chiles has been shown to speed up the pulse, as well as lower blood pressure.

3. Place the tomatillos in a blender, and add the onion, whole chipotles or chipotle powder, and the cilantro. Process until pureed, adding reserved chipotle cooking liquid or water as needed to make a thick, pudding-textured salsa. Taste, and add salt if desired. Serve either warm or cool, as a dip with tortilla chips if you wish, or as desired.

The salsa will keep for 1 week in the refrigerator or up to 6 months in the freezer.

Salsa Roja

🌶 🌶 🌶

Makes 1½ cups

This is a traditional New Mexican table salsa. The hot, spicy edge and hint of cumin reflect the culinary traditions of New Mexico, which blend Native American and Spanish ingredients and flavors.

Salsa Roja is the darling of the restaurant industry because it is so easy to make and because it keeps quite well. I suggest you always keep a batch on hand in the refrigerator—it's not only great as an appetizer, but goes well with many dishes, from scrambled eggs to grilled steaks.

1½ cups chopped fresh tomatoes or diced canned tomatoes (if tomatoes are not in season, canned are best)
1 tablespoon pequin quebrado or other crushed red chile, or to taste
1 tablespoon fresh lime juice
1 tablespoon cider vinegar
½ teaspoon ground Mexican oregano
2 cloves garlic, minced
1½ teaspoons ground cumin
1½ teaspoons coarsely chopped fresh cilantro (optional)

Place all the ingredients in a bowl and stir together until thoroughly blended.

If you plan to refrigerate or freeze the salsa, reserve the cilantro and add it just before serving. Without the cilantro, this salsa will keep for up to 2 weeks in the refrigerator and 6 months in the freezer. Once the cilantro has been added, it will keep for 1 to 2 days in the refrigerator (I do not recommend freezing it with the cilantro).

Black Bean and Corn Salsa

Makes 2½ cups

I absolutely adore this snacking salsa. The contrast of the mellow starch of the black beans and corn with the pickled jalapeños and the fresh tomato makes it special. I developed the salsa for my New York City restaurant, the Pecos River Café, which featured my favorite New Mexican dishes and, of course, my beloved Pecos River Bowl of Red chili (see page 34). At the restaurant, I served this hearty salsa with pan-sautéed chicken livers, of all things! It may sound like an improbable pairing, but the combination of the rich chicken livers with the colorful, spicy salsa made it a customer favorite.

If you're not big on chicken livers, this salsa is great with chips, goes very well with fish and poultry, and is excellent in salads, quesadillas, and scrambled eggs. I also love the tropical variation, which follows.

Prepping Papaya and Mango

If you've never worked with them before, papaya and mango can be intimidating to select and to prepare. Fear not: tackling tropical fruits is easy!

A papaya is ripe when its skin has a greenish-yellow hue and when the fruit yields to gentle thumb pressure. To prepare a papaya, slice the fruit in half lengthwise with a sharp knife. Use a spoon to scoop out and discard the round seeds that fill the center. Then carefully peel away and discard the skin, and chop the flesh as you wish.

To identify a ripe mango, smell the skin—it will be delightfully fragrant. The fruit should feel weighty and soft but not mushy; its skin should easily indent with your thumb. The trick to preparing mango is cutting around the fruit's large central pit. Begin by slicing the mango in vertical thirds—slicing all the way down on either side of the pit. You should end up with two half-moons of fruit and a central piece that consists mostly of the mango's stringy, fibrous pit. With the half moons, score the fleshy side with a knife to create a grid; cut down to the skin but be sure not to slice through it. Scoop these cubes of fruit away from the peel, using a large spoon. Then carefully cut the peel away from the pit section, too, and remove as much of the fruit from the pit as you can.

1 large tomato, stemmed and cut into
   ½-inch cubes
½ cup chopped white or yellow onion
½ cup coarsely diced pickled
   jalapeño chiles
1¾ cups cooked black beans, drained
   (canned is fine)
½ cup cooked whole-kernel corn
½ teaspoon salt
2 cloves garlic, finely minced
¼ cup coarsely chopped fresh cilantro
   (optional)

Combine the tomato, onion, jalapeño, black
beans, corn, salt, and garlic in a large bowl. Stir
well, and then add the cilantro, if using. Serve
immediately or let sit until the flavors meld,
about 15 minutes.

   This salsa will keep in a glass or plastic
container in the refrigerator for 3 to 4 days.

Variation: Black Bean and Tropical Fruit Salsa
Substitute finely diced ripe papaya or mango for
the corn.

Guacamole

Makes about 2 cups

Guacamole at its best! To preserve
avocado's delicate flavor and appearance—
and to help it keep longer—I always cut it
with two knives into coarse 1-inch chunks.
This preserves the fruity, mellow flavor of
the avocado. (When one mashes an avocado,
I like to say that it reflects its punishment:
it becomes somewhat bitter and browns
quickly.)

   This guacamole is terrific served as a dip
with a basket of tortilla chips. If some folks
at your table like things hot and others don't,
keep the guacamole mild and serve a dish
of spicy salsa alongside. Or for something
different, serve it as a salad over chopped
lettuce and sweet cherry tomatoes.

2 ripe avocados (preferably Hass)
½ teaspoon salt, plus more to taste
1 clove garlic, finely minced
1 teaspoon fresh lime juice, or to taste
½ medium-size tomato, chopped
¼ cup finely chopped Spanish onion
1 medium-size jalapeño chile, or to taste,
   stemmed, seeded (if you wish to reduce
   the heat), and minced
2 tablespoons coarsely chopped fresh
   cilantro (optional)
Tortilla Chips (page 2), or chopped lettuce
   and cherry tomatoes, for serving

1. Halve and pit the avocados; scoop the flesh into a bowl. Coarsely chop the avocado, using two knives. Add the salt and garlic. Then slowly add the lime juice, gently folding in the avocado to coat it with the juice.

2. Fold in the tomato, onion, jalapeño, and cilantro if using. Let the guacamole stand for a few minutes to allow the flavors to develop and blend.

3. Taste, and adjust the seasonings if needed, adding more minced jalapeño if you wish it to be hotter.

4. Serve the guacamole as a dip in a pretty bowl (a piece of Mexican pottery will look stunning) surrounded by tortilla chips, garnishing the guacamole with a few chips on top. Or serve it as a salad, dolloped over chopped lettuce and cherry tomatoes.

Guacamole prepared this way will keep for at least 3 days if gently pressed into a vertical storage container with plastic wrap pressed directly onto the surface to remove any air. You can also stir the guacamole into a simple vinaigrette; it will keep for about a week.

Discoloration? It's the Pits

I can hardly count the number of times I've heard that placing an avocado pit in guacamole will keep the green flesh from discoloring. But in all my experience with the fruit, I haven't found that works so well. Instead, I cover a bowl of guacamole with plastic wrap that's pushed down flat against the surface of the dip. Adding something acidic can help prevent discoloration too: sprinkle the guacamole with lime or lemon juice, or add a little of an all-natural ascorbic acid mixture such as Fruit-Fresh (see Sources). Just be careful not to add too much of the ascorbic acid, as it can be slightly sweet.

Watermelon Salsa

Makes 2 cups

The refreshing flavors of watermelon and mint come together in this light, wonderful salsa. You can serve it as a dipping salsa with tortilla chips or cucumber and celery spears, but I also like it with almost any fish or chicken dish, especially one that has some kick.

1 cup seeded, diced watermelon
½ cup chopped sweet onion,
    such as Bermuda, Maui, or Vidalia
1 tablespoon fresh lime juice
¼ cup fresh mint leaves, thinly sliced
¼ cup crushed caribe chile

Combine all the ingredients in a large bowl. Cover the salsa and let it sit at room temperature until the flavors meld, 15 minutes.

This salsa is really of the moment and is best made just before serving—it will not keep for more than a few hours (the watermelon begins to weep and loses its texture).

Creamy Mango Salsa

Makes 1¼ cups

Mangos are my favorite fruit—to me the flavor is of a "gingered peach." This salsa can double as a dressing for fruit salads and tastes fantastic atop a combination of salad greens and fruit. It is also great on almost any grilled or simply prepared seafood, and it makes a zesty, refreshing taco salsa.

I like to serve this salsa with wedges of fruit and grapes and berries; it's a nice break from the chips- or veggies-with-salsa routine. To prevent the cut fruits from browning or oxidizing, sprinkle them with Fruit-Fresh (see Sources) or a similar product.

½ cup sour cream
½ cup mayonnaise
1 large mango, diced (see page 5)
1 tablespoon fresh lime juice, or to taste
½ teaspoon pequin quebrado or other pure ground hot red chile, or to taste
Salt (optional)
Sliced apples, sliced bananas, sliced melon, grapes, and/or berries, for serving (optional)

Place the sour cream, mayonnaise, mango, lime juice, and pequin quebrado in a medium bowl and stir to combine. Taste, and adjust the seasonings, adding salt and more lime juice or ground chile if desired. Serve with fresh fruit, if you wish.

This salsa can be made up to 4 hours ahead and will keep for a day or two in the refrigerator; it does not freeze well.

Confetti Chili Dip

Makes 2 cups

This is my take on the Southwest's most popular hot dip, chile con queso, which usually pairs American cheese with a tomato-and-green-chile mixture, such as the beloved canned Ro-tel. My version ups the ante with fresh onion, garlic, and chiles, Monterey Jack and Cheddar cheeses, and homemade chili. It's a winner.

In the unlikely event that you have leftovers, this dip freezes well for up to 6 months. It is excellent spooned into omelets or served over hot crisp tortilla chips (instant nachos!), hamburgers, and steaks.

⅓ cup vegetable oil

½ cup finely chopped onion, or 3 scallions, including tops, chopped

1 clove garlic, finely minced

1 tablespoon unbleached all-purpose flour

¾ cup evaporated milk

1 medium-size tomato, chopped

1 pound processed cheese food, such as Velveeta, cut into 1-inch cubes

½ cup mixed shredded Monterey Jack and Cheddar cheeses

3 tablespoons finely minced jalapeño chile

½ cup Pecos River Bowl of Red (page 34) or other red chili, preferably without beans

1. Place the oil in a heavy saucepan over medium heat. Add the onions and garlic and sauté the mixture until the onions are soft and slightly translucent, about 5 minutes. Stir in the flour.

2. Gradually stir in the evaporated milk and cook, stirring, until the mixture thickens slightly, about 5 minutes.

3. Add the tomato, cheeses, jalapeño, and chili and cook, stirring, until thick and smooth, about 5 minutes. Serve warm, in a chafing dish over hot water, or with omelets, burgers, or steak.

The dip will keep in the refrigerator for at least 1 week or in an airtight plastic tub in the freezer for up to 6 months (reheat it in a small saucepan over low heat, adding extra evaporated milk as needed to make it creamy).

Preparing Dried, Canned, and Frozen Chiles

Grinding Dried Whole Chiles

Rinse and dry each dried pod, and remove the stem, seeds, and veins. Place about 4 to 6 cleaned pods in a blender or food processor, and process until finely powdered.

Caribe Chile

This is a coarser dried chile that originated in the Caribbean and is named for the Caribe Indians. Starting with dried chiles, rinse and dry the pods, and remove the stems—but not the seeds. Using your fingers, crush or tear the chiles into little pieces, approximately ¼ inch in size.

Red pepper flakes, sold in most supermarkets, have the look of caribe chile, but they are usually an Italian pepper, which imparts a different flavor.

Canned or Frozen Chiles

To use the green chiles that come diced in cans or frozen, just add them to taste. You do not need to defrost the frozen chiles to use them. If you buy canned whole chiles, rinse them and pick out the stems and seeds before using.

San Antonio
Hot Cheese Dip
with Chorizo

🌶️ 🌶️

Serves 6

This Tex-Mexican-style

fondue is very versatile. It can be served as is with warm flour tortillas, or you can spike it with a liquor such as sherry or tequila, or you can make it heartier by adding cooked shrimp or mushrooms. It's delicious in all its variations.

12 to 18 ounces mild Cheddar or Monterey Jack cheese, or a combination
4 ounces chorizo, crumbled, cooked, and drained of fat
2 jalapeño chiles, thinly sliced in rounds, for garnish (optional)
6 to 12 flour tortillas (6 inches each)
Salsa Roja (page 4) or the salsa of your choice, for serving (optional)

1. Cut the cheese into thin slices or shred it. Place the cheese in a heavy skillet that can double as a serving dish. Melt the cheese over low heat, stirring constantly, until it is runny, about 5 minutes. Remove the skillet from the heat and set it on a trivet on the table.

2. Garnish the melted cheese with the crumbled chorizo by scattering it in a line down the center of the skillet.

3. If using the jalapeño, arrange the slices atop the melted cheese in a line perpendicular to the chorizo.

4. Warm the tortillas: Place them in a plastic bag, twist it loosely closed, and microwave on high for 2 minutes. (Alternatively, preheat the oven to 350°F, wrap the tortillas in aluminum foil, and warm them in the oven for 10 minutes.)

5. Fold the tortillas into quarters, pinching the middle to keep them folded, and place them in a basket or on a plate next to the cheese dip for a pretty presentation. Cover the tortillas with a clean cloth to prevent them from drying out. To eat the dip, simply tear off pieces of tortilla and dunk them into the melted cheese, then scoop up some chorizo and jalapeño, if desired. If you wish, serve the salsa of your choice alongside.

Chèvre Bruschetta
with Black Bean Salsa

Serves 8 to 10 (2 to 3 slices per serving)

You have probably come across bruschetta—toasted rounds of crusty bread usually topped with garlicky tomatoes, basil, and a drizzle of olive oil—at your favorite Italian restaurant. Here I'm giving the beloved Italian recipe a delicious *Chili Madness* twist.

If you're making this for a party, you can toast the bread earlier in the day and prepare the salsa a few hours in advance, assembling the bruschetta just before serving.

1 baguette or other long, crisp-crusted, unseeded bread
5 tablespoons olive oil
2 tablespoons fresh lemon juice
2 cloves garlic, minced
¼ cup balsamic vinegar
3 medium-size tomatoes, seeded, diced, and drained
1 cup chopped onion
1 japaleño chile, stemmed, seeded (if you wish to reduce the heat), and minced
1 cup cooked or canned black beans, well drained

½ cup cooked whole-kernel corn
5 leaves fresh basil, thinly sliced
1 cup (8 ounces) goat cheese with Southwestern spices (such as Coonridge brand) or plain goat cheese
Salt and freshly ground black pepper

1. Preheat the oven to 350°F. Slice the bread diagonally into ½-inch-thick slices. Place the slices in a single layer on a baking sheet and lightly brush olive oil over the top of each slice, using 3 tablespoons of the oil.

2. Place the bread in the oven and toast until golden brown, about 6 minutes. Set aside to cool.

3. Meanwhile, combine the lemon juice, remaining 2 tablespoons olive oil, garlic, and balsamic vinegar in a mixing bowl and whisk together thoroughly. Stir in the tomatoes, onion, jalapeño, black beans, corn, and basil. Allow to sit, uncovered, at room temperature until the flavors meld, 5 to10 minutes. Taste the black bean salsa and season it with salt and pepper to taste.

HOT STUFF

Green chiles are very high in vitamin C. Ripe red chiles have high levels of vitamin A.

4. When the bread is cool enough to handle, spread the goat cheese on top of each slice. (If you toasted the bread slices ahead of time, reheat them in a 300°F oven for 3 to 5 minutes before spreading them with the cheese.) Divide the black bean salsa among the bread slices, dolloping a bit in the center of each.

Queso Crema Topped with Jalapeño Jelly

🌶

Serves 4 to 6

This familiar standby takes on terrific flavor when you prepare it with your very own carefully made Jalapeño Jelly. *Queso crema* is, of course, Spanish for "cream cheese."

1 package (8 ounces) regular or
    reduced-fat cream cheese,
    at room temperature
¼ cup Jalapeño Jelly (recipe follows)
24 or more thin party crackers,
    any variety

Place the block of cream cheese in the center of a plate or platter that is large enough to hold it and the crackers. Spoon the Jalapeño Jelly over the cream cheese, spreading it to cover the top of the cheese. Arrange the crackers around the jelly-topped cream cheese.

The jelly-topped cream cheese will keep for about 2 weeks when loosely wrapped and stored in the refrigerator.

Jalapeño Jelly

🌶 🌶 🌶

Makes 5 cups

At least three groups of women entrepreneurs developed successful businesses selling this jelly to specialty food markets. You can capture this same terrific flavor yourself. This jelly is outrageous on freshly baked crusty bread and is wonderful served with cream cheese or with any simply prepared meat dish such as roast leg of lamb. Try it with beef, pork, or chicken, too.

During the holiday season, Jalapeño Jelly makes a great gift. For a festive look, prepare one batch of jelly with red bell peppers and red chiles, and another with green bell peppers and green chiles.

3 large bell peppers, any color,
    stemmed, seeded, and finely
    chopped
3 to 6 medium-size jalapeño chiles,
    stemmed, seeded, and finely
    chopped (use 3 chiles for mild jelly,
    6 chiles for hot)
1½ cups cider vinegar
6½ cups sugar
6 ounces bottled liquid pectin

1. Scrub out five 1-cup jelly jars with resealable lids. Boil the jars in water while preparing the jelly, removing the jars only when ready to fill them.

2. Combine the peppers and chiles with the vinegar and sugar in a large, heavy 5-quart stockpot over high heat. Bring the mixture to a boil and cook, stirring frequently, until it becomes translucent, about 30 minutes.

3. Remove the pot from the heat and let the mixture cool for about 10 minutes. Then stir in the pectin.

4. Place the jelly mixture over high heat again and boil, stirring constantly, for 2 minutes.

5. Remove the pot from the heat, skim the foam off the surface, and allow the jelly to set, stirring it occasionally, until the peppers and chiles are distributed throughout and not floating on top, about 10 minutes. Ladle the jelly into the hot sterilized jars, and seal at once.

Chile-Spiced
Goat Cheese Spread

Makes about 1 cup

Zesty, tangy chile-flavored goat cheese is common in food shops in the Southwest. But I prefer to make my own—and it's not difficult to do. The addition of the chile and olive oil does wonders not only for the flavor of the cheese, but also for its longevity: the cheese lasts up to 6 months, sometimes longer, when stored in a glass jar in the refrigerator.

1 cup (8 ounces) goat cheese,
    at room temperature
2 tablespoons extra-virgin olive oil
1 tablespoon pure ground hot red chile
½ teaspoon ground Mexican oregano
½ teaspoon ground cumin
Dash of salt
Tortilla Chips (page 2), for serving

Place the goat cheese in a medium mixing bowl and stir in all the remaining ingredients, except the tortilla chips, until well blended. Transfer the spiced goat cheese to a small bowl, set the bowl on a large plate, and arrange the tortilla chips on the plate, encircling the bowl.

Green Chile
Pinwheels

◔ ◔

Makes 24 pinwheels; serves 8 to 10

These festive pinwheels look impressive on a plate but are very easy to make. You can prepare them ahead of time, if you wish, and you can vary the ingredients and flavorings to suit your taste and what you have on hand. Try pairing cream cheese with Jalapeño Jelly (see page 12), or flavoring sour cream with a few teaspoons of cabernet and layering it with sliced smoked chicken. Or stir some chopped chipotles into cream cheese and pair it with fresh arugula.

4 flour tortillas (12 inches each)
4 ounces cream cheese, at room
temperature
1 cup chopped parched green chiles,
such as Anaheim/New Mexico
(6 to 8 chiles; see box at right)
1 tablespoon crushed caribe chile or
other hot red chile, for garnish

1. Separate the tortillas and fluff them a bit by shaking them gently; then place them in a plastic bag. Fold down the top of the bag loosely and place it in a microwave oven. Cook on full power until the tortillas are warm and soft, about 30 seconds. (Alternatively, wrap the tortillas in aluminum foil, place them in a

Parching Fresh Chiles

When you cook with fresh green chiles, I recommend that you parch, or roast, them to remove the tough outer skin. The process—intense direct heat on the peel of the chile that nonetheless leaves the flesh uncooked—is easy enough, but if you are not used to the sting of chiles, you may want to wear rubber gloves or to generously butter your hands to prevent a burn from the chiles' irritating oils.

Before parching chiles, first wash them, removing all sand and dirt. Leave the stem on. Then pierce each one with a sharp knife, about 1 inch down from the stem.

To parch one or a few chiles: Set up an ice-water bath in a large bowl next to the stove. Place a chile directly on a medium-hot electric burner, or hold it with tongs or a long-handled fork over a gas burner on medium-high heat. Carefully rotate the chile until the skin is charred on all sides, about 2 minutes. Then plunge the roasted chile into the ice bath. Allow the chile to soak until it is cool to the touch. Then use your fingers to peel away the skin from stem to tip.

To parch large quantities of chiles: If you are using an electric oven, cover the entire top rack with heavy-duty aluminum foil and place it 4 inches from the broiler unit. If yours is a gas oven, cover the broiler rack with foil and place the rack in the closest position to the broiler. (For smaller quantities, cover a baking sheet with foil and place it on an uncovered rack.)

Preheat the broiler. Set up an ice-water bath in the sink or in a very large bowl. When the broiler is hot, carefully place a single layer of chiles on the foil-covered rack (or baking sheet) and cook until the skins begin to blister on top, about 1 to 2 minutes. Carefully turn the chiles, using long tongs or a long-handled metal fork, and continue to cook until the skins are blistered all over, about 1 minute more. Watch the chiles closely—they burn quickly. As soon as the chiles are parched, immerse them in the ice bath. Once the chiles have cooled to the touch, simply pull off the skin in strips, working from the stem to the tip—it should come away easily.

Blot the chiles dry between layers of paper towels. Keep the stems on if preparing chiles rellenos, or remove them if using the chiles in other ways. For a milder roasted chile, slice open the pods and strip out the seeds and veins with the back side of a knife. Once you've prepared your chiles, you can use them right away or freeze them for later use.

Freezing Parched Chiles

To freeze parched chiles, drain them well after removing them from the ice water bath, then place them on cookie sheets and freeze them. (*Do not peel the chiles*—leaving the skin on now gives you more flexibility of use later on.) Package the flash-frozen chiles in plastic freezer bags. To use in a recipe, prep the chiles as needed.

Although freezing does soften the chiles' crisp texture, it does not impair the taste. Because chiles are perishable and seasonal, freezing is often the best option. Frozen parched green chiles keep well for one year.

350°F oven, and bake until they are warm and soft, about 10 minutes.) Meanwhile, tear off four 14-inch-long pieces of waxed or parchment paper.

2. Place a warm tortilla on each sheet of waxed paper. Spread the cream cheese in a thin layer on each tortilla. Blot the green chiles between layers of paper towels to remove any excess moisture, and then sprinkle them evenly over the cream cheese.

3. Roll up each tortilla tightly. Wrap the waxed paper around each roll-up, twisting the ends to hold the paper in place. Place the roll-ups in the refrigerator to firm up the cream cheese and allow the flavors to develop, at least 2 hours. (You can prepare the roll-ups up to this point 3 days in advance, if you wish.)

4. When ready to serve, remove the roll-ups from the refrigerator, unwrap the waxed paper, and use a sharp chef's knife to slice off the ends. Cut each roll-up in half diagonally and then cut each half in half, again on the diagonal.

5. Place the pinwheels, cut side, up on a serving platter, arranging them in groups of four in a cloverleaf pattern. Sprinkle them with the caribe chile, holding your hand at least a foot above the platter to get a confetti effect.

Variation: Sun-Dried Tomato Twirls

Use sun-dried tomato tortillas in place of the plain flour tortillas. Substitute 1 cup chopped sun-dried tomatoes preserved in oil for the parched green chiles, and garnish the pinwheels with sprigs of fresh cilantro instead of the caribe chile.

Nachos Elegantes

Serves 2 to 4

These are one of my favorite appetizers because they are so pretty and have such a yummy blending of flavors. They can also serve as a light meal for two. When artfully arranged, the nachos look like sunflowers. I especially like to serve them on black plates.

In this recipe I give you the option of baking or frying the tortillas. I always bake them, myself, because I prefer the fresh crispness of baked tortillas—and I avoid adding about 25 calories from retained fat for each fried tortilla. That said, some people like fried tortillas better because they like the fried taste, remembering the old adage "Fat is flavor." Personally I believe there is plenty of fat from the cheese in the dish, but do feel free to choose for yourself.

6 corn tortillas (6 inches each)
Vegetable oil, for frying the tortillas (optional)
1 cup shredded mixed Monterey Jack and Cheddar cheeses, or more to taste
¼ cup thinly sliced fresh or pickled jalapeño chiles, or to taste
½ cup Guacamole (page 6)
½ cup refried beans (Refritos, page 131)
2 tablespoons chopped onion, for garnish

2 tablespoons chopped fresh tomato,
      for garnish
2 tablespoons sliced pitted black olives,
      for garnish
2 tablespoons sour cream, for garnish
      (optional)

1. Prepare the tortillas. For both methods, preheat the oven to 425°F.

For baked tortillas: Arrange the tortillas in a single layer on a baking sheet and top them with a smaller baking sheet, which will keep them flat while they bake. Place the tortillas in the oven and bake for 5 minutes. Remove the smaller baking sheet and continue baking the tortillas until they are crisp, about 8 minutes more. Remove the tortillas from the oven and leave the oven on.

For fried tortillas: Place a deep skillet over medium-high heat and add vegetable oil to a depth of 1 inch. When the oil registers 375°F on an instant-read deep-frying thermometer, carefully place a tortilla in the oil and fry until the rapid bubbling subsides, about 20 seconds. Transfer the tortilla to a paper towel to drain, and fry the remaining tortillas, allowing the oil to come back up to 375°F each time.

2. Divide the cheese among the tortillas, sprinkling it atop each one. Place the tortillas on a baking sheet and bake until the cheese melts, about 3 minutes.

3. Transfer the cheese-topped tortillas to a cutting board, and using a large, sharp knife, cut each one into 4 wedges. On a large round platter or on six smaller plates, arrange the pieces of each tortilla in a circle around the edge of the plate, overlapping the points. Scatter the sliced jalapeños over the tortillas. Divide the guacamole and beans among the circles of tortillas, first placing a mound of guacamole in the center of each plate, then spooning some beans around it. Garnish each circle with the onion, tomato, and olives, and top the beans with dollops of sour cream if desired.

Oaxaca Bites

Serves 12

This is my take on a traditional Mexican dish called *clayudas*. I remember first trying them in Santa Maria Atzompa, a delightful village outside Oaxaca that's known for its green pottery. We take an annual trip to Oaxaca, and now every year we go on a culinary tour and watch clayudas being made—and then we sample the delicious results.

I developed this recipe inspired by my experiences in Santa Maria Atzompa, but I changed the dish in two ways: In Oaxaca, this dish is served on tortillas about 14 inches in diameter—a whole meal—whereas I prefer a smaller bite-size version. I also substitute canned black beans for the traditional dried beans cooked from scratch (which you may use, if you wish). These two changes simplify the recipe considerably.

⅓ **cup bacon drippings, lard,**
    or vegetable oil
2 cloves Mexican or large garlic, minced
2 cans (15 ounces each) black beans
Chicken broth (optional)
18 white corn tortillas (6 inches each)
1 cup crumbled queso blanco or feta cheese
2 scallions, thinly sliced on an angle
½ cup crème fraîche, or ½ cup sour cream
    thinned with a bit of milk
1 small bunch cilantro
Chopped pickled jalapeño chiles and/or
    1 cup salsa of your choice, for garnish
    (optional)

1. Warm 1 tablespoon of the bacon drippings in a heavy skillet over medium heat until it melts, about 1 minute. Add the garlic and sauté until it is lightly golden, 2 to 3 minutes.

2. Add the beans, reserving most of the liquid, and cook, mashing most of the beans until the mixture is about as thick as pudding, 5 to 10 minutes. (If the beans get too dry and hard, add

the reserved bean liquid; if this is not enough liquid, add chicken stock or water to soften to pudding consistency.) Remove the beans from the heat and cover them to keep warm.

3. Prepare the tortilla chips: Cut each tortilla almost into quarters, leaving the quarters attached in the center of the tortilla. Line a baking sheet with paper towels.

4. Heat the remaining bacon drippings in a small skillet over medium heat until it is very hot and almost smoking, about 2 minutes. Working with one tortilla at a time, place a tortilla in the skillet and fry it until crisp (it will sound hollow when tapped with tongs and the rapid bubbling of the fat will have subsided), about 20 seconds. Using tongs or a slotted spoon, carefully remove the tortilla and place it on the baking sheet. Repeat with the remaining tortillas, placing them in a single layer on the baking sheet to drain. When the tortillas are cool to the touch, carefully break them into quarters.

5. To assemble, place the tortilla chips on a serving platter. Dollop them with the refried beans, then sprinkle them with the cheese and green onion. Drizzle the crème fraîche over all, and lay the cilantro sprigs on top. Scatter the chopped jalapeños over the top, if desired, and/or serve with the salsa alongside, if you wish.

Variation: Reduced-Fat Oaxaca Bites

Instead of frying the tortillas in step 2, you can bake them: Preheat the oven 425°F. Cut the tortillas into quarters, place them in a single layer on a baking sheet, and top them with a smaller baking sheet (this keeps them flat while they bake). Bake them for 5 minutes. Then remove the smaller baking sheet and continue baking until crisp, 5 to 8 minutes more. Proceed with the recipe from step 5.

Fruity Nachos

Serves 4

Want a departure from the everyday? These unusual nachos are a refreshing break from the traditional hearty flavors of beans, cheese, and jalapeño. You can use almost any firm fruit, alone or in combination—I like nectarines, grapes, apples, and strawberries.

**4 corn tortillas (6 inches each),
    cut into quarters
4 tablespoons cream cheese
    (about half of an 8-ounce package)
At least ½ cup thinly sliced nectarines,
    apples, strawberries, or grapes,
    alone or combined
Juice of ½ lime
¼ teaspoon pequin quebrado**

1. Preheat the oven to 425°F.

2. Place the tortillas in a single layer on a baking sheet, then place a smaller baking sheet on top of them (this keeps them flat as they bake).

Place the tortillas in the oven and bake for 5 minutes. Then remove the smaller baking sheet and continue to bake the tortillas until they are crisp, 5 to 8 minutes more.

3. Spread the cream cheese evenly over the tortilla chips, and arrange the chips on a serving platter. Combine the fruit, lime juice, and pequin quebrado in a bowl, and toss to mix. Then arrange the fruit on top of the cream cheese in an artistic fashion (sometimes I make a face using a strawberry for the mouth, grapes for the eyes, and apple slices for the eyebrows; other times I arrange the fruit in concentric circles or in crisscrossing lines).

New Mexico Tempura

Serves 12

In this delightful Southwestern twist on a favorite Japanese dish, slices of zucchini are dredged in a cornmeal or corn-flour batter and fried until golden and crisp. You can prepare these up to 2 hours in advance, keeping them warm, uncovered, in a 150°F oven. For a fun activity at an informal party, set out a fondue pot full of hot oil and let guests fry their own. Supply a bowl of water-soaked bamboo skewers and a paper-towel-lined baking sheet for draining, and assist the first few people so they know when the tempura is done. Use blue corn flour if you can get it, as it is ground much finer than cornmeal and will supply a finer-textured batter (see Sources).

½ cup unbleached all-purpose flour
½ teaspoon baking powder
¼ teaspoon salt
⅓ cup blue corn flour or cornmeal
1 egg, slightly beaten
½ cup milk
6 small zucchini (1 inch or less in diameter)
1 cup red salsa or enchilada sauce (bottled is fine)
1 quart cooking oil, preferably vegetable or peanut oil

1. Place about 50 bamboo skewers in a large, shallow pan filled with water, and let them soak for at least 30 minutes (this will prevent them from burning when exposed to heat). (Alternatively, use metal skewers.)

2. Meanwhile, place all the dry ingredients in a shallow mixing bowl and stir to combine. Combine the egg and milk in a small bowl, and add this to the dry ingredients, stirring well. (This batter can be made several days ahead; it actually improves when allowed to sit, covered, in the refrigerator. If using chilled batter, allow a slightly longer frying time in step 5.)

3. Cut the zucchini diagonally into ¾-inch-thick slices. Thread each slice onto a bamboo skewer at an angle for an attractive appearance.

4. When ready to serve, heat the enchilada sauce, if using. Spread the salsa over the bottom of a serving plate or platter. Have a paper-towel-lined plate nearby.

5. Pour the oil into a heavy pot and heat it to 340°F. Dip each skewered zucchini slice in the batter just to cover the top side, then fry it in the hot oil until lightly golden, 30 seconds to 1 minute. Carefully remove the skewered zucchini from the hot oil and place on the paper-towel-lined plate to drain. Then arrange the skewers on the salsa or sauce. (You can fry them ahead of time or to order.) Serve warm.

Hot Poppers

🌶 🌶 🌶 🌶

Makes 12 poppers

For those who really like spice, these hot poppers bring on the burn. The cheese helps temper the heat of the jalapeños, but if you wish to tame it further, you can marinate the peppers in fresh lime juice or vinegar before stuffing them with the cheese.

12 whole pickled jalapeño chiles
Fresh lime juice, distilled white vinegar,
 or cider vinegar (optional)
4 ounces Port-Salut, Muenster, or
 Monterey Jack cheese
½ teaspoon pure ground hot or mild red
 chile, for garnish

1. Taste a jalapeño for heat. If it's painfully hot, place the peppers in a large nonreactive bowl and add lime juice to just cover. Marinate the peppers in the lime juice until their heat has diminished somewhat, about 1 hour.

2. Slice the cheese into sticks the length of the jalapeños and about ¼ inch wide.

3. Use a small knife to cut a lengthwise slit down one side of a jalapeño. Carefully insert a stick of cheese through the slit, tucking it firmly inside the pepper. Repeat with the remaining jalapeños and cheese. Sprinkle the ground chile over a serving platter, arrange the stuffed chiles in a spoke pattern, and serve.

Roasted Beets
with Romesco Sauce

Serves 6

Beets are either loved or hated, and many people are in the latter camp. But I have won over dedicated beet haters by serving them this appetizer. You will be amazed at how terrific the roasted beets taste with this creamy, spicy, flavorful sauce. I sampled this dish first as a Spanish tapa, and I have been making it ever since.

The sauce, by the way, can substitute for a rémoulade sauce with seafood such as shrimp, crab, or crayfish, or with vegetables, such as steamed or boiled tiny new potatoes. When roasting, leave 3 inches of stem on the beets to prevent the juice from bleeding too much.

Capsaicin, the chemical responsible for chiles' heat, is an ingredient in some topical pain-relieving creams.

6 to 8 small fresh beets (about 1 bunch)
1 medium-size ripe tomato
2 large cloves garlic
5 blanched almonds
1½ tablespoons red wine vinegar
¼ cup good-quality extra-virgin
 olive oil
½ corn tortilla (6 inch), torn into chunks
1 tablespoon pure ground mild red chile
Generous pinch of pequin quebrado
Salt and freshly ground black pepper

1. Prepare the beets: Preheat the oven to 350°F. Wash and dry the beets, and trim the stems to 3 inches long (you can discard the leaves or reserve them for another use).

2. Place the beets on a baking sheet and transfer them to the oven. Roast the beets until their skins move slightly when touched with a spoon, about 30 minutes for small beets (less than 2 inches in diameter), up to 60 minutes for larger beets.

3. While the beats are roasting, prepare the romesco sauce: Rinse the tomato, remove the core, and cut a very shallow X into the bottom (this will allow you to remove the tomato's skin when it's cooked). Place the tomato, stem end up, the garlic, and the almonds on an ungreased baking sheet and place them in the oven. Roast in the oven along with the beets for about 15 minutes. Remove the garlic and almonds. Then continue to roast the tomato until it is soft, about 15 minutes more. Remove it from the oven. When the tomato and the garlic cloves are cool enough to handle, slip off their skins.

4. Let the beets cool until they're still warm but not hot to the touch. Then peel them by tugging at the skin with a sharp paring knife—the skin and stems should slip off. Any stubborn portions will need to be peeled with a knife. Dice the beets into ¾-inch cubes.

5. Pour ⅓ cup water, the vinegar, and the oil into a blender. Add the roasted tomato, garlic, and almonds, followed by the tortilla chunks, ground chile, pequin quebrado, and salt and black pepper to taste. Process until smooth. Then taste, and adjust the seasonings as needed. Transfer the sauce to a small serving bowl.

6. Center the bowl of sauce on a serving platter and surround it with the diced beets. Provide toothpicks for piercing the beets and dipping them into the sauce.

Tostados con Puerco

Makes 6 tostados

These luscious open-face tacos are pretty to look at and fun to eat, and they're filling enough for a light meal. The meat is seasoned with a spicy Southwestern rub (naturally I'm partial to Gordon's Barbecue Rub, which is offered by my company, Pecos Valley Spice Co.; see Sources).

I make these tostados with pork, but you can substitute beef, chicken, or seafood, or even leave out the meat if you wish. Occasionally I omit the meat and make my vegetarian friends very happy.

6 corn tortillas (6 inches each)
1 pork tenderloin (1½ pounds), trimmed of silver skin
2 tablespoons Southwestern-style seasoning rub
1 recipe Black Bean and Corn Salsa (page 5)
¾ cup mixed shredded Monterey Jack and Cheddar cheeses

1. Preheat the oven to 425°F.

2. Place the tortillas in a single layer on two baking sheets, and top each batch with a smaller baking sheet (this keeps the tortillas flat while they bake). Bake the tortillas for 5 minutes. Then remove the smaller baking sheets and continue baking until the tortillas are crisp, 5 to 8 minutes more. Set them aside. Reduce the oven temperature to 350°F.

3. Place the pork on a large piece of waxed paper and sprinkle it with the seasoning rub; then massage the rub into the meat.

4. Place the pork on a rimmed baking sheet or in a shallow broiler pan, and roast until a meat thermometer registers 160°F when inserted in the thickest portion. Remove the pork from the oven and raise the oven temperature to 425°F. Let the pork cool for at least 20 minutes. Then shred it, using two forks (see Note).

5. To assemble the tostados, place the baked tortillas on a heatproof platter and top them with the shredded pork, salsa, and cheese. Place the platter in the oven and bake the tostados until the cheese melts, about 5 minutes. Serve hot.

Note: The pork can be prepared up until this point a day or two ahead of time and stored in the refrigerator, or it can be placed in freezer bags and frozen. To defrost frozen pork before assembling the tostados, place the plastic bags in warm water until the meat is softened. Reheat the pork by placing it in a covered baking dish and baking it in a 350°F oven until hot, about 5 minutes, or in a microwave oven on high for 2 minutes.

Caliente Carnitas

Serves 24—3 to 4 carnitas each

Pork *carnitas* (which, literally translated, means "little meats") are terrifically tasty and quite easy to make. Traditionally carnitas are dipped into salsas or used as a filling in burritos, tacos, and other dishes; here I suggest serving them as an appetizer with a couple of salsas alongside.

This recipe feeds a crowd, but if you have a smaller group, you can always freeze some of the carnitas for later (see Note). Of course, you can also just divide the recipe by one half or one third.

1 pork shoulder or butt (3 pounds),
    trimmed of any large pieces of fat,
    leaving the marbling
6 cloves garlic, minced
Salt
3 tablespoons pure ground hot red chile,
    or 1½ teaspoons ground chipotle chile
    (chipotle powder)
1 or 2 salsas of your choice, for serving

1. Preheat the oven to 425°F.

2. Using a sharp knife, slice the pork into
2 x ½-inch strips. Place the pork in a large
bowl. In a smaller bowl, combine the garlic
with 1 teaspoon salt (or to taste) and the ground
red chile, and stir well. Sprinkle this mixture
over the pork and stir until thoroughly combined.

3. Place the pork in one or two shallow baking
pans (it should be only one or two layers deep).
Add water to just barely cover the pork, and
transfer the pan(s) to the oven. Roast the pork for
20 minutes. Then reduce the heat to 350°F and
continue cooking the pork, turning it periodically
with a spatula, until all the water has evaporated
and it is crispy and brown, 1 to 1½ hours.

4. Place the roasted pork carnitas on a platter,
and serve immediately with the salsas alongside.

*Note: You can divide the carnitas into smaller
quantities, place them in resealable freezer bags,
press the air out of the bags, and freeze them for
up to 90 days. To reheat the carnitas, place them
in a single layer on a baking sheet in a 350°F oven
and bake until hot and crispy, 10 to 15 minutes.*

Roasted Duck and Portabello Quesadilla

**Makes 1 quesadilla; serves 4 as an appetizer,
1 as an entrée**

Literally translated, *quesadilla*
means "a little detail of cheese." And what
a delicious, versatile detail it is. This version
combines the earthy, sophisticated flavors
of roasted duck and portabello mushrooms
and features my unique grilling technique,
which got rave reviews from the press when
I had my New York City restaurant. Roasted
duck is available at specialty food stores and
some Chinese restaurants; if you can't find it,
substitute roasted chicken or turkey.

1 tablespoon butter, melted, or more as
    needed
1 flour tortilla (10 inches)
¼ cup mixed grated Monterey Jack and
    Cheddar cheeses
4 to 6 slices fresh or pickled jalapeño chiles
2 to 3 tablespoons coarsely chopped
    roasted duck
3 to 4 slices (each about ¼ inch thick)
    grilled or sautéed portabello mushroom
    (see Note)
2 tablespoons cooked black beans
    (canned is fine), rinsed and drained

Assorted flavored cremas (recipe follows),
   for garnish
Red salsa, for garnish
Green salsa, for garnish
Crushed caribe chile, for garnish

1. Place a griddle over medium heat. When it is hot, brush half of the melted butter on an area the size of half a tortilla.

2. Place the tortilla on the griddle so that half of it lies on top of the buttered area. Layer that section of the tortilla with the cheese, jalapeños, duck, mushroom slices, and black beans. Fold the other side of the tortilla over the fillings, carefully pressing down so that the tortilla stays folded. Brush the top of the tortilla with the remaining butter.

3. Continue cooking the quesadilla until the cheese melts and the bottom of the tortilla is golden brown, about 1 minute. Then carefully flip it over with a spatula and cook the other side until golden, about 30 seconds more.

4. Remove the quesadilla to a cutting board. Slice it in half and then in half again, making equal wedges. Place the quesadilla on a platter, garnish with dollops of crema, the salsas, and a confetti sprinkling of caribe chile, and serve immediately.

Note: To grill or sauté portabello mushrooms, gently wipe them clean with a cloth. If grilling, preheat the grill to medium-high and lightly brush the mushrooms with olive oil. Place the mushrooms top side down on the grill and cook, turning once, until tender when pierced with a fork, about 2 minutes per side. If sautéing, place 1 teaspoon of olive oil in a seasoned or nonstick skillet over medium-high heat. When the oil is hot, add the mushrooms top side down and cook, turning, until tender, about 2 minutes per side.

Flavored Crema

Similar to crème fraîche, crema is a thinner version of sour cream. It can be flavored with chiles and other spices and is delicious drizzled over quesadillas, chili, and other dishes for a cool, tangy kick.

1 cup sour cream
1 tablespoon milk, or enough to thin the
   sour cream slightly
1 teaspoon pure ground mild or hot red
   chile, or as desired (for a pink crema);
   or 2 teaspoons flat-leaf parsley
   pureed with 1 teaspoon olive oil
   (for a green crema)

Place the sour cream in a small bowl and thin it with milk until it is slightly runny. Add the flavoring(s) or coloring of your choice, and transfer the crema to a squeeze bottle. Cremas will keep in the refrigerator for up to 1 week. If keeping leftover crema, be sure to clean the tip of the squeeze bottle very well. Remove the top, place plastic wrap over the opening of the bottle, and then secure it by screwing the tip in place over it.

Hot Little Devils

👹 👹 👹 👹

Makes 24 hot little devils

Pigs-in-blankets with attitude, these little devils deliver a spicy twist on an old favorite. The mustard provides a nice sharp tang and the chipotle pepper highlights the hot dogs' already smoky flavor, truly separating these *diablitos* from the traditional pig-in-a-blanket pack.

The devils can be assembled a day before baking, if you wish (see Note).

2 sheets frozen puff pastry
2 tablespoons Dijon mustard
2 teaspoons ground chipotle chile
   (chipotle powder)
24 cocktail franks
1 tablespoon milk or heavy (whipping)
   cream
Mustard, for serving (optional)

1. Remove the puff pastry from the package and lay it out on a counter, uncovered, to thaw, 10 to 15 minutes. Preheat the oven to 400°F.

2. In a small bowl, stir the mustard and ground chipotle together until combined.

3. Cut each piece of puff pastry into strips about 1 inch by 1½ inches (each strip should be long enough to wrap completely around a cocktail frank, and just wide enough that, when

wrapped around the frank, the ends of the frank peek out).

4. Spread a thin layer of the mustard-chipotle mixture on a strip of pastry, place a frank on it, and wrap the pastry around the frank so it forms a belt around the center. Pinch the ends of the pastry together, and place the devils on an ungreased baking sheet. Repeat with the remaining pastry, mustard mixture, and franks.

5. Brush the little devils with a bit of milk and bake for 10 minutes. Then reduce the heat to 375°F and bake until golden, about 10 minutes more. Let cool slightly and serve as is, or with your favorite mustard for dunking.

Note: You can prepare the little devils a day in advance up to step 4. Simply cover the baking sheet with plastic wrap, making sure the plastic seals well—if it doesn't, cover the plastic wrap with aluminum foil—and place it in the refrigerator. Right before serving, unwrap the baking sheet and continue with the recipe as directed in step 5, allowing a slightly longer baking time to account for the colder starting temperature.

Variation: Hot Little Purses

For the same flavor but a different presentation, simply cut the pastry dough differently, into 2½-inch squares. Spread the mustard mixture on each square, allowing a ½-inch margin on all four sides. Place a cocktail frank in the center, and pinch together the opposite corners of the dough to create a little purse shape. Proceed with the recipe from step 5.

Double-Chile
Deviled Eggs

🔥 🔥 🔥

Makes 24 deviled eggs; serves 12

Who doesn't love deviled eggs? If you know anyone who doesn't adore the luscious treats, this version will surely change their mind. The old-fashioned recipe takes really terrifically to spiciness—after all, what's a devil without a little heat?!

12 large eggs
1½ teaspoons salt
1½ tablespoons distilled white or
**   cider vinegar**
¼ cup mayonnaise
1 teaspoon ground chipotle chile
**   (chipotle powder)**
1 teaspoon pure ground mild
**   red chile**
1 tablespoon minced sweet pickle,
**   or to taste**
1 teaspoon Dijon mustard
1 tablespoon minced Italian
**   (flat-leaf) parsley leaves,**
**   for garnish**

1. Cook the eggs: Place the eggs gently in a large saucepan, cover with water, and then gently stir in 1 teaspoon of the salt and 1 tablespoon of the vinegar. Bring the water to a boil over high heat. Then immediately reduce the heat to low, cover the pan, and simmer the eggs until they are hard cooked, 15 minutes. Drain, and immediately place the eggs in a bowl of cold water.

2. While the eggs are cooling, stir the mayonnaise, ground chipotle, ground mild red chile, pickle, and mustard together in a small bowl.

3. When the eggs are cool to the touch, peel them and slice them in half lengthwise. Gently remove the yolks and set them aside; place the whites, cut side up, on a platter. Add the yolks to the mayonnaise mixture and stir well, using a fork to mash them. Taste, and adjust the seasonings as needed.

4. Spoon the yolk mixture into the cavity of the hard-cooked whites, or place the yolk mixture in a pastry bag fitted with a star tip and pipe it into the whites. Sprinkle with the parsley, and serve.

Note: You can prepare these up to 2 days ahead (without the parsley garnish) and store them in the refrigerator, tightly covered with plastic wrap. Remove them from the refrigerator about 30 minutes before serving.

Chile plants first sprouted in South America and then made their way north to Central and North America.

Smoky Scallop and Shrimp "Ceviche"

Serves 6

This is an unusual take on ceviche in that the seafood is quick-smoked and grilled before it is combined to "cook" fully in fresh citrus juice. The additional cooking does add some time to the preparation of the dish, but it gives the ceviche a unique subtly smoky flavor.

8 ounces shucked bay scallops
Salt and freshly ground black pepper
¼ cup fresh lime juice
1 tablespoon black tea leaves,
    or the contents of 1 tea bag
8 ounces medium-size shrimp
    (24 to 36 shrimp), peeled and deveined
½ cup diced onion
2 jalapeño chiles, stemmed, seeded
    (if you wish to reduce the heat),
    and minced
2 cloves garlic, minced
3 tablespoons coarsely chopped fresh
    cilantro leaves
½ cup diced tomato
¼ cup fresh lemon juice
3 tablespoons olive oil
5 corn or flour tortillas (6 inches each)

1. Preheat the oven to 425°F.

2. Rinse the scallops, pat them dry, and season them with salt, pepper, and 1½ teaspoons of the lime juice. Place the scallops on a metal trivet that will easily fit into a large stockpot. Set it aside.

3. Place the tea leaves in the bottom of a large ovenproof stockpot with a tight-fitting lid (choose one that will not be damaged by smoke). Place the lid on the pot and set it over medium-high heat until smoke starts to emerge from under the lid, about 5 minutes. Carefully remove the lid and place the scallop-topped trivet in the pot, working quickly to avoid releasing too much of the smoke. Cover the pot again and transfer it to the oven.

4. Bake the scallops until they are opaque, white, and still somewhat springy, 3 to 5 minutes. Then immediately remove the pot from the oven, take off the lid, and transfer the scallops to a plate. Set it aside.

5. Preheat an indoor or outdoor grill or grill pan.

6. Thread the shrimp onto skewers, piercing both the head and tail ends so the shrimp are held securely. When the grill or grill pan is hot, place the shrimp skewers on it and cook until the shrimp turn light pink, about 2 minutes. Then flip them over and cook until they are somewhat springy to the touch, 2 minutes more. Remove the shrimp from the grill and let cool.

7. When both the shrimp and the scallops are cool, remove the shrimp from the skewers and cut the scallops and shrimp into large dice. Place the seafood in a large bowl.

8. In a small bowl, stir the onion, jalapeño, garlic, cilantro, tomato, lemon juice, remaining lime juice, and olive oil together until combined. Pour the onion mixture over the seafood in the large bowl, and toss well to coat. Cover the bowl and refrigerate it for 30 minutes.

9. Preheat the oven to 425°F.

10. Prepare the tortilla toasts: Cut each tortilla into 6 wedges and place the wedges on an ungreased baking sheet. Bake them until crisp, 5 to 6 minutes.

11. Divide the ceviche mixture among six wine glasses, and place each glass on a small serving plate. Garnish each glass with a tortilla toast, and divide the remaining toasts among the serving plates, encircling the bottom of each glass.

Grilled Serrano-Lime Shrimp

🔥🔥

Serves 6

These zesty shrimp are marinated in freshly squeezed lime juice, then amped up with hot serrano chiles. They're excellent party fare and an elegant appetizer for an intimate dinner. You can double, triple, or even quadruple the recipe as you wish.

½ cup fresh lime juice
2 serrano chiles (or to taste), stemmed, seeded (if you wish to reduce the heat), and finely minced
½ teaspoon salt
2 cloves garlic, minced
24 medium-size shrimp, peeled and deveined
1 teaspoon crushed caribe chile or pequin quebrado, for garnish
1 small bunch fresh cilantro or Italian (flat-leaf) parsley, for garnish

1. Place the lime juice, serranos, salt, and garlic in a large nonreactive bowl and stir to combine. Blot the shrimp dry with paper towels and add them to the marinade. Marinate the shrimp, covered, in the refrigerator for at least 2 hours or up to 1 day.

2. Preheat the grill or broiler to medium-high heat.

3. Thread the shrimp onto metal skewers, 3 or 4 shrimp to a skewer, piercing the center of the shrimp and making sure each shrimp nests under

the previous one and faces the same way. Make sure the shrimp aren't tightly squeezed together, as this will produce uneven cooking.

4. Grill the shrimp until they just turn pink, 2 to 3 minutes per side. (Be careful not to overcook them, or they will become tough and dry.)

5. Transfer the shrimp, still on their skewers, to a serving platter. Sprinkle with the crushed caribe chile, then garnish with the cilantro sprigs. Serve warm.

Chile and Garlic Roasted Peanuts

🐮 🐮 🐮 🐮

Makes 2 cups

These addictive spiced peanuts are often served at parties and at bars in Mexico.

2 cups skin-on salted Spanish peanuts
¼ cup small dried red arbol chiles
¼ cup small cloves garlic
    (about 10 small cloves), unpeeled
2 teaspoons peanut or vegetable oil
Salt (optional)

1. Preheat the oven to 350°F.

2. Place the peanuts in a single layer on an ungreased rimmed baking sheet. Scatter the arbol chiles and garlic over the peanuts, then drizzle them with the oil. Bake for 10 minutes, and then stir. Continue baking until the peanuts are toasty brown and crisp, about 3 minutes more. Be careful not to overcook the peanuts or they will burn.

3. When the peanuts are done, stir them well and taste to see if more salt is needed. Discard the garlic and chiles and transfer the peanuts to a serving bowl.

The peanuts will keep for 3 to 4 months, stored in a well-sealed jar at room temperature.

Small Plates, Big Flavor

I love to throw what I call a "Bite-Size Party," where the whole menu is little appetizers. Here are two of my favorite menus:

South Near the Border Party
• San Antonio Hot Cheese Dip
    with Chorizo
• Fruity Nachos
• Grilled Serrano-Lime Shrimp
• Chèvre Bruschetta with
    Black Bean and Corn Salsa

Mexican Fiesta
• Watermelon Salsa with Tortilla Chips
• Oaxaca Bites
• Smoky Scallop and Shrimp "Ceviche"
• Green Chile Pinwheels
• Tostados con Puerco

2

Chili! Chili! Chili!

This is what you came here for: chili and more chili! Whether you're following one of these recipes to the letter or merely using one as a jumping-off point for your own chili improvisation, it helps to have your chili skills in place before taking the plunge into that pot. Chili-making is an individual sport with a sharp learning curve. Once you've mastered a few basics and been through a short training period, you're ready to start developing your own style and setting your own limits.

In my years as a chili expert—making and sharing chili recipes, judging chili contests, and teaching the art of chili to the thousands of people who have come through my cooking school—I've witnessed many successes and failures 'twixt the pod and the pot. Over the years I've developed what I call my Chili Fitness Plan, an approach that ensures that, no matter how individualized, unconventional, or outrageous your inclinations, your chili will still stand a good chance of being prizewinning quality.

Step one: Find a big ol' pot. Whatever you use, be sure it has a generous open surface for simmering and a heavy bottom for smooth, even cooking. Straight sides are critical—sloping or bulging sides do not produce a chili of uniform consistency.

Once you've found your pot, leave the lid in the cupboard! Covering the pot inhibits the development of flavor and texture. However, with the lid off, you're going to have to check your brew regularly: the liquid will evaporate quickly, and you will probably need to adjust its quantity during the simmering stage.

Step two: Round up your ingredients. Your chili deserves the best ingredients you can muster: pure ground chile pepper coupled with the freshest onions, garlic, and spices. To keep ingredients at their peak, refrigerate or freeze them if you won't be using them all at once. If fresh ground chiles are not available at your local grocery store, they can be ordered online or through the mail and kept cool until use. Check out the list of sources on pages 183 and 184.

Most commercial chili powders are not pure chile: they also contain quite a bit of salt and preservatives, and often ground dehydrated onion and garlic as well, all of which makes for a less-than-fresh flavor. Planning ahead—either making your own chili powder or

SOME LIKE IT HOT . . .
These icons show how fiery each dish is.

MILD

A BIT OF BITE

HOT

HOT ENOUGH
TO MAKE YOU . . .

sourcing a top-notch prepared one—is the key to fresh ingredients and flavors!

Step three: The meat is the meat of the matter. For the chilies in this chapter that stray from the classic beef base, I've included instructions with each recipe. But when it comes to the original bowl o' red or chili con carne—often called true Texas chili—it can only be made with beef. Across the state line in New Mexico, they use pork—but it ain't the same!

The best cut of beef for chili is flavorful chuck roast, cut into ¼- to ½-inch cubes. If you do not want to go to that much trouble, look for chili grind—this is available in most Southwestern markets (you'll sometimes see it marked as "coarse grind" outside that region). Failing all else, pull the butcher aside and ask him to use his ½- to 1-inch blade to coarsely grind some chuck for you.

Step four: Follow the rules. Don't destroy your careful preparations and ingredient sourcing with a haphazard approach once you get over the open flame. Believe me, I have seen haphazard in my time. At chili cookoffs, some contestants try to jazz up their act by tossing ingredients into the pot in alphabetical order, underhand from 6 feet away, or with hired gymnasts doing handsprings over the pot, adding ingredients from midair! That might look pretty, but it's not making the chili its

best. Follow the instructions carefully, adding ingredients as they are called for, when they're called for.

Step five: Keep the fat. Do not drain the fat from the pot at any time during the cooking process. To skim is folly—you will rob the chili of its flavor. Fat is an important flavor catalyst for chili and should not be interfered with until the cooking is finished. Generally there should be no fat to skim, but wait until the very end to make that call.

Step six: Let it simmer. Simmering is vital to most chili recipes: it helps the flavors to get acquainted. Remember to leave the lid off the pot to let the juices cook down to a heavenly—and sometimes wicked—brew.

Step seven: Beans come at the end. Most chili cookoffs do not allow beans in the brew, but if you want beans in your chili, use freshly precooked ones or the best-quality canned ones you can find. Don't put them in until the last half

hour of cooking: if you cook them too long, they'll get mushy and practically disappear.

Step eight: Taste liberally. When your brew has finished simmering, sample your endeavor (if you're like most chiliheads, you'll have been doing so all along) and adjust the seasonings to your taste. If you've gone easy on the chile until this point and you decide to add more, be sure to allow another half hour of simmering time.

Step nine: Revisit the fat situation. Now that the chili has finished cooking, you can assess whether there's some excess fat that needs to be skimmed. Don't get carried away, as you could wind up skimming off most of the flavor. For thorough and easy removal, after your chili is cooked, allow it to cool completely. Refrigerate it for at least 2 hours to give the fat a chance to solidify, and then skim off some of the fat that has risen to the top.

Step ten: Wait a day. Chili only improves with rest, age, and reheating, so I always try to make mine a day in advance of serving. It also freezes well, so be sure to always make enough for at least two meals!

And so, amigo, you have the essential elements—the methods to make this chili madness your slave, not your master!

Pecos River
Bowl of Red

🌶 🌶 🌶 🌶
Serves 8

Pecos River is the name of my spice company and was originally the name of the ranch I owned in New Mexico. I learned my love of chili from my maternal grandfather, who was an executive with the Santa Fe Railroad in the late 1800s. He was charged with giving back surplus land the railroad had claimed for laying tracks, and he clarified land titles from Kansas to New Mexico. My grandfather developed this recipe after spending five years sampling chilies from "cookies," the workers who cooked for the cowboys herding cattle to the railhead.

HOT STUFF

Eat chiles, be healthy! It is believed that consuming chiles 24 days out of 30 can improve health.

2 tablespoons lard, butter, or bacon
    drippings
1 large onion, coarsely chopped
3 pounds boneless chuck roast or
    80% lean beef, cut into ½-inch cubes
3 medium-size cloves garlic, finely chopped
¼ cup pure ground hot red chile,
    plus more to taste
¼ cup pure ground mild red chile,
    plus more to taste

1 tablespoon ground cumin
1½ teaspoons salt, plus more to taste
Fixin's and Mixin's (below), for serving

1. Melt the lard in a large heavy pot over medium heat. Add the onion and cook until it is translucent, about 5 minutes. Remove the pot from the heat.

2. In a large bowl, mix the meat with the garlic, ground chiles, about half of the cumin, and the

Fixin's and Mixin's

When serving chili, I like to offer little bowls of toppings so everyone at the table can doctor their chili as they wish. Not only do they make the chili more flavorful, they add an element of fun—it's always special to be able to customize your own bowl.

The next time you serve chili, try setting out small bowls of these:

• Finely chopped onion

• Sliced pickled jalapeños

• Coarsely grated Cheddar cheese, or mixed grated Cheddar and Monterey Jack cheeses

• Sour cream or Flavored Cremas (page 25)

• Lime wedges lightly dusted with pure ground hot or mild red chile

• Pequin quebrado

salt. Transfer the meat mixture to the pot and immediately add 3 cups water. Stir to combine.

3. Return the pot to the stove, place it over high heat, and bring the meat mixture to a boil. Then lower the heat and simmer, uncovered, stirring occasionally, until the meat is very tender and the flavors are well blended, 2½ to 3 hours.

4. Taste the chili and determine the need for more salt and more chile. Stir in the remaining cumin, and serve with Fixin's and Mixin's alongside.

Pedernales River Chili

Serves 8

Lyndon B. Johnson was a lifelong friend of my husband, Gordon McMeen. Like most Texans, Lyndon really loved chili, and this recipe is reported to have been his favorite. It comes from deep in the heart of Texas.

3 tablespoons lard or bacon drippings
4 pounds coarsely ground lean beef
1 large onion, coarsely chopped
2 medium-size cloves garlic,
    finely chopped
Salt
1 teaspoon dried oregano, preferably
    Mexican
1 teaspoon ground cumin
2 cups boiling water
1 can (28 ounces) whole tomatoes,
    chopped, liquid reserved
¼ cup pure ground hot red chile,
    or to taste
2 tablespoons pure ground mild red chile,
    or to taste

1. Melt the lard in a large pot over medium-high heat. Add the meat, breaking up any lumps with a fork, and cook, stirring occasionally, until it is evenly browned.

2. Add the onion and garlic and cook until the onion is translucent, about 5 minutes.

3. Stir in 3 teaspoons salt, the oregano, ½ teaspoon of the cumin, the boiling water, and the tomatoes with their liquid. Gradually stir in the ground chiles, tasting the mixture after each addition until you achieve the degree of hotness and flavor that suits your palate. Bring the chili to a boil. Then lower the heat and simmer, uncovered, stirring occasionally, until the flavors are well blended, at least 1 hour.

4. Add the remaining ½ teaspoon cumin, and adjust the seasonings to taste.

Carroll Shelby's Chili

🌶 🌶 🌶 🌶

Serves 4

This recipe is the coup de grâce of Grand Prix racer Carroll Shelby. If you use the hot chile in the amount called for, beware! It is truly a pot of fire. It's best to start off with less and add more to taste while the chili is cooking.

8 ounces beef suet, or ½ cup vegetable oil
    (not canola)
1 pound beef round, coarsely ground
1 pound beef chuck, coarsely ground
1 can (8 ounces) tomato sauce
1 can or bottle (12 ounces) beer
¼ cup pure ground hot red chile, or to taste
2 medium-size cloves garlic, finely chopped
1 small onion, finely chopped
1¼ teaspoons dried Mexican oregano
Scant ½ teaspoon paprika
1½ teaspoons ground cumin
Salt
Pinch of cayenne pepper
12 ounces Monterey Jack cheese, grated

1. Melt the suet or heat the vegetable oil in a heavy 3-quart (or larger) pot over medium-high heat. Remove the unrendered suet. Add the meat, breaking up any lumps with a fork, and cook, stirring occasionally, until the meat is evenly browned, 5 to 7 minutes.

2. Add the tomato sauce, beer, about half of the ground chile (unless you are a hothead, in which case add it all), and the garlic, onion, oregano, paprika, 1 teaspoon of the cumin, and 1¼ teaspoons salt. Stir to blend, and bring the mixture to a boil. Then lower the heat and simmer, uncovered, stirring occasionally, for 1 hour.

3. Taste, and adjust the seasonings, adding the cayenne pepper and the rest of the ground chile if desired. Simmer, uncovered, for 1 hour more.

4. Stir in the cheese and the remaining ½ teaspoon cumin. Simmer for 3 minutes, stirring often to keep the cheese from burning.

Buzzard's Breath Chili

🌶

Serves 16

Despite its name, this chili is actually good! The original recipe calls for "dead cow meat, dried red ants, and cigar ashes," but I think the ashes and ants are optional . . . you decide.

The recipe was created when chili cookoffs just started to become popular, and in its original version it took first prize at the Chili Appreciation Society International Cookoff in Terlingua, Texas, in 1971. The masa harina makes for a thicker, somewhat grainy chili—you can add it or omit it as you prefer (for more information, see the box at right).

3 tablespoons lard, butter, or bacon
    drippings
2 large onions, coarsely chopped
8 pounds beef chuck or round,
    coarsely ground
5 cloves garlic, finely chopped
⅓ cup pure ground hot red chile
⅓ cup pure ground mild red chile
1 tablespoon ground cumin
1 teaspoon dried oregano,
    preferably Mexican
3 cans (8 ounces each) tomato sauce
Salt
1 tablespoon chopped parsley (optional)
1 cup masa harina, or to taste (optional)

1. Melt the lard in a large heavy pot over medium heat. Add the onions and cook until they are translucent, about 5 minutes.

2. Combine the beef with the garlic, ground chiles, cumin, and oregano in a large bowl. Add the meat mixture to the pot, breaking up any lumps with a fork, and cook, stirring occasionally, until the meat is evenly browned, about 30 minutes.

3. Add the tomato sauce, 3 cups water, 2 tablespoons salt, and the parsley if using. Bring to a boil. Then lower the heat and simmer, uncovered, for 1 hour.

4. If you are using the masa harina, sprinkle it evenly over the top of the chili (you may use less than 1 cup, if you wish) and stir it well to avoid lumps. Cook the chili, stirring, for 10 minutes more.

5. Taste, and adjust the seasonings.

Masa Harina

Some cooks swear by adding masa harina to their chilies, while others prefer a "pure" chili without it. What is masa harina? Corn treated with ground limestone creates posole, which in turn is ground, creating masa harina (also called just masa).

The starch in the corn acts as a thickener, just like cornstarch or wheat flour, producing a thicker chili overall. It also adds a tortilla-like flavor element. The question of whether to add masa is both a personal and a regional one: masa is used extensively in Mexico and along the border regions, where it has always been available, but farther north and west it is not so popular. It's up to you whether or not to use it. You can buy it at some supermarkets, or see Sources.

Chili
H. Allen Smith

Serves 8

With this recipe, H. Allen Smith—humorist, writer, easterner, and disrespecter of Texas-style chili—entered the first chili cookoff ever held. Sponsored by the Chili Appreciation Society International (CASI), and held in Terlingua, Texas, in 1967, the contest between Smith and Wick Fowler, a Texan and CASI chief cook, ended in a tie.

2 tablespoons olive oil or butter,
    or a combination
4 pounds beef sirloin or tenderloin,
    coarsely ground
1 can (6 ounces) tomato paste
3 medium onions, coarsely chopped
1 green bell pepper, stemmed, seeded,
    and coarsely chopped
4 large cloves garlic, finely chopped
3 tablespoons pure ground hot red chile
1 tablespoon dried oregano, preferably
    Mexican
½ teaspoon dried basil
1 tablespoon cumin seeds or ground cumin
Salt and freshly ground black pepper

1. Warm the oil in a heavy 4-quart pot over medium heat. Add the meat, breaking up any lumps with a fork, and cook, stirring occasionally, until it is evenly browned, about 15 minutes.

2. Stir in the tomato paste, onions, bell pepper, garlic, chile, oregano, basil, about half of the cumin, and 4 cups water. Bring the mixture to a boil. Then lower the heat and simmer, uncovered, stirring occasionally, until the flavors meld, for 2 to 3 hours. Add more water if the chili begins to cook down too much or look too dry.

3. Taste the chili, season with salt and pepper, and add the remaining cumin.

Chili
Woody DeSilva

Serves 8

The original recipe for this super-spicy stew had an extra touch: woodruff. The chili's creator, Woody DeSilva, used this pungent, somewhat sweet-smelling herb because it tied back to his name, but you may want to omit it. Woodruff contains coumarin, which can be toxic in large quantities; if you *do* choose to use it, use only a very small amount. (It may be difficult to find this herb, but try your local specialty food stores and use no more than the amount called for on the package.)

This recipe calls for the chili to be made a day in advance.

2 tablespoons vegetable oil (not canola),
    plus more as needed
5 medium-size onions, coarsely chopped
Salt and freshly ground black pepper
4 pounds beef chuck, coarsely ground
5 medium-size cloves garlic, finely chopped
4 tablespoons dried oregano, preferably
    Mexican
2 tablespoons dried and crushed woodruff
    (optional; see headnote)
1 teaspoon cayenne pepper
2 tablespoons paprika
1 tablespoon ground cumin
½ teaspoon to 1 teaspoon crushed dried
    pequin chile
4 dashes hot pepper sauce
2 cans (15 ounces each) tomato sauce
1 can (6 ounces) tomato paste
¼ cup masa harina (see box, page 37)
    or unbleached all-purpose flour

1. Place the oil in a large heavy skillet over medium heat. Add the onions. Season with salt and black pepper to taste and cook, stirring, until the onions are translucent, about 7 minutes. Transfer them to a large heavy pot.

2. Place the meat in the skillet, adding more oil if necessary. Add the garlic and 1 tablespoon of the oregano, and turn up the heat to medium-high. Break up any lumps of meat with a fork and cook, stirring occasionally, until the meat is evenly browned, about 15 minutes. Transfer this mixture to the large pot as well.

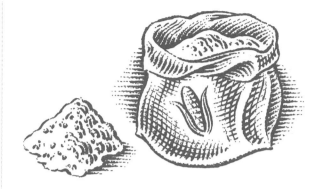

3. In a small plastic or paper bag, shake together the remaining 3 tablespoons oregano, the woodruff if using, and the cayenne pepper, paprika, cumin, and crushed chile. Add the blended spices to the pot and stir in the hot pepper sauce, tomato sauce, and tomato paste.

4. Add enough water to the pot to cover the meat mixture. Place the pot over high heat and bring the contents to a boil. Then lower the heat and simmer, uncovered, for at least 2 hours.

5. Taste, and adjust the seasoning as needed. Cool the chili and refrigerate it overnight. (If the pot is stainless steel, porcelain, or enamel, you can store the chili, covered, in the pot. Otherwise, place it in a covered food storage container.)

6. The next day, skim off the fat that has risen to the top. Mix the masa harina with a little water to make a paste. Reheat the chili to the boiling point, and stir in the masa harina paste. Stir constantly to prevent sticking and scorching, adding water as necessary until the desired texture is achieved.

Dallas Chili

Serves 12

Straight from Big D . . . and

from a very proud chef who modestly
claims it's the world's greatest. It is unusual,
containing no onions but instead ingredients
not ordinarily associated with chili, like
gumbo filé (which is a combination of
ground sassafrass leaves and thyme) and
chicken fat. The original recipe called for
woodruff, which you may be
able to find at a health food
store or specialty spice store,
but which is also considered
toxic in large amounts—I
recommend substituting
chocolate instead.

Try this chili sometime
when you're in an exotic
mood. The brew simmers for
a total of 12 hours.

HOT STUFF

*Like eggplant,
tomatoes, and
potatoes, chiles belong
to the nightshade
family of plants.*

6 pounds beef brisket, coarsely ground
¼ cup pure ground hot red chile
1 tablespoon pure ground mild red chile
½ tablespoon crushed caribe chile
1 teaspoon cayenne pepper
2 tablespoons dried Mexican oregano
8 medium-size cloves garlic, crushed
4 bay leaves, crushed
1 teaspoon gumbo filé (ground sassafras)
3 tablespoons ground cumin

3 tablespoons woodruff, or 2 ounces
   unsweetened chocolate
1 teaspoon paprika
1 tablespoon salt
⅓ cup bacon drippings
2 tablespoons fresh lemon juice
2 tablespoons fresh lime juice
1 tablespoon Dijon mustard
2 tablespoons masa harina
   (see box, page 37)
4 cans or bottles (12 ounces each) beer,
   plus more as needed
1 tablespoon Worcestershire sauce
1 tablespoon sugar
1 tablespoon chicken fat (optional)
Hot pepper sauce (optional)

1. In a large bowl, combine the beef with
the ground chiles, caribe chile, cayenne
pepper, oregano, garlic, bay leaves, gumbo filé,
1½ tablespoons of the cumin, woodruff (but not
the chocolate) if using, paprika, and salt.

2. Place the bacon drippings in a large heavy
pot over medium heat. When they are hot, add
the meat mixture to the pot. Break up any lumps
with a fork and cook, stirring occasionally, until
the meat is evenly browned, about 20 minutes.

3. Stir in all the remaining ingredients,
including the unsweetened chocolate if using and
the chicken fat and hot pepper sauce if you wish.
Bring the mixture to a boil. Then lower the heat
and simmer, uncovered, for 2 hours.

4. Taste, and adjust the seasonings as needed.
Simmer, uncovered, for another 10 hours, stirring

and adding more beer or water if the chili begins to cook down too much or look too dry. Use a large spoon to skim off the fat before serving.

Craig Claiborne's No-Salt Chili con Carne

Serves 2

When the late Craig Claiborne, well-known chef and cookbook author, was put on a no-salt diet, he had two ultimate cravings: one was for a good hamburger and the other was for a good bowl of chili. He developed this recipe, in which the lack of salt is compensated for by the cumin, garlic, and a touch of red wine vinegar.

1 tablespoon peanut or vegetable oil
3 medium-size onions, finely chopped
1 green or red bell pepper, stemmed, seeded, and finely chopped
1¼ pounds veal, beef, or pork shoulder, coarsely ground
2 medium-size cloves garlic, finely chopped
2 tablespoons pure ground hot red chile
1 tablespoon pure ground mild red chile

1 teaspoon ground cumin (see Note)
1 teaspoon dried oregano, preferably Mexican
1 bay leaf
½ teaspoon freshly ground black pepper
4 cups chopped fresh or canned unsalted tomatoes
1 tablespoon red wine vinegar
¼ teaspoon crushed caribe chile, or to taste

1. Place the oil in a deep skillet over medium heat. When it's hot, add the onions and bell pepper and cook, stirring, until the onions are translucent, about 3 minutes.

2. Place the meat in a large bowl and sprinkle it with the garlic, ground chiles, cumin, and oregano. Stir to blend, and then add the meat mixture to the skillet. Break up any lumps with a fork and cook, stirring occasionally, until the meat is evenly browned, about 15 minutes.

3. Add the bay leaf, black pepper, tomatoes, vinegar, and crushed caribe chile, and bring the mixture to a boil. Then lower the heat and simmer for 1 hour, stirring occasionally.

4. Taste, and adjust the seasonings as needed. Remove the bay leaf before serving.

Note: When Craig made this chili, he never divided the cumin—he added it to the cooking chili all at once. However, I've found that dividing the cumin—using half as you cook and half just before you serve the chili—does impart a fresher cumin flavor.

Diet Chili

🌶️ 🌶️

Serves 8

On a waist-trimming regimen?

If so, you can still enjoy that terrific chili taste with this savory stew—there are only 247 calories in each 1-cup serving. There's also less fat in this chili than in many of the other beef chilies—an average of about 12 grams per serving, depending on the leanness of the beef.

1 tablespoon vegetable oil, preferably
   soy or corn oil
2 medium-size onions, finely chopped
2 pounds lean beef, coarsely ground
2 tablespoons pure ground hot red chile
3 tablespoons pure ground mild red chile
1 medium-size clove garlic, minced
1 teaspoon dried oregano, preferably
   Mexican
1½ teaspoons ground cumin
Salt
4 or 5 tomatoes, peeled (see box, page 75),
   stemmed, seeded, and coarsely
   chopped
3 cans (4 ounces each) whole green chiles,
   seeded and chopped, liquid reserved

1. Place the oil in a 4- to 5-quart heavy saucepan over medium heat. Add the onions and cook until they are translucent, about 5 minutes.

2. In a large bowl, combine the meat with the ground chiles, garlic, oregano, ¾ teaspoon of the cumin, and ½ teaspoon salt. Transfer the meat mixture to the pan. Break up any lumps with a fork and cook, stirring occasionally, until the meat is evenly browned, about 15 minutes.

3. Add the tomatoes and the green chiles with their liquid, and bring to a boil. Then lower the heat and simmer, uncovered, stirring occasionally, for 1 hour. Add water if the chili begins to cook down too much or look too dry. Taste, add the remaining ¾ teaspoon cumin, and adjust the seasonings as needed.

4. Remove the chili from the heat and let it cool. Then refrigerate it until the fat has risen to the top and congealed, at least 4 hours or overnight. (Refrigerate the chili, covered, in the pot if the pot is stainless steel, porcelain, or enamel; otherwise, transfer the chili to a covered food storage container before refrigerating.)

5. Before serving, skim off the fat and reheat the chili over medium heat, stirring to prevent sticking. Add water if the chili is too thick.

Jay's Chili

Serves 16

Jay Pennington became the International Chili Society's 1977 World Champion with this vegetable-meat version. It contains four kinds of chiles, mild bell pepper, and a chile salsa.

1 tablespoon vegetable oil (not canola)
3 medium-size onions, finely chopped
2 green bell peppers, stemmed, seeded, and finely chopped
2 stalks celery, finely chopped
3 medium-size cloves garlic, finely chopped
8 pounds beef round, coarsely ground
40 ounces canned tomato sauce
2 cans (14½ ounces each) stewed tomatoes, with liquid
1 can (6 ounces) tomato paste
4 ounces red salsa
1 pickled jalapeño chile (3 inches long), finely chopped
½ cup pure ground hot red chile
¼ cup pure ground mild red chile
1 can (4 ounces) whole green chiles, seeded and finely chopped
1 teaspoon dried oregano, preferably Mexican
3 teaspoons ground cumin
Salt
Freshly ground black pepper

1. Place the oil in a heavy 10- to 12-quart pot over medium heat. Add the onions, bell peppers, celery, and garlic. Cook, stirring, until the onions are translucent, about 5 minutes.

2. Add the meat to the pot a little at a time. Cook, stirring occasionally, until the meat is browned, 20 to 30 minutes.

3. Stir in the tomato sauce, stewed tomatoes with their liquid, tomato paste, salsa, jalapeño, ground chiles, green chiles, oregano, and about 1 teaspoon of the cumin. Add 5 cups water, 3 tablespoons salt, and black pepper to taste. Bring the mixture to a boil. Then lower the heat and simmer, uncovered, stirring often, for 2½ to 3 hours.

4. Taste the chili, add the remaining cumin, and adjust the seasonings as needed.

Reno Red

Serves 12

This recipe, devised by Joe and Shirley Stewart, was the International Chili Society World Championship Chili Cookoff winner in 1979. The added touches of oregano-flavored beer, cider vinegar, and mashed dried chile pods make this chili particularly hearty and different.

1 cup beef suet or vegetable oil
    (not canola)
3 pounds beef round, coarsely ground
3 pounds beef chuck, coarsely ground
Whole black peppercorns, to taste
¾ cup pure ground red chile
    (hot or mild, or a combination)
6 tablespoons ground cumin
6 small cloves garlic, finely chopped
2 medium-size onions, coarsely chopped
½ cup beer
1 tablespoon dried oregano, preferably
    Mexican
6 dried whole red chiles, crushed,
    or ¾ cup crushed caribe chile
2 tablespoons paprika
2 tablespoons cider vinegar
3 cups beef broth
1 can (4 ounces) diced green chiles,
    drained (½ cup)
4 ounces canned stewed tomatoes
1 teaspoon hot pepper sauce
2 tablespoons masa harina
    (see box, page 37)

1. Melt the suet or heat the cooking oil in a large heavy pot over medium-high heat. Remove the unrendered suet. Add the meat and black peppercorns. Break up any lumps of meat with a fork and cook, stirring occasionally, until the meat is evenly browned, about 20 minutes.

2. Stir in the ground chile, cumin, garlic, and onions. Add water to barely cover, and bring to a boil. Then lower the heat and simmer, uncovered, for 30 to 45 minutes, adding more water if the chili begins to cook down too much or look too dry.

3. Meanwhile, heat the beer in a small saucepan over low heat. When it is hot, add the oregano, turn off the heat, and let the oregano-beer "tea" steep for 5 minutes. Then drain the tea, discarding the oregano leaves.

4. Stir the crushed red chiles into the meat mixture. Stir in the oregano-beer tea, paprika, vinegar, 2 cups of the beef broth, and the diced chiles, tomatoes, and hot pepper sauce. Simmer, uncovered, stirring often, for 30 to 45 minutes.

5. Dissolve the masa harina in the remaining 1 cup broth. Stir it into the pot and simmer, uncovered, for 30 minutes. Taste, and adjust the seasonings as needed.

Mike Roy's
Housebroken Chili

Serves 4

Mike Roy was a fixture in broadcast journalism in the San Francisco area for a number of years. His spicy chili is "housebroken" by the addition of orange liqueur and given an extra twist with the tablespoon of orange zest. It's an interesting and delicious beef chili.

1½ tablespoons lard or bacon drippings
1 medium-size onion, coarsely chopped
1 medium-size clove garlic, finely chopped
1 tablespoon grated orange zest,
   preferably from an organic orange
2 pounds lean beef, preferably sirloin or
   round steak, coarsely ground
3 tablespoons pure ground mild red chile
3 teaspoons ground cumin
1 tablespoon salt
½ teaspoon freshly ground black pepper
1 cup beef broth
2 tablespoons orange-flavored liqueur,
   such as Cointreau
1 teaspoon hot pepper sauce

1. Melt the lard in a large heavy skillet over medium-high heat. Add the onion, garlic, and orange zest and cook, stirring, until the onion is translucent, about 5 minutes.

2. Add the beef to the skillet. Break up any lumps with a fork and cook, stirring occasionally, until the meat is evenly browned, about 15 minutes.

3. Stir in the ground chile, 1½ teaspoons of the cumin, the salt, the black pepper, 2 cups water, and the broth. Bring to a boil. Then lower the heat and simmer, uncovered, stirring occasionally, for 3 to 4 hours. Add water if the chili begins to cook down too much or look too dry.

4. Add the remaining 1½ teaspoons cumin, the orange liqueur, and the hot pepper sauce. Taste, adjust the seasonings as needed, and cook, uncovered, for 15 minutes longer.

Housebreaking Chili

For a *really* fun party, offer jiggers of tequila to "housebreak"—or tame the spiciness of—chili. You can stir the shot into your bowl of chili or, if you prefer, just toss it back! For added excitement, offer different qualities and brands of tequilas. It's really amazing how the tequila affects chili's spicy flavor, creating a mellower, less piquant taste.

Chipotle Chili

Serves 6 to 8

This chili is for serious hot chili lovers who like the smokiness of chipotles. Chipotles always add a depth of flavor and richness that is truly habit-forming. Instead of morita chipotles, which are mechanically dried and flavored, I much prefer to reconstitute dried traditional chipotles, which are slowly smoked in banana leaves and impart a much smokier and more authentic taste. If these are unavailable, I use chipotle powder ground from the traditional chipotles (to find both, see Sources).

1 tablespoon bacon drippings
2 large onions, chopped
4 cloves garlic, minced
3 pounds boneless beef chuck, cut into
    ½-inch cubes with some fat left on
4 dried chipotle pods, reconstituted
    (see Note) and chopped, or 2 teaspoons
    chipotle powder
½ cup pure ground hot red chile
2 tablespoons ground cumin
¼ cup dry red wine
Fixin's and Mixin's (page 34), for serving

1. Melt the bacon drippings in a large pot over medium heat. When the drippings are hot, add the onions and cook until they are translucent and starting to brown, about 5 minutes. Remove the pot from the heat and stir in the garlic and beef. Then add the chipotles, ground chile, 1 tablespoon of the cumin, and water to cover by 1 inch.

2. Return the pot to the stove over high heat. When the mixture just begins to bubble, reduce the heat to low and simmer until the meat is very tender and the flavors have blended, 2 to 3 hours.

3. Add the remaining 1 tablespoon cumin and the wine, and cook briefly. Taste, and adjust the seasonings as needed. Serve with Fixin's and Mixin's.

Note: To reconstitute the dried chipotles on the stovetop, place them in a small pot and add a dash of vinegar and water to just cover. Simmer them over low heat until soft, 30 minutes. Alternatively, place the chipotles, vinegar, and water in a quart-size microwave-safe liquid measuring cup, cover with plastic wrap, and microwave on full power for 5 minutes.

When the chiles are fork-tender, discard the water. Chop the chiles before adding them to the brew.

Texas/Two Fingers Chili

Serves 6

The recipe for this chili was given to me at a San Francisco Pillsbury Bake-Off in the mid-1970s. I cooked it up and liked the unusual taste. Tequila seems to impart a subtle tang that most brews don't possess. The recipe was prepared to promote Two Fingers, a brand of tequila—hence the name.

2 tablespoons vegetable oil (not canola)
3 pounds lean beef, coarsely ground
2 medium-size cloves garlic, finely chopped
5 tablespoons pure ground mild red chile
3 teaspoons ground cumin
1½ teapoons cayenne pepper
1 tablespoon dried Mexican oregano
Salt
2 cups silver or light tequila
½ cup masa harina (see box, page 37)
1 dried whole red chile, crushed, or
    2 tablespoons crushed caribe chile
    (optional)
1 teaspoon hot pepper sauce (optional)

1. Place the oil in a large heavy pot over medium-high heat. When it is hot, add the meat. Break up any lumps with a fork and cook, stirring occasionally, until the meat is evenly browned, about 15 minutes.

2. Stir in the garlic, ground chili, 1½ teaspoons of the cumin, the cayenne pepper, the oregano, 1 tablespoon salt, the tequila, 6 cups water, and the masa harina. Bring the mixture to a boil. Then lower the heat and simmer, uncovered, for about 1½ hours. Add more water if needed, depending on the desired texture.

3. Add the remaining 1½ teaspoons cumin. Then taste, and adjust the seasoning. If desired, add the crushed chile and the hot pepper sauce and simmer, uncovered, for 30 minutes. (If you are not adding the optional ingredients, go ahead and serve the chile without the extra cooking time.)

Nevada Annie's
Cowboy Chili

Serves 16

Laverne Harris, a.k.a. Nevada Annie, won the International Chili Society's 1978 cookoff with this delicious recipe. She urges cooks to add the most important ingredient of all: "lots of love."

⅓ cup lard
3 medium-size onions, coarsely chopped
2 green bell peppers, stemmed, seeded, and coarsely chopped
2 stalks celery, coarsely chopped
1 tablespoon finely chopped pickled jalapeño chiles (approximately 2 chiles)
8 pounds beef chuck, coarsely ground
2 cans (14½ ounces each) stewed tomatoes
1 can (15 ounces) tomato sauce with mushrooms
1 can (6 ounces) tomato paste
½ cup pure ground hot red chile
¼ cup pure ground mild red chile
2 teaspoons ground cumin
3 bay leaves
1 tablespoon hot pepper sauce
Garlic salt to taste
Onion salt to taste
Salt and freshly ground black pepper to taste
½ cup beer

1. Melt the lard in a large heavy pot over medium-high heat. Add the onions, bell peppers, celery, and jalapeños and cook, stirring, until the onions are translucent, about 5 minutes.

2. Add the meat to the pot. Break up any lumps with a fork and cook, stirring occasionally, until the meat is evenly browned, 20 to 30 minutes.

3. Stir in all the remaining ingredients, add enough water to cover, and bring the mixture to a boil. Then lower the heat and simmer, uncovered, stirring often, for 3 hours.

4. Taste, and adjust the seasonings as needed.

Wheat & Meat Chili

🌶 🌶

Serves 4

Having little meat but lots of wheat on hand, an Ogden, Utah, chili cook "stretched the stew" with wheat and liked it well enough to let me know about it. Try it if you yen for something different. Whole wheat kernels, also known as wheat berries, are available in health food stores.

1 cup whole wheat kernels, soaked
    overnight in water to cover
4 ounces beef suet, finely chopped,
    or ¼ cup lard
2 medium-size onions, coarsely chopped
1½ pounds beef, coarsely ground
2 tablespoons pure ground hot red chile
2 tablespoons pure ground mild red chile
3 medium-size cloves garlic, crushed
½ teaspoon dried Mexican oregano
2 teaspoons ground cumin
Salt
½ teaspoon crushed caribe chile
1 can (8 ounces) diced green chiles
1 can (6 ounces) tomato paste
1 jar (28 ounces) tomato juice

1. Place the wheat kernels and their soaking water in a heavy saucepan over high heat and bring to a boil. Cover and simmer for 1 hour, adding more water as the kernels cook, if necessary. Set aside.

2. Melt the suet in a large heavy pot over medium-high heat. Remove and discard the unrendered suet pieces. Add the onions to the pot, and cook until they are translucent, about 5 minutes.

3. In a large bowl, combine the beef with the ground chiles, garlic, oregano, 1 teaspoon of the cumin, and 1 teaspoon salt. Add this beef mixture to the pot. Break up any lumps of meat with a fork and cook, stirring occasionally, until the meat is evenly browned, about 10 minutes. Stir in the caribe chile, green chiles, tomato paste, and tomato juice.

4. Drain the wheat kernels, reserving their cooking liquid, and stir them into the chili. Bring to a boil. Then lower the heat and simmer, uncovered, for 1 hour, adding some of the reserved wheat liquid if the chili begins to get too dry. Taste, and adjust the seasonings as needed.

Authentic Texas Border Chili

🌶 🌶 🌶 🌶

Serves 10 to 12

The creator of this gastronomic epic hails from Brownsville, Texas, and insists that you follow his recipe to the letter!

3 medium-size tomatoes, peeled (see box, page 75), stemmed, and seeded

1 large Bermuda onion, finely chopped

¼ teaspoon dried Mexican oregano

2 teaspoons paprika

5 large cloves garlic, one whole, the rest finely chopped

4 pounds beef sirloin or round steak, coarsely ground

1 tablespoon lard, butter, or bacon drippings

4 bunches (about 24) scallions, chopped

5 green bell peppers, stemmed, seeded, and coarsely chopped

5 serrano or jalapeño chiles (fresh or pickled), stemmed, seeded, and finely chopped

1 pound cooked, sliced, drained chorizo sausage or other spicy hot sausage (not Italian sausage)

Salt

¼ cup pure ground hot red chile

¼ cup pure ground mild red chile

3 tablespoons whole cumin seeds, toasted and crushed (see Note)

Beer (optional)

1. Combine the tomatoes, onion, oregano, paprika, and 1 clove of the garlic in a blender, and puree. Scrape the mixture into a large heavy pot, add the beef, stir to combine, and set it aside.

2. Melt the lard in a heavy skillet over medium heat. Add the scallions, bell peppers, serrano chiles, chorizo, and the remaining garlic, and cook until the scallions are translucent, about 5 minutes.

3. Stir the scallion mixture into the beef-and-tomato mixture. Add 2 teaspoons salt, the ground chiles, half of the crushed cumin seeds, and enough water or beer to cover. Bring to a boil over medium-high heat. Then lower the heat and simmer, uncovered, for 4 to 6 hours.

4. Add the remaining cumin. Taste, and adjust the seasonings as needed.

Note: To prepare the cumin seeds, place them on a rimmed baking sheet and toast in a preheated 300°F oven for a few minutes, until lightly browned. Transfer the seeds to a bowl and crush them with a mallet, or crush them with a mortar and pestle.

HOT STUFF

Chili was once banned from San Antonio, Texas, schools because it was considered prison food and thus the "soup of the devil."

Hy Abernathy's Georgia Chain-Gang Chili

Serves 20

I can't guarantee that this recipe has prison chain-gang roots, but ideally it should be cooked over a 2- to 3-day period—thereby chaining you to your stove! Seriously, make sure to allow at least 4 hours of cooking time. If you go the 3-day route, marinate the beef overnight, and then on the first day, prepare the chili and cook it very slowly for 5 or 6 hours. Let it sit overnight again. Then cook it for 3 hours on the second day and again for 3 hours on the third.

This chili is hot, but not overly so. As the creator of the recipe, Hy Abernathy—a 1979 Terlinga International Chili Championship contestant—once said, "I don't think chili should bring tears to your eyes, but it should produce a few beads of sweat on the brow."

1 cup dry Burgundy wine
½ teaspoon dried thyme leaves
2 bay leaves
4 medium-size cloves garlic, finely chopped
½ teaspoon freshly ground black pepper
3 pounds beef (any cut), coarsely ground
3 pounds extra-lean beef, coarsely ground
2 large whole skinless, boneless chicken
    breasts
Salt
2 tablespoons vegetable oil (not canola)
2 medium-size onions, coarsely chopped
3 large boneless pork chops, or 1 small
    pork roast (about 2½ pounds),
    trimmed of all fat, coarsely ground
¼ to 1 cup pure ground mild red chile
1 teaspoon cayenne pepper
1 teaspoon dried Mexican oregano
½ teaspoon ground cumin
Dash of crushed dried rosemary
1½ cups canned crushed Italian-style
    tomatoes
1 can (16 ounces) tomato sauce
1 can (8 ounces) tomato sauce, preferably
    with jalapeños

1 can (4 ounces) whole mild green chiles,
    seeded and chopped
1 can (4 ounces) diced pickled jalapeño chiles
1 to 2 tablespoons hot pepper sauce
1 tablespoon butter
3 fresh whole green chiles, parched
    (see box, page 14), peeled, seeded, and
    chopped
½ cup chopped fresh mushrooms
½ cup Sauterne wine
1 can or bottle (12 ounces) beer

1. Combine the Burgundy, thyme, bay leaves, garlic, and black pepper in a large nonreactive bowl to make a marinade. Place all the beef in the bowl and mix lightly to coat the meat well. Cover, and refrigerate overnight. (If time is short, marinate for 2 hours at room temperature.)

2. Place the chicken breasts in a saucepan and add water to cover. Add 1 teaspoon salt and simmer over low heat for 30 minutes. Remove the chicken, reserving the liquid. Finely chop the chicken breasts and set aside.

3. Place the oil in a large heavy pot over medium heat. Add the onions and cook until they are translucent, about 5 minutes.

4. Meanwhile, drain the beef, straining and reserving the marinade. Mix the beef and pork together in a large bowl. Then mix in the ground chile, cayenne pepper, oregano, cumin, rosemary, and 2 teaspoons salt. Transfer the meat mixture to the large pot. Break up any lumps of meat with a fork and cook, stirring occasionally, until the meat is evenly browned, 20 to 30 minutes.

5. Add half of the reserved marinade, the reserved chicken, and the tomatoes, both tomato sauces, mild green chiles, jalapeños, and 1 tablespoon of the hot pepper sauce.

6. Place the butter in a heavy skillet over medium heat. When the butter has melted, add the parched chiles, mushrooms, and a small amount of the Sauterne and cook for 3 minutes. Transfer this to the chili pot.

7. Bring the chili to a boil. Then reduce the heat and simmer, uncovered, for at least 3 hours. While the chili is cooking, from time to time gradually stir in the remaining reserved marinade, the remaining Sauterne, and the beer. If the chili begins to cook down too much or look too dry, stir in the water the chicken was cooked in. Taste, and adjust the seasonings as needed, adding the remaining hot sauce if desired.

Australian Dinkum Chili

Serves 8

We may think chili madness is a uniquely American affliction, but it has affected another country with a cowboy culture: our friends "down under" have the same passion for chili as we Yanks. Why, they even have a National Chili Archives in Tibooburra, New South Wales, and an entire cult of chili-eaters on the auto-racing circuit.

This recipe for dinkum chili (*dinkum* is Australian slang for "authentic") won the Annual Western Australian Winter Championship Chili Cookoff at Kunanaggi Well in the late 1970s. It was created by Australia's auto-racing team. I've adapted it here for American ingredients.

8 slices bacon
2 tablespoons vegetable oil
2 medium-size onions, coarsely chopped
1 stalk celery, coarsely chopped
1 green bell pepper, stemmed, seeded, and coarsely chopped
2 pounds boneless top beef sirloin, cut into 1-inch cubes
1 pound ground beef
1 pound ground pork
¼ cup pure ground hot red chile
3 tablespoons pure ground mild red chile
2 medium-size cloves garlic, finely chopped
1 tablespoon dried Mexican oregano
1 teaspoon ground cumin
2 cans or bottles (12 ounces each) beer, preferably Australian
1 can (14½ ounces) whole tomatoes
1 boomerang (optional but authentic)
1 tablespoon brown sugar

1. Lay the strips of bacon in a large heavy skillet over medium-low heat. Fry the bacon until crisp;

then drain it on a paper-towel-lined plate. Cut the bacon into ½-inch pieces, and reserve.

2. Place the oil in a large heavy pot over medium heat. Add the onions, celery, and bell pepper, and cook until the onions are translucent, about 5 minutes.

3. In a large bowl, combine the beef and pork with the ground chiles, garlic, oregano, and cumin. Transfer the meat mixture to the pot. Break up any lumps with a fork and cook over medium heat, stirring occasionally, until the meat is evenly browned, 15 to 20 minutes.

HOT STUFF

The hottest chile in the world is India's Bhut Jolokia. Its name means "ghost chile."

4. Add the beer, tomatoes, and reserved bacon to the pot and bring to a boil. Then lower the heat and simmer, uncovered, for 1 hour.

5. Wave the boomerang over the pot 14 times, and then cook for 30 minutes. Stir the chili constantly for 3 minutes. Then taste, adjust the seasonings, and add more beer if the chili has cooked down too much or looks too dry.

6. Simmer for 2½ hours more (waving the boomerang 14 times at every 1-hour interval).

7. Stir in the brown sugar and simmer for 15 minutes longer, vigorously waving the boomerang over the pot.

The "Dinkum" Deal

Here's a list of authentic chili ingredients the likes of which you've probably never seen before. They are listed as they appear in the original recipe for Dinkum Chili.

- 500 grams wallaroo bacon
- 2 tablespoons vegetable oil
- 1 medium-size brown onion, chopped
- 1 white onion, chopped
- 2 stalks celery, chopped
- 1 green pepper, diced
- 1 kilogram coarsely chopped red kangaroo shank
- 500 grams coarsely chopped gray kangaroo steak
- 500 grams ground emu ham
- 2 cloves garlic
- 31½ grams Tasmanian light red chile
- 31½ grams Woororooka chile
- 140 grams oregano
- 1 fluid gram cumin
- 1 bottle (740m/l) Australian beer
- 1 can (0.41 liter) whole tomatoes
- 1 boomerang

First-Love Chili

⚫

Serves 2

This recipe is highly recommended for chili newcomers. It has been known to warm the cockles of the heart and secure long-lasting devotion. The cinnamon and cloves add a particularly nice flavor, but remember to remove them before serving. Although the proportions listed produce a chili-for-two (enough for one chili devotee plus one novice), they can be doubled to serve four.

1 tablespoon lard
1 large onion, finely chopped
2 medium-size cloves garlic, finely chopped
1 pound lean beef, coarsely ground
2 tablespoons pure ground red chile
    (hot or mild, or a combination to taste)
1 teaspoon celery salt
¼ teaspoon cayenne pepper
1 teaspoon ground cumin
½ teaspoon dried basil
Salt
1 can (14½ ounces) plum tomatoes,
    chopped, liquid reserved
1 small bay leaf
1 small stick cinnamon
2 whole cloves
1 green bell pepper, stemmed, seeded,
    and coarsely chopped
1 can (16 ounces) red kidney beans,
    rinsed and drained

1. Melt the lard in a large heavy pot over medium-high heat. Add the onion and garlic and cook until the onion is translucent, about 5 minutes.

2. Add the meat to the pot. Break up any lumps with a fork and cook, stirring occasionally, until the meat is evenly browned, about 5 minutes.

3. Stir in the chile, celery salt, cayenne pepper, ½ teaspoon of the cumin, the basil, 1 teaspoon salt, the tomatoes and their liquid, the bay leaf, cinnamon stick, and whole cloves. Add 3 cups water and bring the mixture to a boil. Then lower the heat and simmer, uncovered, stirring occasionally, for 2½ hours.

4. Stir in the bell pepper and kidney beans, and simmer, uncovered, for 30 minutes longer.

5. Remove the cinnamon stick, bay leaf, and if possible the cloves. Add the remaining ½ teaspoon cumin. Then taste, and adjust the seasonings as needed.

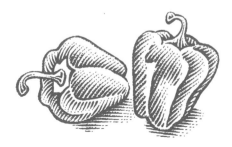

Bert Greene's
Peppered Chili

◉ ◉

Serves 4 to 6

Bert Greene, the popular food writer, contributed this recipe to the 1980 edition of *Chili Madness.* It originally appeared in his book *Kitchen Bouquets.* He considered this oven-made recipe the best of his chili collection. Serve it to strong friends—and proceed with some caution with the serrano chiles. For a real treat, layer it over the Lime Rice on page 135.

7 tablespoons butter

2 medium-size cloves garlic, finely chopped

4 onions, finely chopped

1 large green bell pepper, stemmed, seeded, and finely chopped

1¼ pounds ground beef round

1 tablespoon vegetable oil (not canola)

1½ pounds boneless beef shoulder or chuck, trimmed and cut into strips 2 inches long and ½ inch thick and wide

3 tablespoons pure ground mild red chile

3 large tomatoes, peeled (see box, page 75), stemmed, and chopped

1 teaspoon sugar

1 bay leaf, crumbled

4 fresh basil leaves, chopped, or a pinch of dried basil

Pinch of dried thyme leaves

½ teaspoon paprika

½ teaspoon cayenne pepper

½ teaspoon ground allspice

1 dried whole red chile, crushed, or 2 tablespoons crushed caribe chile

1 teaspoon soy sauce

½ teaspoon hot pepper sauce

6 serrano or jalapeño chiles (fresh or pickled), stemmed and finely chopped

½ cup dry red wine

¾ cup beef broth

1 teaspoon salt

½ teaspoon freshly ground black pepper

3 cups cooked or canned red kidney beans, rinsed and drained

1. Melt 3 tablespoons of the butter in a large heavy skillet over medium heat. Add half the garlic, half the onions, and all the bell pepper and cook until the vegetables have softened somewhat and the onion is translucent, about 7 minutes.

2. Make a large well in the center of the vegetables and place the ground beef in it. Raise the heat and cook, stirring the beef and scraping the skillet with a metal spatula. Gradually stir in the surrounding vegetables and cook until the meat is evenly browned, about 5 minutes. Transfer this mixture to a Dutch oven.

3. Place the vegetable oil and 1 tablespoon of the butter in the skillet over high heat. Reduce the heat to medium-high and add the beef shoulder, a few strips at a time. Cook, stirring, until it is well browned, 15 to 20 minutes. Transfer the strips to a plate as they are done. Lower the heat, and wipe out the skillet with a paper towel. Return the beef strips to the skillet, stir in the ground chile, and cook for 3 minutes. Transfer to the Dutch oven.

4. Melt the remaining 3 tablespoons butter in the skillet over medium heat. Add the remaining onions and garlic and cook until fragrant, 3 minutes. Stir in the tomatoes, sugar, and bay leaf and cook for 10 minutes more. Transfer the mixture to the Dutch oven.

5. Preheat the oven to 300°F.

6. Stir all the remaining ingredients, except the kidney beans, into the Dutch oven. Bake, covered, for 3 hours.

7. Stir the beans into the chili, and bake for another 30 minutes.

Cookout Chili

Serves 2

Charbroiling the meat and roasting the peppers over an open fire adds a real outdoor taste to this chili-studded brew. It can be wildly hot if spicy chiles are used, but of course, the hot-ness of the chili really depends on the heat of the peppers. If you are looking for more sizzle, choose chiles with pointy tips and narrow shoulders. For a milder brew, select broad-shouldered, blunt-tipped chiles. When preparing this chili, you'll need an outdoor grill or a grill rack set over a fire pit. Either way, it should be large and sturdy enough to support a Dutch oven.

1 pound ground beef chuck
1 green bell pepper, stemmed, seeded, and chopped
4 fresh domestic green chiles, such as Anaheims, parched (see box, page 14), stemmed, seeded, and finely chopped
1 fresh or pickled jalapeño chile, chopped
2 scallions, including tops, coarsely chopped
1 can (16 ounces) tomato sauce
½ teaspoon dried oregano, preferably Mexican
½ teaspoon ground cumin
1 teaspoon pure ground hot red chile
1 teaspoon crushed caribe chile
1 can (16 ounces) red kidney beans, rinsed and drained

1. Form the meat into 3 or 4 hamburger patties.

2. Preheat an outdoor grill to medium-high heat or about 400°F, or build a fire in a fire pit fitted with a sturdy grill rack. If building a fire, you can use firewood or charcoal. Allow about 30 minutes for the fire to become hot; when it's ready, the coals will be gray on their edges and you should be able to hold your hand over the fire only for a count of three.

3. Place the hamburgers on the grill and cook them until they are medium rare on the inside and nicely crisp on the outside, about 3 minutes per side. Set them aside to cool.

4. Lower the gas or electric grill to low heat or 250°F; or, if using a campfire, scatter the coals to cool them down. Crumble the hamburgers into a Dutch oven or large skillet, and place the Dutch oven on the grill, or over the campfire at the edge of the grill rack. Add the bell pepper, green chiles, jalapeño, scallions, tomato sauce, oregano, cumin, ground hot red chile, crushed caribe chile, and kidney beans. Simmer over the fire, stirring occasionally, until the flavor has developed and the peppers and scallions are soft, at least 30 minutes. (If cooking over a campfire, you may need to return the pot to the center of the grill rack.)

5. Taste, and adjust the seasonings as needed before serving.

Clyde's Chili

🌶 🌶 🌶
Serves 6 to 8

Easternized and somewhat

"conveniencized," the chili at Clyde's—a Washington, D.C., restaurant chain—is a favorite of the Capitol Hill set. When I used to travel frequently to the D.C. area in the late 1970s, I came to like their chili so much that I asked for the recipe. I've cut this quick-cooking recipe down from its gargantuan restaurant proportions but kept its irresistible taste.

3 tablespoons vegetable oil (not canola)
2 large onions, coarsely chopped
3 pounds beef, coarsely ground
2 tablespoons Worcestershire sauce
3 medium-size cloves garlic, finely chopped
¼ cup pure ground hot red chile
¼ cup pure ground mild red chile
2 teaspoons ground cumin
1 teaspoon dried Mexican oregano
Salt
1 can (16 ounces) kidney beans in chili sauce
1¾ cups (15 ounces) chili sauce (ketchup type)

1. Place the oil in a Dutch oven or heavy 5-quart saucepan over medium heat. Add the onions and cook until they are translucent, about 5 minutes.

2. Add the beef to the pot. Break up any lumps with a fork and cook, stirring occasionally, until the meat is evenly browned, 7 to 10 minutes. Add the Worcestershire sauce and garlic, and cook for 3 minutes.

3. Stir in the ground chiles, 1 teaspoon of the cumin, the oregano, and 2 teaspoons salt. Cook, uncovered, for 5 minutes.

4. Add the beans and chili sauce and simmer, uncovered, for 1 hour.

5. Add the remaining 1 teaspoon cumin. Taste, and adjust the seasonings as needed.

Agreeing to Disagree

Chili cookoffs and debates grow out of feuds, spats, and heated rivalries—not to mention knock-down, drag-out fights. All to answer the burning question: Who really makes the greatest chili?

New Mexicans are committed to the idea that chili must be pure: everything-but-the-kitchen-sink concoctions are unheard of, hissed and booed at and generally ignored. Traditionally, New Mexicans serve a saucy red chili puree or a green chili stew with sizable chunks of meat, usually pork, with stewed pinto beans on the side. Heavy on the chile and light on the meat, New Mexican chili never contains any additional vegetables.

Next door in Texas (and elsewhere), however, chili nearly always contains lots of coarse-ground beef, chile, garlic, cumin, and onions. It's clear that many chili heads' deeply held beliefs about the "right" brew stem from regional loyalties. Still, as chili evolves over time, you'll surely find a New Mexican who'll throw a veggie into the pot, or a Texan who'll sneak in a bean or two—just don't ask them to admit it!

Serendipity's Southern Chili

🌶 🌶

Serves 6 to 8

Eastern chili lovers flock to the Serendipity 3 general store and restaurant in New York City for this spicy chili. You can make it yourself, or visit Serendipity 3 when you're in the Big Apple.

4 tablespoons (½ stick) butter
1 large onion, coarsely chopped
3 to 4 pounds ground lean beef
½ cup pure ground hot red chile
¼ cup pure ground mild red chile
3 tablespoons ground cumin
3 medium-size cloves garlic, minced
1 tablespoon freshly ground black pepper
1 tablespoon salt
1 tablespoon sugar
1 can (14½ ounces) peeled whole tomatoes
4 cans (16 ounces each) red kidney beans, with liquid

1. Melt the butter in a Dutch oven over medium heat. Add the onion and cook until it is translucent, about 5 minutes.

2. In a large bowl, combine the meat with the ground chiles, about half of the cumin, the garlic, and the black pepper. Transfer the meat mixture to the Dutch oven. Break up any lumps with a fork and cook, stirring occasionally, until the meat is evenly browned, about 15 minutes.

3. Stir in the remaining ingredients and bring to a boil. Then lower the heat and simmer, uncovered, stirring occasionally, for at least 4 hours but as long as 8 if possible.

4. Taste and adjust the seasonings as needed, adding the remaining cumin.

ESQUIRE FORTNIGHTLY'S Eastern Establishment Chili

Serves 10 to 12

My company, Pecos Valley Spice, introduced its chile seasonings in *Esquire* magazine's 1979 chili cookoff, held at Bloomingdale's in New York City. This chili took first prize at the cookoff, in which an East Coast cook representing *Esquire* was pitted against a Texan from *Texas Monthly* magazine. I think the easterner won because he used our pure ground chiles instead of chili powder, which has a less fresh flavor.

2 cups dried red kidney beans, rinsed and picked over
⅓ cup olive oil or lard, plus more as needed

5 pounds beef brisket, cut into ½-inch cubes
2 large onions, coarsely chopped
6 large cloves garlic, finely chopped
2 green bell peppers, stemmed, seeded, and coarsely chopped
2 tablespoons dried basil
1 bay leaf
2 tablespoons pure ground mild red chile
1 tablespoon cayenne pepper
1 tablespoon crushed caribe chile
2 tablespoons ground cumin
2 tablespoons masa harina (see box, page 37)
6 cups canned tomatoes, chopped, liquid reserved
Salt and freshly ground black pepper
½ cup freshly brewed coffee

1. Place the beans in a bowl, cover with water, and soak overnight.

2. Drain and rinse the beans, discarding the soaking liquid. Place the beans in a heavy saucepan, add water to cover by 2 to 3 inches, and bring to a boil over high heat. Then lower the heat and simmer, uncovered, stirring occasionally, until tender, about 1 hour. Set the pan aside.

3. Heat the oil or melt the lard in a large heavy flameproof casserole over medium heat. Pat the brisket dry and add it to the casserole. Cook, stirring the beef often, until is quite brown on all sides, 20 to 30 minutes. Remove it from the casserole using a slotted spoon; set it aside.

4. Add more oil or lard to the casserole if needed. Then add the onions and garlic and cook until

the onions are translucent, about 5 minutes. Stir in the bell peppers, basil, bay leaf, ground chile, cayenne pepper, caribe chile, and 1 tablespoon of the cumin. Cook for about 1 minute. Then add the masa harina and cook for 1 to 2 minutes longer.

5. Return the brisket to the casserole, and add the tomatoes and their liquid. Bring the mixture to a boil. Then lower the heat and simmer, uncovered, stirring occasionally, for 2 hours.

6. Stir in salt and black pepper to taste, and adjust the other seasonings as needed. Add the coffee and simmer, uncovered, for 1 hour.

7. Add the kidney beans to the chili. Simmer, uncovered, for 30 minutes.

8. Taste and adjust the seasonings again, adding the remaining 1 tablespoon cumin. Remove the bay leaf before serving.

Gringo Chili

Serves 4

This easy recipe makes a mild chili that kids love; in bigger batches it's particularly good for children's parties.

It's a great change from the usual fare, and a fun recipe to put together with help from the kids.

2 teaspoons lard, butter, or bacon drippings
½ medium-size onion, coarsely chopped
1 pound lean beef round, coarsely ground
2 tablespoons pure ground hot red chile
1 tablespoon pure ground mild red chile
¾ teaspoon dried oregano, preferably Mexican
¾ teaspoon ground cumin
2 medium-size cloves garlic, finely chopped
2 cans (10½ ounces each) condensed tomato soup
1 can (10½ ounces) condensed onion soup
2 cans (16 ounces each) red kidney beans, rinsed and drained

1. Melt the lard in a heavy 4- to 5-quart pot over medium heat. Add the onion and cook until it is translucent, about 5 minutes.

2. In a large bowl, combine the meat with the ground chiles, oregano, cumin, and garlic. Transfer the meat mixture to the pot. Break up any lumps with a fork and cook, stirring occasionally, until the meat is evenly browned, about 5 minutes.

3. Stir in the tomato soup, onion soup, and beans, and bring to a boil. Then lower the heat and simmer, uncovered, until the liquids cook down and the mixture thickens, 30 minutes. Taste, and adjust the seasonings as needed.

Jeanne Owen's
Chili con Carne

Serves 6

Sesame, caraway seeds, and olives combine to create a unique flavor in this brew. Still very much a chili, the nutty taste brings to mind Europe and a Bavarian Octoberfest. It's a perfect dish to sit down to sometime in the autumn—maybe after raking the leaves. The preparation technique is totally Jeanne's, and she won many contests with this chili. It breaks all the rules—browning the meat and then covering it as it cooks—but the flavor is good and totally original!

⅓ cup olive oil
3 pounds lean beef round, cut into
    1-inch cubes
2 medium-size onions, finely chopped
3 medium-size cloves garlic, finely chopped
Salt
4 cups boiling water
1 teaspoon caraway seeds
2 teaspoons sesame seeds
½ teaspoon ground oregano, preferably
    Mexican
2 to 4 tablespoons pure ground red chile
    (hot, mild, or a combination)
1 cup pitted green olives
2 cans (16 ounces each) red kidney beans,
    rinsed and drained

1. Heat the oil in a large sauté pan or 6-quart braising pan over medium heat. Add the beef, a few pieces at a time, stirring to brown them evenly. As the beef browns, transfer it to a plate.

2. Add the onions to the pan and cook, stirring, for about 2 minutes. Then add the garlic. Cook until the onions are translucent, about 3 minutes longer.

3. Return the beef cubes to the pan, season with salt to taste, and then add the boiling water, caraway seeds, sesame seeds, and oregano. Bring to a boil. Then lower the heat, cover the pan, and simmer for 1 hour.

4. Gradually stir in the ground chile, tasting until you achieve the degree of heat and flavor that suits your palate. Add the olives and simmer, covered, for 1 hour.

5. Taste, and adjust the seasonings as needed. Then stir in the kidney beans and heat through.

Chocolaty Chili

Serves 2 to 3

This recipe comes from the company that brought you those great chocolate chips: Nestlé. Adding chocolate to the chili mixture gives it a Mexican mole-like flavor. We can thank the Aztecs for discovering chocolate and then adding chile to it.

2 tablespoons vegetable oil
(not canola)
1 medium-size onion, finely chopped
2 cloves garlic, finely chopped
1 pound lean beef, coarsely ground
1 can (16 ounces) red kidney beans,
rinsed and drained
1 can (16 ounces) tomato puree
1 can (6 ounces) tomato paste
4 fresh domestic green chiles,
such as Anaheims, parched
(see box, page 14), peeled, seeded,
and chopped, or 1 can (4 ounces)
chopped green chiles
2 ounces bittersweet chocolate, halved
2 tablespoons pure ground red chile
(hot, mild, or a combination)
1 teaspoon ground cumin
1 beef bouillon cube

1. Place the oil in a large skillet over medium heat. Add the onion and garlic and cook until the onion is translucent, about 5 minutes.

2. Add the meat to the skillet. Break up any clumps with a fork and cook, stirring occasionally, until the meat is evenly browned, about 5 minutes.

3. Stir in the kidney beans, tomato puree, tomato paste, green chiles, ½ cup water, 1 ounce of the chocolate, the ground chile, ½ teaspoon of the cumin, and the beef bouillon cube. Mix well and bring to a boil. Then lower heat and simmer, uncovered, stirring occasionally, for 30 minutes.

4. Stir in the remaining 1 ounce chocolate and continue cooking until it is thoroughly blended, adding water if the chili begins to cook down too much or look too dry. Taste, add the remaining ½ teaspoon cumin, and adjust the seasonings.

HOT STUFF

Much like chocolate, chile gives the body a rush similar to that from sex or a runner's high.

Murray's Girlfriend's Cincinnati Chili

Serves 6

Don Singleton, an erstwhile reporter for the New York *Daily News*, discovered Cincinnati folks to be enthusiastic "chili mavens." He gives this spicy specialty a "six-Rolaid" rating.

2 tablespoons butter
2 pounds ground beef
6 bay leaves
1 large onion, finely chopped
6 medium-size cloves garlic,
    finely chopped
1 teaspoon ground cinnamon
2 teaspoons ground allspice
4 teaspoons vinegar (any kind),
    plus more as needed
1 teaspoon crushed caribe chile
1½ teaspoons salt
2 tablespoons pure ground red chile
    (hot, mild, or a combination),
    plus more as needed
1 teaspoon ground cumin
½ teaspoon dried oregano, preferably
    Mexican
1 can (6 ounces) tomato paste
1 can (16 ounces) red kidney beans,
    rinsed and drained
8 ounces vermicelli
½ cup grated Cheddar cheese,
    for serving
1 small onion, finely chopped,
    for serving

1. Place the butter in a large heavy skillet over medium-high heat. Add the meat to the skillet. Break up any lumps with a fork and cook, stirring occasionally, until the meat is evenly browned, 5 to 7 minutes.

2. Stir in the bay leaves, onion, garlic, cinnamon, allspice, vinegar, caribe chile, salt, ground red chile, cumin, oregano, tomato paste, and 6 cups water. Taste, and adjust the seasonings: if the flavor is too sweet, add a small amount of vinegar; if it is not spicy enough, add a small amount of chile.

3. Bring the mixture to a boil. Then lower the heat and simmer, uncovered, until the flavors are well blended and the chili is thick, 2 to 4 hours.

4. Thirty minutes before serving, add the kidney beans to the mixture and continue to simmer the chili.

5. Bring a pot of salted water to a boil, add the vermicelli, and cook according to the package directions until just tender.

6. Drain the pasta and divide it among six bowls. Spoon a generous amount of chili over the pasta, removing the bay leaves as they appear. Top each bowl with grated cheese and raw onion, or pass them separately in serving bowls.

Sun Dance Chili

Serves 6

Straight from Scottsdale, Arizona—real sun country—where the sun dance is a popular Native American art motif, this veggie-heavy brew is a subtle version appealing to those who don't like chili too hot or pure (i.e., Texan: without beans, tomatoes, or other foreign objects)!

2 tablespoons lard, butter,
    or bacon drippings
1 large onion, coarsely chopped
½ stalk celery, finely chopped
1 red, green, or yellow bell pepper,
    stemmed, seeded, and finely chopped
½ cup sliced fresh mushrooms
3 pounds beef, coarsely ground
2 tablespoons pure ground hot red chile
1 tablespoon pure ground mild red chile
½ teaspoon dried Mexican oregano
1 teaspoon ground cumin
3 medium-size cloves garlic, finely chopped
1 teaspoon salt
1 can (14½ ounces) whole tomatoes,
    chopped, liquid reserved
1 can (6 ounces) tomato paste
1 can (4 ounces) whole green chiles, seeded
    and chopped
2 cans (16 ounces each) red kidney beans,
    with liquid

1. Melt the lard in a large heavy pot over medium heat. Add the onion, celery, and bell pepper and cook until the onion is translucent, about 5 minutes. Add the sliced mushrooms and cook for an additional 5 minutes.

2. In a large bowl, combine the meat with the ground chiles, oregano, ½ teaspoon of the cumin, and the garlic. Transfer the meat mixture to the pot. Break up any lumps with a fork and cook, stirring occasionally, until the meat is evenly browned, 5 to 7 minutes.

3. Stir in the salt, tomatoes and their liquid, tomato paste, and green chiles, and bring to a

Chiles: Too Hot to Handle

Before you get up to your elbows in chile peppers, fresh or dried, let me warn you: Handling those dynamos with your bare hands can lead to painful results. The capsaicin that gives the peppers their spicy flavor can also work its fiery magic on your bare skin. Remember, it's an acid!

Although folk wisdom says that buttering your hands before you get started will prevent chile burn, I haven't found this to work all that well with the spicier chiles. The one thing that does work, all the time, is wearing rubber gloves. After working with chiles, wash both your hands and your rubber gloves thoroughly with soap and water. And never, ever touch your hands to your eyes, nose, or mouth if you've been handling chiles.

If you're stubborn, as many a chilihead is, and you've ignored my warning, treat the burn as you would any other: doctor it up with a paste of baking soda and water or with a commercial burn ointment. If you have an aloe plant, break off a piece and rub the cut end against your sore skin for natural relief. But don't forget that it's always less unpleasant to prevent a burn than to treat one.

boil. Then lower the heat and simmer, uncovered, stirring occasionally, for 1½ hours.

4. Add the beans and their liquid and simmer, uncovered, for 30 minutes. Add the remaining ½ teaspoon cumin. Taste, and adjust the seasonings as needed.

Midwest Chili

Serves 10 to 12

This easy-to-prepare chili recipe calls for a combination of coarsely ground and finely ground beef, giving the finished product a nice varied texture. You might like to substitute butter beans for the pinto beans, as some midwesterners do.

3 pounds beef chuck, coarsely ground
   or cut into ½-inch cubes
2 pounds ground beef chuck
2 large onions, coarsely chopped
5 medium-size cloves garlic,
   finely chopped
1 tablespoon pure ground hot red chile
5 tablespoons pure ground mild red chile
3 tablespoons ground cumin
3 teaspoons salt
2 cans (15 ounces each) tomato sauce
2 cans (28 ounces each) diced tomatoes,
   with liquid
4 cups freshly cooked pinto beans,
   or 2 cans (16 ounces each), rinsed
   and drained

1. Place the beef, onions, and garlic in a heavy 5-quart pot or Dutch oven. Break up any lumps of meat with a fork and cook over medium heat, stirring occasionally, until the meat is evenly browned, 20 to 30 minutes.

2. Stir in the ground chiles, about half of the cumin, and the salt, thoroughly incorporating everything. Add 3 cups water, the tomato sauce, and the tomatoes, mashing them with a fork. Bring the mixture to a boil. Then lower the heat and simmer, uncovered, stirring occasionally, for about 1½ hours.

3. Add the remaining cumin. Taste, and adjust the seasonings as needed. Stir in the beans and simmer, uncovered, for 30 minutes.

Chili à la Franey

Serves 4

Well-known late chef and author
Pierre Franey devised this excellent recipe
for a chili that can be prepared in practically
no time at all. He suggested garnishing the
finished brew with sour cream and lime
wedges.

The chili is made with two types of meat:
lean beef and lean pork. If possible, ask your
butcher to grind them together.

1 pound **very lean beef, coarsely ground**
1 pound **very lean pork, coarsely ground**
1 tablespoon **olive oil**
3 large **onions, finely chopped**
1 green **bell pepper, stemmed, seeded,**
    and finely chopped
2 stalks **celery, finely chopped**
1 tablespoon **finely chopped garlic**
1 tablespoon **dried Mexican oregano**
2 **bay leaves**
2 teaspoons **ground cumin**
3 cups **tomatoes with tomato paste**
    (sometimes labeled stewed tomatoes
    in heavy puree; if unavailable,
    use 2½ cups stewed tomatoes and
    3 ounces tomato paste)
1 cup **beef broth**

½ teaspoon **crushed caribe chile**
2 tablespoons **pure ground red chile**
    (hot, mild, or a combination)
Salt and freshly ground black pepper
2 cups **cooked red kidney beans, drained,**
    or about 1 can (16 ounces), rinsed and
    drained

1. If you were unable to get the beef and
pork ground together, place the meats in a
large bowl and mix them together with your
hands to just combine.

2. Place the oil in a large heavy pot over
medium heat. Add the meat to the pot. Break
up any lumps with a fork and cook, stirring
occasionally, until it is evenly browned, 5 to
7 minutes.

3. Add the onions, bell pepper, celery, garlic,
oregano, bay leaves, and 1 teaspoon of the cumin.
Mix well. Then add the tomatoes, broth, 1 cup
water, the caribe chile, ground chile, and salt and
pepper to taste, and bring to a boil. Lower the
heat and simmer, uncovered, stirring often, for
about 20 minutes.

4. Add the beans and simmer for 10 minutes
longer. Add the remaining 1 teaspoon cumin.
Taste, and adjust
the seasoning as
needed. Remove
the bay leaves
before serving.

Santa Clara Chili

🌶 🌶 🌶 🌶
Serves 6

Pueblo Indians in New Mexico were perhaps the first chile aficionados. They were enjoying the pepper pod centuries before the Spanish arrived in the 1500s.

3 tablespoons lard
2 pounds lean beef chuck, cut into
    ½-inch cubes
3 tablespoons unbleached all-purpose flour,
    in a paper bag
1 medium-size onion, coarsely chopped
2 medium-size cloves garlic, finely chopped
5 tablespoons pure ground hot red chile
3 tablespoons pure ground mild red chile
1½ teaspoons salt
½ teaspoon dried oregano, preferably
    Mexican
Pinch of ground cumin
4 cups beef broth
6 cups Gordon's Fabulous Frijoles
    (page 130), or 6 cups canned pinto
    beans heated with 2 cloves finely
    chopped garlic, for serving

1. Melt the lard in a large heavy skillet over medium heat. Place the beef in the paper bag containing the flour, and shake the bag to coat the beef. Shake the excess flour off the beef cubes, transfer them to the skillet, and cook, stirring, until the meat is evenly browned, 15 to 20 minutes.

2. Add the onion and garlic and cook until the onion is translucent, about 5 minutes.

3. Remove the skillet from the heat and stir in the ground chiles, coating the beef-and-onion mixture evenly. Add the salt, oregano, and cumin and stir. Then add about 1 cup of the broth. Return the skillet to low heat and cook, stirring, until the mixture is smooth and thick, about 30 minutes.

4. Continue to add broth, a little at a time, stirring until all is incorporated. Cook, uncovered, until the mixture is thick and the flavors are well blended, 1 to 2 hours. Taste, and adjust the seasonings as needed.

5. Traditionally the beans are spooned into bowls and topped with the chili, but you can serve them alongside if you prefer.

A Red Chili Nightmare

🌶 🌶 🌶 🌶
Serves 4

If you're an adventurous cook and you want a batch of chili that will fill the house with fragrant wonderfulness, this gourmet delight is for you—despite its "nightmarish" ingredients list. The pinto beans must be soaked overnight before you begin.

1 cup dried pinto beans, rinsed and
    picked over
2 tablespoons lard
1 tablespoon bacon drippings
1 medium-size onion, coarsely chopped
12 ounces hot country-style pork sausage
1 pound lean beef, coarsely ground
4 cloves garlic, crushed
1 teaspoon anise seeds
½ teaspoon coriander seeds, crushed
½ teaspoon fennel seeds
½ teaspoon ground cloves
1 cinnamon stick (about 1 inch long), ground
1 teaspoon freshly ground black pepper
1 teaspoon paprika
1 whole nutmeg, ground
1 teaspoon ground cumin
2 teaspoons dried Mexican oregano, crushed
12 dried whole red chiles, or 1½ cups
    crushed caribe chile
¼ cup sesame seeds
1 cup blanched almonds, crushed fine
1½ ounces milk chocolate, broken into
    small pieces
1 can (6 ounces) tomato paste
2 tablespoons vinegar, any kind
1 tablespoon fresh lemon juice
1 soft corn tortilla (6 inches), chopped
Salt

1. Place the beans in a large bowl, add 2 to 3 cups water (enough to cover them), and soak overnight. Check the beans occasionally and add water as necessary to keep them moist.

2. Drain and rinse the beans, discarding the soaking liquid. Place them in a heavy saucepan, and add 3 to 4 cups water (enough to make a chunky soup). Bring to a boil over medium-high heat. Then lower the heat and simmer, partially covered, until the beans are cooked but still firm, about 45 minutes. Check occasionally and add more water if necessary. Drain the beans, reserving the cooking liquid.

3. Melt the lard in a heavy skillet over medium heat. Add the beans and fry them lightly in the lard until they're glossy and flecked with brown, about 10 minutes. Set the beans aside.

4. Melt the bacon drippings in a large heavy pot over medium heat. Add the onion and cook until it is translucent, about 5 minutes.

5. In a large bowl, combine the sausage and beef with the garlic, anise seeds, coriander seeds, fennel seeds, cloves, cinnamon, black pepper, paprika, nutmeg, cumin, and oregano. Add the meat mixture to the onion in the pot. Break up any lumps of meat with a fork and cook, stirring occasionally, until well browned, 12 to 15 minutes.

6. Meanwhile, if you are using the dried whole chiles, crush them and discard the stems. Place them in a small bowl, add hot water to cover, and soak until they're softened, about 30 minutes. Drain the chiles and set them aside.

7. Add the reserved bean cooking liquid to the pot. Stir in the reconstituted chiles or caribe chile and all the remaining ingredients except the salt. Bring to a boil. Then lower the heat and cook, uncovered, for 30 minutes.

8. Add the beans and simmer, uncovered, stirring occasionally, for another 30 minutes, adding water as necessary to maintain the consistency of a chunky soup.

9. Taste when your curiosity becomes unbearable. Add salt to taste, and adjust the other seasonings as needed.

New Mexican Pork Chili

🌶 🌶 🌶 🌶
Serves 6 to 8

In New Mexico, the chili meat of historic choice was pork, which was brought to the region in the early 16th century. Beef was basically not available then. As time passed and tastes evolved, many New Mexicans continued to prefer the flavor of pork with chiles—it creates a sweeter dish. I like to serve this chili in the typical New Mexican style: ladled over pinto beans, or with the beans on the side. For tradition's sake—to say nothing of great flavor—accompany the meal with hot tortillas or the sopaipilla-like Indian Fry Bread on page 143.

HOT STUFF

Mouth on fire after one chile too many? Drink milk, eat ice cream, or try something starchy, like rice or bread.

3 pounds pork shoulder, fat and bone removed (reserve the fat), cut into ½-inch cubes
1 teaspoon salt
2 medium-size cloves garlic, finely chopped
½ cup pure ground mild red chile (or a combination of mild and hot)
½ teaspoon dried oregano, preferably Mexican
3 cups chicken broth
2 teaspoons ground cumin
4 cups Gordon's Famous Frijoles (page 130), or 2 cans (16 ounces each) cooked or refried pinto beans, heated

1. Melt the pork fat in a heavy pot over medium-high heat until there is enough melted fat to coat the bottom of the pan. Remove and discard the unmelted fat.

2. Add the meat, then the salt and garlic, stirring well. Remove the pot from the heat and stir in the ground chile and oregano, coating the meat evenly with the spices. (If you are using a combination of mild and hot chiles, reserve the hot chile until step 4.) Add about 1 cup of the broth and stir well.

3. Return the pot to medium-high heat, add the remaining broth, bring to a boil, and stir. Reduce the heat and simmer, uncovered, for about 1 hour.

4. Taste, and adjust the seasonings as needed. Remove the pot from the heat, sprinkle the cumin and hot chile (if using) over the top, and stir well. Serve the chili with the frijoles on the side.

Navajo Green Chili

🌶 🌶 🌶 🌶

Serves 8 t o 12

Beware, chili novices—you may be too green for this green chili. It is a favorite of the Navajos and they like it *hot.* Go light on the chiles when starting out—you can always add more. Serve this with Bear Paw Bread (page 144) or generously buttered hot flour tortillas.

3 pounds pork shoulder, fat and bone removed (reserve the fat), cut into ½-inch cubes
⅓ cup unbleached all-purpose flour
2½ teaspoons salt
3 medium-size onions, coarsely chopped
4 medium-size cloves garlic, finely chopped
2 cans (14½ ounces each) whole tomatoes, chopped, liquid reserved
20 fresh green chiles, parched (see box, page 14), peeled, and cut crosswise into 1-inch-wide strips (to equal about 4 cups; see Note)
½ teaspoon dried Mexican oregano

1. Melt the pork fat in a heavy straight-sided 5-quart pot over medium-high heat.

2. Combine the flour and salt in a paper bag. Add the pork cubes and shake the bag to coat them with the flour. Shake the excess flour off the pork cubes. Add the pork to the pot, a third

Red vs. Green

What's the difference between red chiles and green chiles? It all depends on when in their growing cycle they were harvested. The old line about chiles is that they "all start life green." At the height of the summer growing season, green chiles appear on the plants. As summer turns to fall and the chiles ripen, their color deepens to red. Green chiles tend to be hotter on the tongue, whereas red chiles have a more pungent flavor but slightly mellower heat.

Way long ago, when chili con carne became popular with the cattle drivers, green chiles were too perishable to transport over long distances, and so they were generally unavailable. Thus the popularity of green chiles was basically restricted to the growing areas, such as New Mexico, where tons of green chiles have traditionally been consumed. It's only recently, with the wide availability of refrigerated transport, that fresh green chiles have been so easily obtained.

As with most things concerning chili and chiles, there is a huge controversy over which is best. In New Mexico, there is even the state question: "Red or green"? Waiters in traditional restaurants always ask this and natives have strong opinions about which is better. The simple answer? They are both delicious!

at a time, and cook, stirring, until the cubes are evenly browned on all sides, 2 to 3 minutes per side. As they are browned, transfer the pork cubes to a bowl and set aside.

3. Add the onions and garlic to the pot and cook, stirring occasionally, until the onions are translucent, about 5 minutes.

4. Return the pork to the pot, stir in the tomatoes, their liquid, and 3 cups water, and bring to a boil. Then lower the heat, cover the pot, and simmer for 30 minutes.

5. Uncover the pot, add the chiles and oregano, and cook for another 30 minutes. Taste, and adjust the seasonings as needed.

Note: If you can't find fresh chiles, use 2 cans (16 ounces each) whole green chiles. Drain them, seed them, and cut them crosswise into 1-inch slices.

Amarillo Chili

🌶 🌶
Serves 4

A marriage of pork and beef creates a full-flavored chili fiesta. This meaty, quasi-traditional Texan chili reflects the geography of its namesake. Amarillo is in the Texas panhandle, close to the New Mexico border, where green chiles are very popular, and also close to Oklahoma, where tomatoes and beans became staples in the chili made on long cattle drives. As you'll see, this chili incorporates those ingredients, and more.

4 slices bacon, cut into ½-inch pieces
2 medium-size onions, coarsely chopped
1 medium-size clove garlic, finely chopped
8 ounces lean pork shoulder, coarsely ground
1 pound beef round, sliced into ½-inch cubes
8 ounces beef chuck, coarsely ground
4 canned whole green chiles, seeded and chopped, or 1 can (4 ounces) chopped green chiles
1 tablespoon pure ground hot red chile, or to taste
2 tablespoons pure ground mild red chile
1 teaspoon dried oregano, preferably Mexican
1½ teaspoons ground cumin
Salt
2 cans (6 ounces each) tomato paste
1 can (16 ounces) pinto beans, rinsed and drained

1. Line a plate with paper towels. Place the bacon in a large deep, heavy pot over medium heat and fry until the bacon has rendered most of its fat, about 5 minutes. Use a slotted spoon to remove the cooked pieces to the paper-towel-lined plate, and set aside.

2. Add the onions and garlic to the bacon fat and cook until the onions are translucent, about 5 minutes.

3. Add the pork and beef to the pot. Break up any lumps of ground meat with a fork.

4. Stir in the green chiles, ground chiles, oregano, about half of the cumin, 1½ teaspoons salt, the tomato paste, and 3 cups water. Bring to a boil. Then lower the heat and simmer, uncovered, stirring occasionally, for 2 hours.

5. Taste, and adjust the seasonings as needed. Stir in the remaining cumin, the beans, and the bacon, and simmer for another 30 minutes.

Big Chief Posole Chili

Serves 12 or more

The Big Chief truck stop en route to the Four Corners region of New Mexico, just north of Albuquerque, is very near the turnoff for the Zia Indian Pueblo. For years the Big Chief has been known for its posole, which is a hearty stew of pork, chewy posole kernels (limestone-treated corn; see Sources), chiles, and spices. Posole is a dish revered by most western Native Americans and Mexican Indians. In Mexico and other regions, it is often spelled with a z instead of an s.

At the truck stop they serve it simply, as a soup with crackers. I have embellished the recipe, adding the Mexican toppings, which you won't find at the truck stop.

1 pound dry posole (use hominy in a pinch)
1½ pounds boneless pork shoulder or butt, excess fat trimmed and discarded, cut into ½-inch cubes
3 cloves garlic, minced
½ cup pure ground hot red chile, preferably from New Mexico
3 teaspoons ground cumin
1 tablespoon salt
2 cups thinly shredded fresh cabbage, for garnish (optional)
2 limes, cut into wedges, for garnish (optional)
1 avocado, pitted, peeled, and cut into cubes, for garnish (optional)
1 bunch cilantro, torn into small sprigs, for garnish (optional)

1. Place the posole in a 6-quart or larger pot and cover it with water to a depth of at least 4 inches. Bring to a boil. Then reduce the heat to medium and cook at a lively simmer, adding more water as needed to maintain a souplike consistency, until the kernels pop, 3 hours or more. (Do not add any seasonings at this point, as they can prevent the bursting of the kernels.) When the kernels are soft, remove the pot from the heat.

2. Place the pork in a cold seasoned skillet, set it over medium-high heat, and cook, without stirring, until the meat is evenly browned on the first side, about 15 minutes. Flip it over and brown on the second side for about 5 minutes. Add the pork to the posole.

3. Pour ½ inch of water into the skillet and deglaze it over medium heat, scraping up the browned bits with a spoon. Pour the browned bits and the deglazing liquid into the posole. Add the garlic, red chile, 1½ teaspoons of the cumin, and the salt. Add water to maintain a souplike consistency. Return the pot to medium heat, and simmer until the flavors blend well, at least 30 minutes.

4. Just before serving, stir in the remaining 1½ teaspoons cumin. Serve the chili in individual bowls, with the toppings in separate bowls alongside. Or serve it without the toppings, as a side dish.

Wild Game Chili

🌶 🌶 🌶 🌶
Serves 6

This is a takeoff on my favorite chili, Pecos River Bowl of Red (page 34). It's a great chili to make when out in a cabin in the woods, perhaps after hunting game. Lacking game, beef round steak, rump roast, or London broil can be substituted.

I have added lots of spices and seasonings to balance any gaminess from the meat. You can also boost the chili's flavor by "housebreaking" it with a shot of tequila just before eating it (see box, page 45)!

¼ cup bacon drippings, salt pork,
   or lard
1 large onion, chopped (about 1½ cups)
3 pounds boneless venison or antelope
   meat, cut into ½-inch cubes
6 large cloves garlic, minced
2 tablespoons pure ground mild red chile
¼ cup pure ground hot red chile,
   preferably from New Mexico
2 tablespoons crushed caribe chile,
   or to taste
1 can or bottle (12 ounces) beer
1 cup beef broth
1½ tablespoons ground cumin seeds
½ cup red dry wine
Salt
6 shots tequila (optional)
Fixin's and Mixin's (page 34),
   for serving
6 to 12 flour tortillas, warmed and
   buttered, for serving

1. Melt the drippings in a large saucepan or pot over medium-high heat. Add the onion and cook until translucent, about 5 minutes. Remove the pan from the heat and add the meat, garlic, chiles, beer, and beef broth. Stir well, and then add half of the cumin (about 2 teaspoons).

2. Return the pot to medium heat and bring to the first bubbles of a boil. Then reduce the heat and simmer, uncovered, checking the liquid and adding water as necessary to maintain a liquid broth, for 3 to 4 hours. (At this point the chili can be cooled to room temperature, covered, and refrigerated for serving later, or frozen in freezer bags or storage containers.)

3. Before serving, stir in the wine and remaining 2½ teaspoons cumin. Cook until the flavors blend, about 30 minutes. Add salt to taste and adjust the seasonings as needed. Ladle the chili into bowls, and serve each bowl with a shot of tequila on the side, if desired. Pass the Fixin's and Mixin's and the hot tortillas at the table.

Fall Veggie Chili

🌶 🌶 🌶 🌶

Serves 8

I use a beef brisket in this chili, but you can substitute almost any full-flavored cut, such as London broil, sirloin, or flank steak. Long, slow simmering is the key here—it develops the flavor of the fall vegetables. I like this hearty chili with crusty bread or warm tortillas oozing with butter.

3 tablespoons vegetable oil (not canola),
  plus more if necessary
½ cup unbleached all-purpose flour
2 teaspoons salt
Several grinds of black pepper
3 pounds beef brisket, trimmed of excess
  fat, cut into 1-inch cubes
2 cups coarsely diced carrots
3 cups coarsely diced celery
2 cups coarsely chopped onion
3 fresh green chiles, parched
  (see box, page 14), peeled, and
  coarsely chopped (about ½ cup), or
  ½ cup canned or frozen chopped
  green chiles
3 large russet potatoes, halved and
  cut into large chunks
¼ cup pure ground mild red chile
¼ cup pure ground hot red chile

1. Place the oil in a large pot over medium-high heat. Stir the flour, salt, and pepper together in a wide, shallow dish. Dredge the beef pieces in the seasoned flour, dusting off the excess, and carefully lower them into the hot oil. Cook the beef, in batches, until it is browned on all sides, allowing each side to brown before turning it, about 10 minutes for the first side and 5 minutes for each of the other sides. (To enhance the browning, do not overcrowd the pot; brown only as many pieces as will fit in a single layer.) When the beef is browned, transfer it to a plate and repeat with the next batch, adding more oil if necessary.

2. Return the browned beef to the pot. Add 8 cups water and the carrots, celery, onion, and green chiles. Bring to a boil. Then reduce to a simmer and cook, uncovered, for 2 hours.

3. Add the potatoes and the ground chiles, and cook for 30 minutes more. Taste the chili and adjust the seasonings as needed.

Chickie Veggie Chili

Serves 6 to 8

This chili has a wonderful flavor that's reminiscent of gumbo but without the okra or filé. I made it the first time with end-of-the-season garden vegetables, of which I had considerable amounts. If you want to double up some of the vegetables or use substitutes, it will still be very good!

2 tablespoons olive oil
2 large whole boneless, skinless chicken
    breasts, cut into ¾-inch dice
    (about 6 cups)
1 large onion, chopped
3 cloves garlic, minced
2 stalks celery, sliced crosswise into
    ¼-inch pieces
8 to 10 fresh green chiles, parched
    (see box, page 14), peeled, and cut
    crosswise in ½-inch pieces, or 2 cups
    canned or frozen chopped green chiles
6 large ripe tomatoes, peeled
    (see box, page 75) and chopped
4 chicken-apple (or similar) sausages, sliced
2 cups whole-kernel corn (from 2 to 3 ears
    fresh, or use canned or frozen)
1 head broccoli, chopped
1 can (15 ounces) black beans
    (about 2 cups), rinsed and drained
2 cups chopped cabbage
    (about ½ small head)
2 large carrots, sliced into ¼-inch-thick
    rounds
2 cups chicken broth, plus more if needed
Crusty bread, for serving
Olive oil or butter, for serving

1. Place the oil in a large pot (5 quarts or larger) over medium-high heat. Add the chicken pieces and cook, stirring occasionally, until lightly browned, 5 minutes. Add the onion and garlic, and cook until the onion is translucent, about 5 minutes.

2. Add the remaining ingredients, except the bread and oil, cover the pot, and cook over medium-low heat until the vegetables are done, about 30 minutes. If the chili is too thick, stir in water or additional chicken broth until the desired consistency is achieved. Cook for 5 minutes more.

3. Taste the chili and adjust the seasonings as needed. Serve with the crusty bread and olive oil or butter.

How to Peel Tomatoes

The easiest way to get tomatoes out of their notoriously thin, delicate skins is with a method called blanching—quickly submerging the tomatoes in boiling water—which loosens the skin just enough to let the flesh slip away easily.

Bring a large pot of water to a boil. While the water is heating, prepare an ice water bath: Fill a large bowl or pot about halfway with cold water and ice cubes, leaving room for the tomatoes to eventually be added.

When the water reaches a boil, cut a shallow X in the bottom of each tomato, just breaking through the skin. When all the tomatoes have been cut, plunge them in the boiling water for 15 to 20 seconds. Using a tool such as a spider, a mesh strainer, or a slotted spoon, immediately transfer the tomatoes to the ice water bath to halt the cooking. When the tomatoes are cool to the touch, peel off their skins with your fingers or with the tip of a knife.

If you're peeling a large quantity of tomatoes, work in batches: Too many tomatoes added to the hot water at once will lower the temperature, minimizing the effect of the blanch. When working in batches, be sure to maintain the temperature of the ice water bath, as well—add new ice cubes as the old ones melt.

Blue Heaven Chili

Serves 2 to 4

Blue cheese is an unlikely ingredient in conventional chili, although other types of cheese have long been chili "tamer downers" and a favorite fixin' and mixin' (see page 34). Since I have always really liked blue cheese in any form, I decided to see if its wonderful flavor would give a great-tasting "edge" to chili—and it sure does. Try it!

2 tablespoons bacon drippings
    or butter
1 cup chopped onion
2 cloves garlic, minced
1 large whole boneless, skinless
    chicken breast, cut into ½-inch dice
    (2 to 2½ cups)
3 cups rich chicken broth (see Note)
4 to 6 fresh green chiles, parched
    (see box, page 14), peeled, and coarsely
    chopped, or 1 cup canned
    or frozen chopped green chiles
1 medium russet potato, unpeeled, diced
½ teaspoon salt, or to taste
½ cup crumbled blue cheese
    (blue cheese, Gorgonzola, Roquefort,
    or Stilton will work well)

1. Melt the bacon drippings in a large pot over medium heat. Add the onion and cook until it is translucent, about 5 minutes.

2. Add the garlic and chicken and cook, stirring, until the chicken begins to brown, about 4 minutes.

3. Add the broth, green chiles, and potato to the pot. Simmer until the chicken is cooked through and the potatoes can be pierced with a fork, 30 to 40 minutes.

4. Taste the chili and adjust the seasonings as needed, adding salt to taste (many chicken broths and bouillons are so loaded with salt that none is needed). Spoon the chili into individual bowls, and scatter the blue cheese over the top of each serving.

Note: To make "rich" chicken broth, simply simmer regular chicken broth (canned or homemade) over medium heat until it is reduced by half, 15 to 20 minutes (in this case you would begin with 6 cups broth and cook it down to 3).

Chili Talks Turkey

😈 😈

Serves 4 to 6

Leftover turkey lends itself to spices. The only trick to incorporating it in chili is to avoid overcooking it. In this chili the turkey is added during the last 5 minutes or so of cooking time, just before serving. If you don't have leftover turkey on hand, you can use ground turkey sautéed in a bit of oil until cooked through, or diced turkey tenders simmered in chicken broth for about 15 minutes, until just done.

2 tablespoons vegetable oil
   (not canola)
1 medium-size onion, chopped
   (about 1 cup)
2 cloves garlic, minced
3 or 4 fresh green chiles, parched
   (see box, page 14), peeled,
   and chopped, or ½ cup canned
   or frozen chopped green chiles
¼ cup crushed caribe chile, preferably
   from New Mexico (see Sources)
3 cups chicken broth
1 can (15½ ounces) pinto beans,
   rinsed and drained
2 teaspoons ground cumin
3 cups cooked diced or ground turkey
   (about 1½ pounds; see headnote)
8 to 12 corn tortillas, warmed,
   for serving (optional)

1. Place the oil in a large pot over medium heat. Add the onion and cook until it is translucent, about 5 minutes. Add the garlic, green chiles, caribe chile, broth, beans, and 1 teaspoon of the cumin. Cook, uncovered, until the flavors blend, about 15 minutes.

2. Add the turkey and cook for about 5 minutes. Add the remaining 1 teaspoon cumin, taste, and adjust the seasonings as needed. Serve with warm corn tortillas if desired.

Chorizo Turkey Chili

🌶️ 🌶️

Serves 4 to 6

When you have leftovers

around Thanksgiving time, consider making this spicy turkey chili—it's perfect for cold fall nights. You can create your own turkey stock from the leftover bones or, if you feel pressed for time, use prepared turkey or chicken broth. Vary the other ingredients to suit your taste, or add a starchy vegetable, corn, or beans to make this a satisfying one-bowl dinner.

8 ounces chorizo sausage, casings removed
    and discarded, meat coarsely chopped
1 large onion, chopped
2 cloves garlic, minced
6 cups turkey or chicken stock
1 can (15 ounces) garbanzo, pinto,
    or black beans, rinsed and drained
1 can (14½ ounces) diced tomatoes,
    with their liquid
2 tablespoons chopped pickled jalapeño
    chiles, or to taste
3 tablespoons mild or hot pure ground
    red chile
3 teaspoons ground cumin
3 corn tortillas (6 inches each),
    sliced into thin strips, for garnish
    (optional)
3½ cups coarsely chopped cooked turkey
2 tablespoons coarsely chopped fresh
    cilantro, for garnish (optional)

1. Place the chorizo in a large saucepan or pot over medium heat and cook until nicely browned, about 5 minutes. Drain off most of the visible fat, leaving a thin coating on the bottom of the pan.

2. Add the onion and cook, stirring, until it is translucent, about 5 minutes. Stir in the garlic, followed by the stock, beans, tomatoes, jalapeños, ground chile, and 1½ teaspoons of the cumin. Simmer, uncovered, for about 15 minutes.

3. Meanwhile, if you are using the optional tortilla garnish, preheat the oven to 425°F.

4. Arrange the tortilla strips, if using, in a single layer on a baking sheet and bake until crisp, 8 to 10 minutes.

5. Add the turkey to the chili and simmer until the flavors blend, about 5 minutes. Add the remaining 1½ teaspoons cumin and simmer briefly.

6. Spoon the chili into bowls, and garnish with the cilantro and tortilla strips if you wish.

A World of Innovations

Chile has come a long way since the first cookoffs of the late 1960s. The tried-and-true red chile–flavored ground beef brews have given way to a variety of eccentric concoctions. Even at the most old-fashioned chili cookoffs, you can find chilies containing all manner of ingredients from seafood to poultry, not to mention a whole range of vegetables and cheeses. And with our shrinking world, ethnic influences from the far corners of the globe have found their way into chili. For a far-flung twist on the classic pot, try the Clam and Green Chile Chili (facing page) or the Moroccan Chili (page 86).

Turkey Tetrazzini Chili

🌶️ 🌶️

Serves 4

A favorite leftover turkey dish—tetrazzini—with a chili twist. Tetrazzini is a casserole in which turkey or chicken is layered with cooked thin spaghetti and a sherried mushroom sauce (according to legend, it was first created as a treat for an opera singer of the same name). This souplike chili has the same basic ingredients, plus green chile. I really prefer using fresh chiles here—they're more attractive than the canned or frozen varieties.

1 tablespoon olive oil
1 medium-size onion, chopped (about 1 cup)
1 clove garlic, minced
6 to 8 fresh green chiles, parched (see box, page 14), peeled, and sliced into ¾-inch-wide ribbons (to equal 1 cup), or 6 to 8 ounces canned or frozen chiles (see headnote)
3 cups chicken broth
1 cup sliced fresh mushrooms
4 ounces vermicelli or thin spaghetti
3 teaspoons ground cumin
¼ cup dry sherry
3 cups diced cooked turkey (about 1½ pounds)
1 wedge Romano or Parmesan cheese (4 ounces)
4 sprigs Italian (flat-leaf) parsley, for garnish
8 grissini (thin, seedless Italian bread sticks), for garnish

1. Place the oil in a large pot over medium heat. Add the onion and cook, stirring, until it is translucent, about 5 minutes. Add the garlic, chiles, broth, mushrooms, vermicelli, and 1½ teaspoons of the cumin. Cook, uncovered, until the flavors blend, about 15 minutes. Stir in the sherry.

2. Add the turkey and cook for about 5 minutes. Then add the remaining 1½ teaspoons cumin. Taste, and adjust the seasonings as needed.

3. Ladle the chili into bowls, and use a vegetable peeler to slice curls of cheese over the chile. Garnish each serving with a sprig of parsley and 2 grissini, crisscrossed and poking out of the bowl.

Clam and Green Chile Chili

Serves 4 to 6

Clams are definitely an unusual chili ingredient! I have always loved New England–style clam chowder and thought, why not marry those flavors with the mild taste of green chiles and the spicy pep of chorizo? The combination works, and I think you will enjoy it, too.

8 ounces Mexican chorizo sausage, casings removed and discarded, meat chopped
1 cup chopped onion
2 large russet potatoes, unpeeled, diced
3 large fresh green chiles, parched (see box, page 14), peeled, and chopped, or ½ cup canned or frozen chopped green chiles
2 jalapeño chiles, stemmed, seeded (if you wish to reduce the heat), and minced
3 cloves garlic, minced
2 teaspoons ground cumin

1 can (15 ounces) whole-kernel corn
2 cups chicken broth
6 corn tortillas (6 inches each), cut into very thin strips, for garnish
2 cans (6 ounces each) chopped clams
Salt (optional)
Pequin quebrado (optional)

1. Place the chorizo in a 5-quart pot over medium heat and cook, stirring, until it begins to brown and render some of its fat, about 5 minutes. Remove most of fat with a spoon, leaving a thin layer on the bottom of the pot.

2. Add the onion to the pot and cook, stirring, until it is translucent, about 5 minutes. Add the potatoes, both chiles, garlic, 1 teaspoon of the cumin, the corn, and the chicken broth. Simmer until the potatoes are tender, about 20 minutes.

3. While the chili is simmering, preheat the oven to 425°F.

4. Arrange the tortilla strips in a single layer on a baking sheet and bake until crisp, 8 to 10 minutes. During the first few minutes of baking time, twist the strips with a large fork to make them spiral. Set aside.

5. Add the clams and remaining 1 teaspoon cumin to the chili and simmer for 5 minutes more. Taste, and adjust the seasoning as needed, adding salt if desired. To serve, ladle the chili into soup bowls and top each serving with a stack of tortilla strips. Then sprinkle with pequin quebrado if desired. Or pass the pequin at the table for those who wish to spice things up themselves.

White Lobster Chili

Serves 4

Lobster is such an elegant seafood—it should be handled carefully and never overcooked. Before adding the lobster, take great care with the chili to get the base well prepared, making sure it's seasoned just right (if you play with the seasonings while the lobster simmers, you risk overcooking it).

2 lobster tails (6 to 8 ounces each),
    fresh or frozen (see Note)
2 teaspoons butter
2 tablespoons vegetable oil
    (not canola)
1 large onion, chopped
2 cloves garlic, minced
1 bunch fresh kale or spinach,
    well washed and cut into
    1-inch-wide ribbons (about 2 cups)
2 cans (15 ounces each) cannellini
    Great Northern beans, or navy beans,
    rinsed and drained
2 teaspoons pequin quebrado
3 cups chicken broth or fish stock

1. Preheat the broiler. If you are using an electric broiler, position the rack 3 to 4 inches from the heat; if using a gas broiler, position the rack 1 inch from the heat.

2. Using a sharp, heavy knife or kitchen shears, cut down the underside of each lobster tail all the way through the meat and almost to the upper shell. Spread 1 teaspoon of the butter on the exposed meat of each lobster tail. Place the tails, shell side down, on a small rimmed baking sheet. Broil until the lobster meat just turns white and is no longer translucent and the shell is red, 3 to 4 minutes. Be careful not to overcook.

3. Set the lobster tails aside until they are cool enough to handle. Then pull the meat out of the shells and cut it into ½-inch cubes. Set it aside.

4. Heat the oil in a large pot over medium-high heat. Add the onion and garlic and cook until the onion is translucent, about 5 minutes.

5. Stir in the kale, cover the pot, and cook until the greens are soft, about 15 minutes (about 3 minutes if using spinach). Add the beans, pequin quebrado, and stock and simmer, uncovered, to marry the flavors, about 5 minutes. Taste and adjust the seasonings as needed.

6. Stir the lobster into the vegetable mixture and cook until it is heated through, about 5 minutes. Serve immediately.

Note: If using frozen lobster, thaw it in the refrigerator for a day; or if you need it sooner, thaw it in cold water until the flesh is somewhat soft, about 2 hours.

Mexican Tortilla Chili

Serves 4 to 6

Similar to tortilla soup, this spicy veggie chili is delicious. It is made in the Mexican style, whereby the vegetables are grilled prior to being added to the soup—the grilled veggies have deeper, mellower flavors than their raw counterparts. The soup is made in two parts: the flavorful broth is prepared first and then poured over the vegetables.

If you wish to make this a vegetarian dish, simply substitute vegetable broth for the chicken broth.

FOR THE CHILI BROTH:
8 large tomatoes, stemmed
2 large Spanish onions, peeled
    and halved
6 large Mexican garlic cloves, peeled
    (see Note)
1 quart chicken or vegetable broth
    (canned is fine)
1 teaspoon chipotle powder, or
    2 dried chipotles, reconstituted
    (see Note)
1 piece (2 inches) cinnamon, preferably
    canela (see Sources)
Salt (optional)

FOR THE CHILI VEGETABLES:
2 pounds butternut squash (1 medium
    squash), peeled, seeded, and cubed
1 teaspoon ground dried Mexican oregano
1 can (15 ounces) black beans, drained
    and rinsed
1 can (15 ounces) garbanzo beans
    (chickpeas), with liquid
1 small bunch Swiss chard, stemmed,
    sliced into 1-inch-wide ribbons
    (about 1 cup)
1 teaspoon ground cumin

FOR SERVING:
1 lime
Corn tortillas, warmed (optional)

1. Prepare the broth: Score an X into the bottom of each tomato, cutting just through the skin. Place the tomatoes, onions, and garlic on a comal or other heavy griddle over medium-high heat and cook, turning, until the vegetables char on all sides, about 10 minutes. (Remove the garlic as soon as it browns a bit.) Transfer the vegetables to a plate and set them aside.

2. Place the chicken broth in a large Dutch oven or small stockpot over high heat. Add the chipotle powder and bring to a boil. Then reduce the heat, cover the pot, and simmer for 5 minutes.

3. Meanwhile, peel and chop the tomatoes. Chop the onions, removing any blackened spots, and mince the garlic.

4. Add the tomatoes, onions, and garlic to the broth, along with the canela. Simmer to blend the flavors, about 10 minutes. Remove the canela, taste the broth, and adjust the seasonings as needed, adding salt if desired. Keep warm.

5. Prepare the chili vegetables: Bring 4 cups salted water to a boil in a large saucepan. Add the squash and oregano, cover the pan, and simmer until the squash is tender, about 15 minutes. Add the black beans, garbanzo beans, chard, and cumin and cook, uncovered, until the chard is limp and tender, about 10 minutes. Drain the vegetables, reserving the cooking water.

6. Cut the lime into quarters or sixths, depending on the number of servings. Squeeze a wedge of lime into the bottom of each individual bowl. Divide the vegetables among the bowls, and ladle the broth over them, covering the vegetables. (If the broth has become too stewlike, use the reserved vegetable cooking liquid to thin it to a soupier consistency.) Serve with warm corn tortillas, if desired.

Notes: Before using dried chipotles, you must reconstitute them. To do so on the stovetop, place them in a small pot and add a dash of vinegar and water to just cover. Simmer them over low heat until soft, 30 minutes. Alternatively, place the chipotles, vinegar, and water in a quart-size microwave-safe liquid measuring cup, cover with plastic wrap, and microwave on full power for 5 minutes.

When the chiles are fork-tender, discard the water (or reserve it for later use in marinades and salad dressings) and mince the chiles.

I've called for Mexican garlic here because it has a complex flavor and its large cloves are easy to peel.

Vegetarian Chili

Serves 6 to 8

What to do when vegetarian friends or relatives are coming to dinner? Good news: they need not go chili-less. This recipe provides the hearty, spice-infused taste of chili plus the benefit of complete protein from the combination of beans and bulgur. It's also full of flavorful, healthful vegetables: onions, garlic, celery, carrots, bell peppers, and tomatoes. Serve this brew topped with crumbly cheese, such as queso blanco or feta, for additional protein and flavor.

2½ cups dried kidney beans, soaked overnight in water to cover
3 teaspoons salt
1 cup tomato juice
1 cup bulgur (see Note)
2 tablespoons olive oil
2 medium-size onions, coarsely chopped
4 medium-size cloves garlic, minced
3 stalks celery, coarsely chopped
3 carrots, coarsely chopped
3 or 4 tomatoes, peeled (see box, page 75), seeded, and coarsely chopped
1 tablespoon fresh lemon juice
2 tablespoons pure ground hot red chile
3 tablespoons pure ground mild red chile
½ teaspoon dried Mexican oregano
1 teaspoon dried basil
1 teaspoon ground cumin
Freshly ground black pepper
1½ green bell peppers, stemmed, seeded, and coarsely chopped
4 ounces queso blanco or feta cheese, crumbled, for serving (optional)

1. Drain the kidney beans, place them in a large heavy pot, and add water to cover. Add 1 teaspoon of the salt and bring to a boil over high heat. Lower the heat and simmer the beans, partially covered, until tender, about 1 hour. Watch the water level and add more water, if necessary, to keep the beans from scorching.

2. Meanwhile, place the tomato juice in another saucepan and bring to a boil over medium heat. Once it has reached a boil, immediately remove it from the heat and add the bulgur. Cover and let stand until the bulgur softens but is still slightly crunchy, 15 minutes.

3. Heat the olive oil in a large heavy pot over medium heat. Add the onions and garlic and cook until the onions are translucent, about 5 minutes. Stir in the celery, carrots, tomatoes, lemon juice, ground chiles, oregano, basil, ½ teaspoon of the cumin, black pepper to taste, and the remaining 2 teaspoons salt. Cover the pot and cook until the vegetables are nearly tender, 10 to 15 minutes. Add the bell peppers, cover, and cook for another 10 minutes.

4. Add the kidney beans, the water in which they cooked, and the bulgur to the vegetables. Stir the mixture thoroughly, cover the pot, and simmer over low heat, stirring occasionally to make sure the bulgur does not stick to the bottom of the pot, for 30 minutes. The chili may be thick—add more water as necessary.

5. Taste the chili and adjust the seasonings as needed. Ladle the chili into bowls and sprinkle the cheese on top, if desired.

Note: Bulgur is available at some supermarkets and most health food stores. If bulgur is not available, cracked wheat can be substituted.

Butternut Squash and Black Bean Chili

Serves 6

This vegetarian chili is definitely a far cry from the hearty beef red chili often known as chili con carne. The butternut squash, which just happens to be the most nutritious of all squash varieties, is a flavorful accent to the black beans and kale, and makes this brew as healthy as a multivitamin. This chili is already pretty quick to put together, and if you use a pressure cooker, you'll be enjoying it in no time!

HOT STUFF

If you haven't got time for the pain but love that chile taste, try mild chiles like cherry peppers and pepperoncini.

¼ cup vegetable or olive oil
1 medium-size butternut squash, peeled, seeded, and diced (about 4 cups)
1 medium-size onion, chopped
4 cloves garlic, minced
4 cups vegetable broth
1 can (15½ ounces) black beans, drained and rinsed
1 medium-size bunch kale, well rinsed and sliced crosswise into 1-inch-wide ribbons (about 1½ cups)
3 jalapeño chiles, stemmed, seeded (if you wish to reduce the heat), and minced
½ teaspoon coriander seeds
½ teaspoon dried Mexican oregano, or to taste
½ teaspoon pequin quebrado, or to taste
1½ teaspoons ground cumin, or to taste
2 tablespoons sour cream, or to taste, for garnish
6 lime wedges, for garnish

1. Place the oil in a pressure cooker or in a large heavy pot over high heat. Add the squash, onion, and garlic and cook, stirring, until the onion is translucent, about 5 minutes.

2. Add the broth, beans, kale, jalapeños, coriander, oregano, pequin quebrado, and ¾ teaspoon of the cumin. If using a pressure cooker, seal the cooker, reducing the heat to low or to maintain steam, and cook according to the manufacturer's instructions for vegetables. If the kale is not tender when you remove the lid of the pressure cooker, continue cooking, without sealing the cooker, until it is soft, 5 to 10 minutes more.

If using a standard pot, bring the mixture to a boil. Then reduce the heat, cover the pot, and simmer for 30 minutes. Check the kale: if it is not quite tender, re-cover the pot and continue cooking until it is soft, 5 to 10 minutes.

3. Add the remaining ¾ teaspoon cumin and adjust the seasonings as needed. Ladle the chili into individual bowls, and serve each with a dollop of sour cream and a lime wedge.

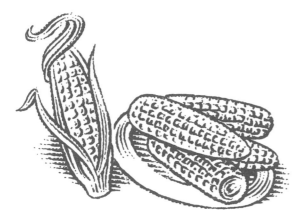

Corn and Bacon Chowder-Chili

🌶️ 🌶️

Serves 2 to 4

The smoky flavor of bacon adds character to almost any chili, soup, or stew, and here, paired with corn and potatoes, it makes this chili extra-special. For a veggie version, simply skip the bacon, use 3 tablespoons olive or vegetable oil to sauté the vegetables, and add a drop or two of liquid smoke.

6 slices bacon, cut crosswise into
 ½-inch-wide pieces
2 cups chopped onions
3 cups diced unpeeled russet potatoes
 (2 to 3 potatoes)

4 fresh green chiles, parched, peeled,
 stemmed, and chopped, or 1 can
 (4 ounces) chopped green chiles
4 fresh red chiles, parched
 (see box, page 14), peeled,
 stemmed, and chopped (see Note)
2 cups fresh, frozen, or canned corn
 (if fresh, cut from 1 large ear of corn)
2 cups chicken broth
2 cups whole milk
½ cup heavy (whipping) cream or
 evaporated skim milk
1½ teaspoons ground cumin
1 teaspoon salt, or to taste
Hot pepper sauce (optional)
1 teaspoon crushed caribe chile

1. Place the bacon in a large saucepan or pot over medium to medium-low heat, and cook until it is crisp, 3 to 5 minutes. Transfer the bacon to a paper-towel-lined plate and set it aside.

2. Drain most of the bacon drippings from the saucepan, leaving just a thin layer on the bottom. Add the onions and potatoes and cook, stirring, until the onions are translucent and the potatoes are slightly browned around the edges, 5 to 7 minutes.

3. Add the green and red chiles, corn, broth, milk, and cream and stir well. Add the cumin and salt, cover the pan, and simmer until the potatoes are tender, about 10 minutes.

4. Stir in the bacon. Taste the chili and adjust the seasonings as needed, adding hot pepper sauce to taste (you can also pass it at the table, if you prefer). Serve sprinkled with the caribe chile.

Note: If you can't find fresh red chiles, chop 1 jar (4 ounces) drained pimiento strips and add several drops hot pepper sauce.

Moroccan Chili

Serves 4

A simple Middle Eastern lentil soup-stew, this is great for vegetarians. It can also be a winner for meat-lovers—simply add a ham hock while the lentils cook in step 2, and then stir some chopped ham into the pureed lentils in step 3.

1 tablespoon olive oil
1 cup chopped onion
3 large cloves garlic
8 ounces red lentils, rinsed and
**   picked over**
1 teaspoon salt, or to taste

Freshly ground black pepper
2 teaspoons ground cumin
Hot pepper sauce
¼ cup plain yogurt, for garnish
8 to 12 cilantro sprigs, for garnish

1. Place the oil in a large saucepan over medium-high heat. When the oil is hot, add the onion and cook, stirring, until it is browned, 7 to 10 minutes. Add the garlic and cook briefly.

2. Add the lentils and enough water to cover them by 1 inch. Add the salt, a few grinds of pepper, and 1 teaspoon of the cumin. Stir well, cover the pan, and simmer until the lentils are tender, at least 20 minutes.

3. When the lentils are tender, carefully transfer them, and their cooking liquid, to a blender and process until smooth. Return the pureed lentils to the pan and simmer for about 5 minutes. Add the remaining 1 teaspoon cumin. Taste the chili and adjust the seasonings as needed, adding hot pepper sauce to taste (if you prefer, you can pass the hot sauce at the table).

4. Ladle the chili into bowls, and top each serving with a dollop of yogurt and a few sprigs of cilantro.

3

Chili Encores

Chili is festive party and family food. It's best suited to be made in large batches—often gargantuan ones! The savory simultaneity of flavors is perfect for large proportions, big crowds, and endless servings. And so there will come a time when you, as every chili-maker does, open the fridge and find yourself confronted with a big pot of cooled-down goodness, just waiting to be warmed back up and eaten. Although there's nothing wrong (and a whole lot right) with just reheating the leftovers for another round of bowls of blessedness, there's plenty you can do to reincorporate your leftovers (or, as I like to think of them, encores waiting to happen) into something that takes on a slightly different form.

That's what this chapter is here for: inspired ideas for taking your chili and re-serving it in a new context. From simple and perfect Chili Scramble—good for breakfast any time of day—to refined platters of Green Chili Fettucine, chili turns out to be as much a versatile ingredient as it is a starring player in its own right. Here you'll find chili encores that take you everywhere—across the map, throughout the day, to any occasion. Make weeknight dinners easy with

Chili-Chile Farfalle Toss, a quick and simple dish that's as zesty as it is comforting. For a casual barbecue, Chili Burgers Supreme just can't be topped. Of course, classic chili casseroles—Enchilada Casserole with its rich saucy flavor, Crazy Chili Casserole, and Baked Chili with Beans—all prove that when that spicy chili meets a hot oven, it becomes a thing of magic. And there's a phalanx of pies: Texas-Style Tamale Pie, Upside-Down Chili Pie, and that undeniable American classic, the Frito Pie.

As far as I'm concerned, you can't do a taco or burrito much better than to fill it up with chili, so just to make sure things are done right, here you'll find recipes for Chili Tacos, Navajo Tacos, Texas-Style Burritos, and more.

It's a rare exception that one of these recipes relies exclusively on one type of chili and no other, but when one does, I've made a point of noting it. Since chili is such a matter of personal taste, most of these recipes can be used with any sort of bowl o' red (or bowl of any other color) that you've had made up. What matters is that you're keeping the chili ball rolling.

SOME LIKE IT HOT . . .
These icons show how fiery each dish is.

MILD

A BIT OF BITE

HOT

HOT ENOUGH TO MAKE YOU . . .

Chili Scramble

Serves 4

I grew up eating this dish for breakfast, or in the afternoon as a light meal. When I was a child, my mother would buy a product called Chili Stick in the cold cuts section of the grocery store, and she would incorporate it into this dish. Chili Stick was a somewhat fatty, compressed chili con carne; there's now something called chili brick (which is quite similar) on the market. If you don't have homemade chili on hand—I like red chili here—and if you can find chili brick, you can still make this dish by substituting the chili brick measure for measure. This flavorful scrambled egg dish can be served as is or wrapped in a flour or corn tortilla.

8 eggs
2 tablespoons milk
1 tablespoon butter
½ cup red chili or chili brick
Sour cream, for garnish (optional)
Chopped scallions, including tops,
    or onion, for garnish (optional)
Grated Cheddar or Monterey Jack
    cheese, or a combination,
    for garnish (optional)

1. Place the eggs in a medium bowl and beat until scrambled. Add the milk and beat to incorporate it.

2. Melt the butter in a skillet over medium-low heat. Add the eggs and stir them a bit with a spatula. When the eggs begin to set, stir in the chili and cook, stirring, until the eggs are cooked to your liking.

3. Top the scramble with sour cream, chopped scallions, and grated cheese, if you wish. Serve immediately.

Migas

Serves 4

Migas is a dish that originated in the Andalusian region of Spain. In its Spanish form, leftover crumbs or chunks of bread (*migas* means "crumbs" in Spanish) are fried with garlic and combined with ham or chorizo. In Tex-Mex cooking, migas has evolved into a popular dish that still incorporates crumbs—in the form of tortilla chips or broken stale tortillas—that are mixed into scrambled eggs, often along with onions, chiles, and cheese. Traditionally, Tex-Mexican migas have been a breakfast or brunch dish, but now they're also commonly served as a light meal later in the day.

In this recipe I offer the Tex-Mex version with a Spanish twist, where meaty chili stands in for the Spanish ham or chorizo. To make these migas vegetarian, simply substitute the Vegetarian Chili on page 82.

2 tablespoons olive oil or butter
⅓ cup finely chopped onion
4 corn tortillas (6 inches each),
    torn into small pieces
8 eggs, beaten
½ cup thick, meaty chili, such as
    Pecos River Bowl of Red (page 34)
    or Amarillo Chili (page 70)
⅔ cup grated mixed Monterey Jack
    and Cheddar cheeses
2 fresh green chiles, stemmed, seeded
    (if you wish to reduce the heat), and
    chopped (about ¼ cup), or half of a
    4-ounce can of chopped green chiles
1 small avocado, pitted, peeled, and
    coarsely chopped, for garnish (optional)
¼ cup salsa, for garnish (optional)
Sour cream, for garnish (optional)
Cilantro sprigs, for garnish (optional)
Chopped tomato, for garnish (optional)

1. Place the oil in a large sauté pan over medium heat. Add the onion and tortilla bits and cook, stirring, until the onion is translucent and the tortilla bits are somewhat crisp, about 5 minutes.

2. Stir in the eggs. Then add the chili, cheeses, and green chiles. Cook, stirring, until the eggs are done to your liking.

3. Serve each portion topped with the garnishes of your choice.

Chili Cheesy Grits Soufflé

Serves 6 to 8

Chile grits soufflé in one form or another has long been a personal favorite. It is a casserole made with cooked grits, garlic, grated cheese, sour cream, and green chiles, all baked together until the top is crisp. In this recipe I'm taking it to another level by adding hearty red chili. It's delicious, satisfying, and great as part of a buffet. Even better, it can be made ahead of time and refrigerated or frozen (see box, facing page).

Salt
1 cup quick-cooking grits
1 teaspoon butter, for greasing the
   baking dish
2 cloves garlic, finely minced
1¼ cups shredded easy-melting cheese
   (a combination of Monterey Jack and
   Cheddar cheeses is good)
½ cup chopped fresh or parched green chiles
   (see page 14; from 4 whole chiles), or
   ½ cup canned or thawed frozen chopped
   green chiles
½ cup meaty red chili, such as Pecos River
   Bowl of Red (page 34)
2 eggs, well beaten

1. Bring 4 cups water and ½ teaspoon salt to a boil in a heavy saucepan. Add the grits, stirring constantly, and cook until the mixture returns to a boil. Then reduce the heat to a simmer and cook, stirring, until the grits have softened and the mixture is very thick or until all the water has been absorbed, 5 to 7 minutes. Remove from the heat and let cool for a few minutes.

2. Meanwhile, butter a 2-quart casserole or an 8 × 8-inch baking dish.

3. When the grits have cooled a bit but are still warm, stir in the garlic, ¼ cup of the cheese, and the chiles, chili, eggs, and additional salt if you wish. Transfer this mixture to the casserole and sprinkle with the remaining 1 cup cheese. (You can make the scramble up to this point and cover and refrigerate it for up to 3 days, or freeze it for up to 3 months.)

4. Preheat the oven to 350°F.

5. Place the casserole in the oven and bake until the top is crispy and the cheese has melted, 30 minutes. If you're serving the scramble as part of a buffet, you can keep it warm on a hot tray or in a chafing dish for up to 3 hours.

Crazy Chili Casserole

🌶 🌶 🌶

Serves 6 to 8

This yummy casserole

was inspired by a favorite version of chilaquiles from the Yucatan. Similar to migas, chilaquiles are broken-up tortillas that are cooked with meat and cheese in a chile sauce. When I taught a class on Mexican cuisine at the Melia Mayan resort in Cozumel, I happily ate chilaquiles almost daily at the resort's breakfast buffet. Here I present my take on their dish, using chili for the meat to wonderful effect.

12 corn tortillas (6 inches each)
1 teaspoon butter, for greasing the
    baking dish
1½ cups chili, any kind (if thick, thinned to
    gravy consistency with chicken broth)

1¼ cups grated or crumbled white cheese,
    such as queso blanco, feta,
    Monterey Jack, or mozzarella
1 cup sour cream
2 tablespoons finely chopped onion

Freezing, Refrigerating, and Reheating Casseroles

If you want to freeze a casserole for use later in the day (or on another day altogether), try this little trick: Line an unbuttered baking dish with two sheets of aluminum foil, crisscrossing the foil and allowing it to extend about 6 inches outside the dish on all sides. Then grease the foil with butter or nonstick cooking spray. Assemble the casserole in the dish, bring up the sides of the foil to cover it, and place it in the freezer. When you are ready to bake the casserole, pop the frozen-solid block out of the foil (discard the foil), butter the baking dish, put the frozen block back into the buttered dish, and bake it for 1½ times longer than called for in the recipe (so if the original recipe calls for a baking time of 30 minutes, you'd bake the frozen casserole for 45 minutes).

If you are reheating a refrigerated casserole, simply add 5 to 10 minutes to the baking time.

1. Preheat the oven to 425°F.

2. Quarter the tortillas and place them on a large cookie sheet. Bake the tortillas until they are crisp, 12 to 15 minutes. Set them aside and reduce the oven heat to 350°F.

3. Butter a 2-quart or 8 × 8-inch baking dish. Cover the bottom of the dish with a layer of crisp tortillas, overlapping them slightly. Top the tortillas with half of the chili, then half of the cheese. Dollop half of the sour cream over the cheese layer. Repeat the layers, beginning with the remaining tortillas and ending with the remaining sour cream. Sprinkle the onion over the top.

4. Place the casserole in the oven and bake until bubbly and lightly browned on top, 30 minutes.

Enchilada Casserole

😋 😋 😋

Serves 4

This is a very old-fashioned

dish—we made this in my childhood. It uses enchilada flavors but layers them like a lasagna . . . quite a treat. With the addition of chili, this casserole is very hearty and delicious, and typically Texan with its use of beef and so much cheese. You can make the dish ahead of time and refrigerate or freeze it until serving (see box, page 91).

1 pound American cheese,
   cut into 1-inch cubes
1 can (12 ounces) evaporated milk
1 tablespoon butter, for greasing the
   baking dish
12 corn tortillas (6 inches each)
2 cups beef chili
½ cup chopped onion

1. Heat the cheese and the evaporated milk in a 3-quart saucepan over medium heat, stirring until the cheese melts.

2. Preheat the oven to 350°F. Butter a 2-quart casserole.

3. Cover the bottom of the casserole with half of the tortillas, overlapping them slightly. Top the tortillas with half of the chili and half of the onion. Repeat the layers, beginning with the remaining tortillas and ending with the remaining onion. Pour the cheese mixture over the layers, and cover the dish with aluminum foil.

4. Place the casserole in the oven and bake until the top is bubbly and has golden spots, 25 to 30 minutes.

Variations:

Add 2 cups cooked pinto beans for extra flavor. If preferred, you could use a green-chile chili, such as the Navajo Green Chili on page 69.

Baked Chili
with Beans

🌶 🌶 🌶 🌶

Serves 4

Beef and beans go together perfectly, so why do so many people say that "real" chili doesn't contain beans? Well, chili con carne was first cooked up as trail food on long cattle drives, and cattle drives, naturally, were all about beef. There was more beef than there was a market for it, so making all-beef chili made sense. Also, cooked beef keeps longer than cooked beans do; adding beans to the chili brew would make it spoil faster. So as the popularity of traditional chili con carne spread, the answer to the beef-and-beans question became: serve the beans on the side or layered under the chili.

Here you get the best of both worlds: beans layered with the chili and more chile—green chile, that is—and everything baked and bubbled together. To prepare this ahead of time, see the box on page 91.

2 teaspoons butter, for greasing the skillet
2 cups beef chili
1 cup stewed pinto beans, such as Gordon's Fabulous Frijoles (page 130)
½ cup green chiles, parched (see box, page 14), peeled, and coarsely chopped
½ cup chopped onion
½ cup grated sharp Cheddar cheese

1. Preheat the oven to 350°F.

2. Butter a 9-inch cast-iron skillet or a 2-quart casserole. Spread the chili in the bottom of the skillet. Then layer on the beans, chiles, onion, and cheese.

3. Place the skillet in the oven and bake until the cheese is melted and the mixture is bubbly, about 20 minutes.

HOT STUFF

Red chiles have the highest antioxidant properties of all chiles and help maintain the freshness of foods they are added to.

Texas-Style
Tamale Pie

🌶 🌶 🌶 🌶

Serves 4

This typically Texas-style casserole is a favorite for entertaining because it can be made well ahead of time—2 to 3 days—and then baked just before serving (see box, page 91). It combines the spicy, savory flavors of Southwestern cooking and highlights three popular Tex-Mex ingredients: chili, corn, and cheese. You can vary the ingredients to suit your taste and to use what you have on hand. Add a green salad such as the Spinach Mango Salad with Lemony Mustard Dressing (page 112), and perhaps some Garlic Sticks (page 148), and you have a very tasty meal.

1 teaspoon salt
1 cup white, yellow, or blue cornmeal
1 teaspoon butter, for greasing the
    casserole
2 cups chili, preferably beef
½ cup cooked, canned, or thawed frozen
    whole-kernel corn
1 tomato, stemmed and diced
1 medium-size onion, chopped
¼ cup thinly sliced pimiento-stuffed
    green olives
½ cup mixed grated Monterey Jack
    and Cheddar cheeses, or to taste

1. Place 3 cups water and the salt in a large
saucepan over high heat. In a medium bowl,
combine 3 cups water with the cornmeal. When
the salted water boils, gradually pour in the
cornmeal, stirring constantly. Cook over low heat,
stirring often, until thick, about 30 minutes.

2. Meanwhile, preheat the oven to 350°F. Butter
the bottom and sides of a 3-quart casserole.

3. While the cooked cornmeal is still warm,
spread it over the bottom and sides of the
casserole, smoothing it out to a thickness of about
½ inch. Spread the chili over the cornmeal on the
bottom of the casserole. Then add the remaining
ingredients in layers, ending with the cheese.
Bake until the crust is crisp and lightly browned,
30 to 45 minutes.

Upside-Down Chili Pie

🌶 🌶 🌶
Serves 6 to 8

The spicy flavors of chili have
always paired well with cornbread. This pie
is actually somewhat similar in taste to the
Tamale Pie on page 93, but here the chili
flavor is more up-front and prominent, and
the cornbread is a light layer. You can use
any leftover chili for this one. (To make it
ahead of time, see the box on page 91.)

1 teaspoon butter, for greasing the
    casserole
3 cups chili, any kind
½ cup chopped onion
¼ cup chopped pickled jalapeño chiles
1 recipe batter for Bacon Crumble
    Cornbread, bacon omitted (page 141),
    or batter prepared from 1 box
    (8½ ounces) Jiffy corn muffin mix
½ cup mixed grated Monterey Jack and
    Cheddar cheeses

1. Preheat the oven to 350°F. Butter a 3-quart
casserole or baking dish.

2. Spread the chili over the bottom of the
casserole. Then layer with the onion and
jalapeños. Spread the cornbread batter on top,

smoothing it to the corners of the casserole. Sprinkle the cheese over the batter.

3. Bake until the top is golden brown and a toothpick inserted in the center of the pie comes out clean, 35 minutes.

Frito Pie
🌶 🌶 🌶
Serves 4

These are quite popular at fundraisers, sporting events, and lunch counters because they're tasty, handy, and easy to eat on the go. Traditionally, the "pie" was made in a small bag of Fritos, with the chips serving as the bottom layer of the pie. Tourists visiting Santa Fe always used to love buying the pies from the take-out window at Woolworth's on the Plaza, which sadly is long gone (and which many New Mexicans consider the birthplace of this delicious dish). Since the new Fritos bags aren't safe to bake in, I recommend making the pie in a casserole dish instead—it tastes just as good as it did at Woolworth's.

1 teaspoon butter for greasing the
    casserole
4 cups Fritos corn chips
2 cups chili, any kind
½ cup chopped onion
¾ cup grated Cheddar cheese, or mixed
    Monterey Jack and Cheddar cheeses

1. Preheat the oven to 350°F (see Note). Butter the bottom and sides of a 1-quart casserole dish.

2. Spread half of the Fritos on the bottom of the casserole. Top with the chili, then the onion, and finally the cheese. Top with the remaining chips. Place the casserole in the oven and bake until the cheese melts, about 15 minutes.

Note: If you prefer, you can prepare the pies in individual microwave-safe bowls and bake them in a microwave oven on high for 2 minutes.

Chili Tacos
🌶 🌶 🌶
Serves 4

Some say the word "taco" comes from *tago,* Mexican slang for "take it and go." Tacos started as a children's snack in northern Mexico a long time ago. In that desperately dry area, where food was always scarce, Mexican mothers began serving the first tortillas they made to their hungry children, to keep the childrens' hands full and leave the mothers free to get the rest of the meal prepared. Then the mothers began to fill the fresh tortillas with any available leftovers, such as beans or cheese, and the taco as we know it was born.

8 fresh corn tortillas (for soft tacos) or
taco shells (for crisp tacos)
2 cups thick chili, such as Pecos River
Bowl of Red (page 34) or
Reno Red, (page 43), reheated
(see box, facing page)
1 cup thinly shredded cabbage
½ cup sour cream or grated cheese,
such as sharp Cheddar, Monterey Jack,
or Mexican queso blanco
2 limes, quartered
½ cup salsa, or more to taste, for serving

1. If you are using fresh corn tortillas, place a
griddle, comal, or skillet over medium-high heat
and warm each tortilla briefly, flipping it as soon
as it starts to blister, about 3 seconds per side.
Wrap the heated tortillas in a clean kitchen towel
to keep them warm. If you are using crisp taco
shells, bake them in a preheated 300°F oven until
just warm, 8 to 10 minutes.

2. Spoon ¼ cup of the chili into each warmed
tortilla or taco shell, and top the chili with
2 tablespoons of the shredded cabbage and
1 tablespoon of the sour cream or cheese. Serve
each taco with a lime wedge, and pass the salsa
at the table.

Navajo Tacos

Serves 6

These delicious tacos are so much
fun! They are very popular at events in the
Southwest—from the prestigious Arabian
Horse Show in Scottsdale, Arizona, to nearly
every fair and festival in New Mexico. No
wonder—the warm, chewy, sopaipilla-like
bread is the perfect basis for a taco.

2 cups Gordon's Fabulous Frijoles
(page 130) or other cooked pinto beans
1 recipe Indian Fry Bread (page 143;
also see Note)
2 cups thick red chili, such as Santa Clara
Chili (page 66) or Carroll Shelby's
Chili (page 36), reheated (see box,
facing page)
⅓ cup chopped onion
1½ cups finely shredded iceberg or
romaine lettuce
1 large tomato, stemmed and chopped
Salsa, for serving (optional)

Place the beans in a saucepan over medium
heat and cook, stirring, until warmed through,
about 5 minutes. Place a disk of fry bread on
each of six plates, and then layer each one with
⅓ cup of the beans and ⅓ cup of the chili. Top
each taco with some onion and a small pile of
lettuce. Scatter the chopped tomato over the
lettuce. Serve immediately, with salsa if desired.

Note: If you don't feel like making the fry bread, yet yearn for tacos with a rich fried flavor, you can lightly fry flour tortillas instead. The tacos will not be the same, but they'll be close. To prepare them, pour vegetable oil to a depth of about ½ inch in a skillet of the same diameter as the flour tortillas. Heat the oil over medium-high heat until a small piece of tortilla quickly sizzles and turns light brown when slipped into the oil. Fry each tortilla only until it begins to puff, about 1 minute. Then layer the beans, chili, and other ingredients as described.

Reheating Chilled Chili

Warming up leftover chili is a pretty simple endeavor. If using the stovetop, lightly coat the bottom of a saucepan with vegetable oil spray (which will help prevent the chili from sticking to the pan), add the chili, and cook, stirring occasionally, over medium heat. It should take about 5 to 10 minutes to heat the chili through, depending on how much of the brew you have in the pan.

If you'd rather use a microwave oven (which will eliminate the burnt-to-the-bottom factor), place the chili in a microwave-safe dish, cover it with a lid or plastic wrap, and microwave on high power for 1 to 2 minutes, pausing halfway through to give the chili a quick stir.

Chili con Carne Burritos

Makes 4 burritos

These burritos are wonderful filled with almost any kind of beef or pork chili. While the recipe is of course called Chili con Carne Burritos, which would imply that you should only use *meat* chili, these are truly just as good with any of the chicken, turkey, or veggie chilies in Chapter 2.

4 flour tortillas (10 to 12 inches each)
1 cup Refritos (page 131) or canned
    refried beans
2 cups traditional-style beef chili,
    such as Pecos River Bowl of Red
    (page 34), Santa Clara Chili (page 66),
    or Hy Abernathy's Georgia Chain-Gang
    Chili (page 49)
¾ cup shredded Cheddar cheese, or
    mixed Cheddar and Monterey Jack
4 tablespoons chopped onion
4 tablespoons sliced pickled jalapeño chiles
4 leaves romaine or iceberg lettuce,
    for serving
Grated Monterey Jack and/or Cheddar
    cheese, for garnish (optional)

1. Preheat the oven to 450°F, or preheat the broiler.

2. Place the tortillas in a plastic bag and heat them in a microwave oven on high for 1 minute. (Alternatively, wrap them in aluminum foil and warm them in the oven for 2 minutes while heating the chili and beans.)

3. Place the beans and the chili in separate saucepans over medium heat, and cook, stirring, until warmed through, about 5 minutes (or place them in microwave-safe bowls and heat them in the microwave for 1 to 2 minutes).

4. Place a tortilla on a large baking sheet. Spread ¼ cup of the beans in the center of the tortilla, and then top the beans with ½ cup of the chili, 3 tablespoons of the cheese, 1 tablespoon of the onion, and 1 tablespoon of the jalapeños. Fold the lower third of the tortilla away from you, to cover the filling slightly, and then fold in the sides of the tortilla, making sure they overlap. (Thus the burrito should be "sealed" at the bottom and sides, and open at the top.) Repeat with the remaining tortillas, beans, chili, cheese, onions, and jalapeños.

5. Place the baking sheet in the oven or under the broiler, and cook until the burritos are crisp and lightly browned, 7 to 10 minutes.

6. Arrange each burrito on a lettuce leaf, garnish the burrito with a "belt" of the grated cheese, if using, and serve.

HOT STUFF

Many birds feed on chiles—unlike mammals, their mouths don't have receptors for capsaicin and thus don't feel the peppers' heat.

Texas-Style Burritos

🌶️🌶️

Makes 4 burritos

Texas has historically been long on beef, starting with the Europeans who took advantage of the free land to raise their prized cattle in the early 19th century. Once in Texas, these settlers discovered, to their dismay, that there was no market for the beef because the area was so remote. So beef was eaten liberally right at home until the advent of the railroads, which spurred the famous cattle drives to the railheads in Kansas. These meaty burritos are Texas-size and yield that true Texas taste: beef. You can make them with leftover chili or with shredded roasted brisket or chuck.

4 flour tortillas (10 to 12 inches each)
1 cup Refritos (page 131) or canned
   refried beans
2 cups beef chili or shredded cooked beef
½ cup crumbled white Mexican cheese,
   such as queso blanco or quesillo,
   or feta
4 tablespoons chopped onion
4 leaves romaine or iceberg lettuce,
   for garnish
1 cup Red Chile Sauce (recipe follows),
   for garnish

1. Preheat the oven to 450°F, or preheat the broiler.

2. Place the tortillas in a plastic bag and heat them in a microwave oven on high for 1 minute. (Alternatively, wrap them in aluminum foil and warm them in the oven for 2 minutes while heating the chili and beans).

3. Place the beans and the chili in separate saucepans over medium heat and cook, stirring, until warmed through, about 5 minutes (or place them in microwave-safe bowls and microwave on high for 1 to 2 minutes).

4. Place a tortilla on a large baking sheet. Spread ¼ cup of the beans over the center of the tortilla, and top the beans with ½ cup of the chili, 2 tablespoons of the cheese, and 1 tablespoon of the onion. Fold the lower third of the tortilla away from you, to cover the filling slightly, and then fold in the sides of the tortilla, making sure they overlap. (Thus the burrito should be "sealed" at the bottom and sides, and open at the top.) Repeat with the remaining tortillas, beans, chili, cheese, and onion.

5. Place the baking sheet in the oven or under the broiler and cook until the burritos are crisp and lightly browned, about 10 minutes.

6. Arrange each burrito on a lettuce leaf, garnish the burrito with a "belt" of the sauce, and serve.

Red Chile Sauce

Makes 2½ cups

This basic red chile sauce is as versatile as it is flavorful. It can be layered into enchiladas and served over burritos, and it goes fabulously with store-bought or homemade chiles rellenos, tamales, and chimichangas. It freezes well in freezer bags or food storage containers for up to 6 months.

**2 tablespoons butter, lard, or bacon
     drippings
2 tablespoons unbleached all-purpose flour
¼ cup pure ground hot red chile
¼ cup pure ground mild red chile
2 cups beef broth or water
1 clove garlic, minced
Pinch of dried Mexican oregano
Pinch of cumin
¾ teaspoon salt**

1. Melt the butter in a medium saucepan over low heat. Add the flour and cook, stirring constantly, until the mixture is smooth and slightly golden, 3 to 4 minutes.

2. Remove the pan from the heat, add the ground chiles, and stir to blend them into the butter mixture. Return the pan to low heat and gradually stir in the broth. Add the garlic,

Burritos Unwrapped

Legend has it that the burrito—which means "little donkey" in Spanish—got its name from the Spanish conquistadores who raided Mexico in the 1500s. At that time, young boys used to ride little gray burros (donkeys) while tending their parents' flocks. The boys' most common snack was a corn tortilla wrapped around pinto bean refritos. As the conquistadores rode across the countryside on horseback, they often came across these young boys and, feeling hungry after a long day's ride, would swoop down from their horses and snatch the food the boys were eating. As the story goes, the conquistadores referred to these stolen treats as burritos, naming them after the burro-riding boys they had pilfered them from.

I often think that the burritos served in restaurants look rather boring—they are white and unadorned and rolled like a cigar. I've been folding them in a triangular shape. But despite my burritos' unusual appearance, I often fill them in the traditional manner, starting with a layer of refried beans—though at times I have used cole slaw, grilled zucchini, or peppers and onions.

The beauty of a burrito is that it can be whatever you want it to be—a triangle or a cylinder, filled with beans or with vegetables, topped with sour cream or with guacamole. Be creative!

oregano, cumin, and salt (if you used water instead of broth). Raise the heat to medium and cook, stirring, until the flavors blend and the sauce thickens and becomes very smooth, about 15 minutes.

Variation: Meaty Red Chile Sauce

Cook 1 pound ground beef or finely cubed beef in a 9- to 10-inch sauté pan (omit the butter) over medium heat. Sprinkle the flour directly onto the meat and stir to combine. Once the flour is well incorporated, cook for 1 to 2 minutes. Then remove the pan from the heat and stir in the chiles. Return the pan to the heat, add the broth or water, garlic, oregano, cumin, and salt (if you used water, not broth). Cook, stirring, until the sauce is moderately thick. Taste, and adjust the seasonings as needed.

New Mexico—Style Chili-and-Cheese Enchiladas

🌶 🌶 🌶

Serves 4 as a very hearty meal, 6 as a hearty meal

This is one of my very favorite dishes, especially when made with blue corn tortillas. A few years ago, everyone lightly fried the tortillas that went into enchiladas, whether they were flat New Mexico–style enchiladas or the rolled variety common elsewhere in the United States and in Mexico. (I offer the flat New Mexico style here, but if you prefer rolled enchiladas, see the variation that follows.) However, to reduce calories and fat—and especially to save time—I have been teaching people to make enchiladas with un-fried tortillas. Since the cheese and sauce bubble into the enchiladas while they bake, I don't think the fried flavor is missed.

It is a popular New Mexico custom to place a soft-fried egg on top of each stack of enchiladas as soon as it comes out of the oven—I recommend giving it a try.

2 cups thick red or green chili, such as Reno Red (page 43) or Navajo Green Chili (page 69)
8 to 12 white, yellow, or blue corn tortillas (6 inches each)
1 onion, chopped
About 1 cup shredded Monterey Jack or Cheddar cheese, or a combination
1 tablespoon butter (optional)
4 to 6 eggs (optional)
3 leaves romaine lettuce, sliced crosswise into ½-inch-wide ribbons, for garnish
3 leaves red-leaf lettuce, sliced crosswise into ½-inch-wide ribbons, for garnish
2 ripe tomatoes, stemmed and sliced into thin wedges (16 pieces total), for garnish

1. Preheat the oven to 350°F.

2. Spread a small spoonful of chili on each of four or six ovenproof dinner plates. Place a tortilla on each chili-spread plate, and top it with some more chili, some onion, and a scattering of cheese. Repeat these layers once or twice more (so each stack has 2 or 3 tortillas), ending with a topping of onions, chili, and, finally, cheese.

3. Place the plates in the oven and bake until the cheese melts and the chili bubbles slightly, 10 to 15 minutes.

4. If you wish to top the enchiladas with fried eggs, just before removing the enchiladas from the oven, place the butter in a large skillet over medium-low heat. When the butter sizzles, crack the eggs into the skillet, 2 to 4 at a time (depending on the size of the skillet), and fry until the whites are firm and the yolks are just beginning to set at the edges, about 4 minutes.

5. Carefully remove the enchiladas from the oven, and top each with a fried egg if desired. Garnish each plate, encircling the enchiladas first with the romaine, then with some red-leaf lettuce. Divide the tomato wedges among the plates, spacing them evenly apart.

Variation: Rolled Chili-and-Cheese Enchiladas
Pour vegetable oil to a depth of ½ inch in a small skillet or sauté pan and set it over medium-high heat. When the oil is hot, add a tortilla and lightly fry it until it is golden but still soft, a few seconds per side. Drain the tortilla on paper towels. Repeat with the remaining tortillas. Dip the fried tortillas into the chili to coat about half of each tortilla, and divide half of the cheese and all of the onion among the tortillas, scattering them in

a strip down the center. Beginning at the dipped end, roll up the tortillas around the filling and place them, seam side down, on ovenproof plates (2 to a plate) or in an oblong baking dish. Top with the remaining chili and cheese. Place in a preheated 350°F oven and bake until the cheese melts, 10 to 15 minutes. Garnish the enchiladas with the lettuces and tomatoes before serving.

Chili 'n' Fixin's
Quesadilla

Makes 1 quesadilla; serves 1

This is the best way to make
quesadillas—much easier than sandwiching the filling between two tortillas. Here you grill the quesadilla in a small amount of sweet butter, lending a yummy buttery taste to the tortilla.

This quesadilla incorporates all the flavors of a bowl of chili topped with fixin's and mixin's. The fixin's included here are my favorite—cheese, onion, and pickled jalapeños. You can play with the filling as you like, improvising from the Fixin's and Mixin's on page 34.

1 teaspoon unsalted butter, melted,
    or more as needed
1 flour tortilla (10 inches)

¼ cup mixed grated Monterey Jack and
    Cheddar cheeses
4 to 6 slices fresh or pickled jalapeño
    chiles
2 to 3 tablespoons thick red or green chili,
    such as Pecos River Bowl of Red
    (page 34) or Midwest Chili (page 64)
2 tablespoons Gordon's Fabulous Frijoles
    (page 130), or other cooked pinto beans
    (optional)
2 teaspoons chopped onion
¼ small avocado, pitted, peeled,
    and thinly sliced
Assorted Flavored Cremas (page 25),
    for garnish
Red salsa, for garnish
Green salsa, for garnish
Crushed caribe chile, for garnish

1. Place a griddle over medium heat. When it is hot, brush half of the melted butter on an area the size of half a tortilla.

2. Place the tortilla on the griddle so half of the tortilla lies on top of the buttered area. Layer that section of the tortilla with the cheese, jalapeños, chili, beans if using, onion, and avocado. Fold the other side of the tortilla over the fillings, carefully pressing down so that the tortilla stays folded. Brush the top of the tortilla with the remaining melted butter.

3. Continue cooking the quesadilla until the cheese melts and the bottom of the tortilla is golden brown, about 1 minute. Then carefully flip it with a spatula and cook until the other side is golden, about 30 seconds more.

4. Transfer the quesadilla to a cutting board. Slice it in half and then in half again, making 4 equal wedges. Place the quesadilla on a platter, garnish it with dollops of crema, the salsas, and a confetti sprinkle of caribe chile, and serve immediately.

Chili Burgers Supreme

Makes 4 burgers

Traditional-style chili is

fabulous on hamburgers, and even better on cheeseburgers. I personally like to top burgers with beefy red chilies, such as Pecos River Bowl of Red (page 34), or green-chile varieties, such as Navajo Green Chili (page 69).

1½ pounds ground lean choice or prime
    beef, such as sirloin
1 teaspoon salt
Generous pinch to ½ teaspoon freshly
    ground black pepper
1 clove garlic, minced
4 hamburger buns
1 cup traditional chili, reheated
    (see box, page 97)
½ cup grated Cheddar or Monterey Jack
    cheese, or a combination
½ cup chopped onion

Classic Chili Combos

The farther you get from Texas, chili's birthplace and the region of its greatest popularity, the more the variations. New Mexico and the other Southwestern states all have their iconic versions, but chili has spread its magic far beyond the chile's natural growing areas. All over the country, chili lends a zing to those familiar favorites: the ubiquitous frankfurter (the chili dog, of course) and the humble hamburger (the all-American chili burger). But consider these regional variations:

- Cincinnatians sometimes add lettuce to their chili bowls, and are famous for serving chili over a bed of spaghetti.

- Louisvillians stir in broken-up tamales, usually the canned variety, to add texture and flavor.

- Kansas Citians go totally American and serve chili over macaroni, sometimes even baking the chili and noodles together in a casserole, in a dish well known to school kids as chili-mac.

Variations even pop up within Texas itself! Dallasites and New Mexicans both stake claim to the beloved dish know as Frito Pie. It's a concoction of chili over Fritos, cheese, and onions—and you can find the recipe on page 95.

1. Preheat a barbecue grill to medium-high. (If you are cooking indoors, see the Note.)

2. In a large bowl, mix the ground beef with the salt, black pepper, and garlic. Form it into 4 burgers, each about ¾ inch thick.

HOT STUFF

Chiles are popular in hot climates, possibly because they increase perspiration, which cools the body down.

3. Place the burgers on the grill and cook to the desired doneness, allowing about 4 minutes per side for medium. (To judge the doneness of the burgers, press them with the end of a spatula or tongs: if the burger is rather firm, it is medium. You can also check the juices: if bloody, the burger is rare; if clear, it is medium to well-done.) Place the buns face down on the grill until just lightly toasted.

4. Transfer the hamburger buns to plates and place a burger on the bottom half of each bun. Spoon some of the chili, cheese, and onion over each burger, and serve immediately.

Note: If you prefer to fry the burgers indoors, select a heavy griddle or frying pan. Preheat the griddle over medium-high heat, and spray it with a bit of vegetable oil spray or oil it lightly with peanut or vegetable oil. When the griddle is hot and a few drops of water scattered on it dance into steam, place the burgers on the hot surface and cook as described.

Portabello Mushroom Chili 'n' Cheese Steaks

Serves 4

I don't know about you, but anytime I see mushrooms on the menu, I take a second look. I adore mushrooms and am especially fond of the meaty, delicious flavor of portabellos. If possible, choose portabellos with caps that are still cupped, not opened all the way, and with gills that have not turned black. The richness of the portabellos provides a yummy contrast with the spicy chili. If you're serving this dish to vegetarians, simply use a veggie-only chili, such as Butternut Squash and Black Bean Chili (page 84) or Vegetarian Chili (page 82).

4 medium portabello mushroom caps, stems removed
4 tablespoons (½ stick) unsalted butter, or more as needed
2 cloves garlic, minced
2 cups chili
½ cup crumbled goat cheese (4 ounces)
1 jalapeño chile, stemmed and sliced into thin rounds

1. Preheat the oven to 375°F.

2. Gently clean the mushrooms with a soft, dry brush or cloth, removing any dirt or grit. Leave the mushroom caps whole if they are still cupped. If they have fully opened, cut them crosswise into ½-inch-thick slices.

3. Melt the butter in a heavy skillet over medium heat. Add the mushrooms, top side down, and cook until that side is somewhat softened, about 5 minutes. (If using sliced mushrooms, place them cut side down in the hot butter.) Add the garlic to the skillet and stir it in and around the mushrooms. Turn each mushroom or slice over and cook a few minutes more, until there is no light color showing.

4. Place each mushroom, gill side up, on an ovenproof plate (or, if using sliced mushrooms, place them on a rimmed baking sheet in 4 equal portions). Spoon ½ cup of the chili over each mushroom cap (or sliced mushroom portion), top each one with 2 tablespoons of the cheese, and

place in the oven. Bake until the cheese bubbles into the chili, about 15 minutes.

5. Remove the plates from the oven, top each "steak" with some jalapeño slices, and serve immediately.

Spinach Wrap
with Veggie Chili

Makes 1 large serving or 12 appetizers

I adore the combination of tangy herbed goat cheese, savory vegetarian chili, and zingy pickled chiles in this delicious wrap. It makes a great lunch for one, but it's also a pretty party appetizer—and it's especially good for gatherings because it can be made ahead of time and the recipe can be doubled or tripled. You can make the wrap up to 2 days in advance, keeping it in a tightly covered container in the refrigerator and slicing it just before serving. I like to cut the wrap diagonally and arrange the pieces in clusters so they look like flower petals on the plate. You can vary this recipe many different ways, substituting different chiles and cheeses, such as cream cheese, Boursin cheese, or another spreadable cheese, and just about any of the thick chilies, such as the Chorizo Turkey Chili (page 77) or the Chickie Veggie Chili (page 74).

1 spinach-flavored flour tortilla (12 inches)
2 tablespoons low-fat or nonfat herbed
   goat cheese, at room temperature
3 tablespoons vegetarian chili, such as
   Vegetarian Chili (page 82) or Butternut
   Squash and Black Bean Chili (page 84)
5 or 6 slices pickled jalapeño chiles
1 tablespoon chopped tomato, for garnish
   (optional)
Fresh cilantro sprigs, for garnish (optional)

1. Place the tortilla in a plastic bag and warm it in a microwave oven on high until it is soft and pliable, about 30 seconds. (Alternatively, wrap it in aluminum foil and place it in a preheated 350°F oven until soft, about 3 minutes.) Meanwhile, tear off a 12-inch square of waxed paper.

2. Lay the warmed tortilla on the waxed paper. Spread the goat cheese over it, spoon the chili on top, and sprinkle with the jalapeños.

3. Roll the tortilla up tightly, wrap the waxed paper around it, and twist the ends together to seal. Place the waxed-paper-covered wrap in the refrigerator to firm up, at least 2 hours and up to 2 days.

4. When you're ready to serve the wrap, remove it from the refrigerator, peel off the waxed paper, and use a sharp chef's knife to slice off the ends. Cut the wrap in half diagonally and then cut each half in half, again on the diagonal. If serving it as a single wrap, stack the pieces artfully on the plate. If serving it as appetizers, cut each quarter into 3 pieces, allowing at least a ½-inch margin on the short side of each quarter so the wrap pieces

will not fall apart. Place the wrap pieces, cut side up, on a serving platter, arranging them in groups of four in a cloverleaf pattern.

5. Garnish with the chopped tomato and cilantro sprigs, if desired.

Green Chili and Three Cheeses Quick Pizza

Makes 1 individual pizza

Navajo Green Chili is a fantastic topping for this easy-to-make pizza, which you can prepare in just minutes. The cheeses really tame the chili's spicy edge. The tortilla makes an excellent quick and crispy base and looks exactly like a thin-crusted pizza when finished. If you prefer a puffier crust, use a prebaked variety such as a Boboli, or make your own from my favorite pizza dough recipe, which follows. For a more nutritious quick crust with a nacho-like flavor, substitute a corn tortilla.

1 flour tortilla (10 to 12 inches); or 1 ball
   Make-Ahead Pizza Dough (recipe
   follows), at room temperature
¼ cup grated mozzarella cheese

½ cup Navajo Green Chili (page 69); or
    4 fresh green chiles, parched (see box,
    page 14), peeled, stemmed, seeded
    (if you wish to reduce the heat), and
    coarsely chopped; or ½ cup canned or
    thawed frozen chopped green chiles
2 cloves garlic, minced, if using green chiles
¼ cup grated smoked Gouda, mozzarella,
    Cheddar, or other easy-melting smoked
    cheese
2 tablespoons grated Romano or Parmesan
    cheese

1. Preheat the oven to 425°F.

2. Place the tortilla on a baking sheet or pizza
pan, and sprinkle the mozzarella over it. (If
you are using the pizza dough, sprinkle a work
surface with semolina flour and roll the dough out
to form a 10-inch disk, as described in the dough
recipe. Place the dough on the baking sheet, and
sprinkle the mozzarella over it.)

3. Spoon the Navajo Green Chili (or scatter the
chopped green chiles and the garlic) over the
mozzarella. Then sprinkle the Gouda and Romano
cheeses on top.

4. Place the pizza in the oven and bake until
the crust is crisp and the cheeses are melted
and bubbling, 10 to 15 minutes if using a tortilla,
20 minutes or longer if using pizza dough. Serve
immediately.

Make-Ahead Pizza Dough

Makes enough for 12 individual 10-inch pizzas

I like this dough very much
because you can prepare it in advance and
then keep it on hand for making quick,
fresh, delicious pizzas in minutes, without
any fuss or muss. Put the dough together
when you have time, rolling it into balls and
refrigerating or freezing them for later use.

3½ cups lukewarm water
1 scant tablespoon (1 packet) active
    dry yeast
1 tablespoon salt
1 tablespoon sugar
7 cups unbleached all-purpose flour,
    plus extra for kneading
1 cup semolina flour (if not available,
    substitute unbleached all-purpose flour)
¼ cup olive oil

1. Pour ½ cup of the lukewarm water into a
small bowl and add the yeast, beating with a
whisk or fork until it is fully dissolved. Set aside.

2. Pour the remaining 3 cups lukewarm water
into a medium bowl and stir in the salt and sugar.

3. Place the flour and semolina in a large bowl, or in the bowl of a stand mixer fitted with the dough hook. Add the olive oil to the sugar-salt-water mixture, and add this to the flour all at once. Mix on low speed until the flour is combined with the liquid. Then add the dissolved yeast and mix on medium-low to medium speed until the dough is smooth, 2 to 3 minutes.

HOT STUFF

Some people can better bear the intense spice of certain chiles because they have fewer heat receptors on their tongue.

4. Turn the dough out onto a very lightly floured wood or marble surface, and knead by hand until it is very springy, smooth, and resilient when pressed with a finger, 3 to 5 minutes. If necessary, add more flour to the board, a little bit at a time, to get a stiff dough that yields thin threads when pulled between two fingers (keep in mind that the least possible amount of flour will yield the best dough).

5. Leave the kneaded dough on the board, cover it with the mixing bowl, and let it rise until doubled in bulk, about 1 hour (if the room is warm, it will rise faster).

6. When a finger pressed into the dough goes in easily, knead the dough again until it is satiny and smooth, a few seconds; then divide it into 12 equal portions. Shape them, creating balls of dough—pinching the edges of each ball and stretching the dough and sealing it firmly together to form a round ball of dough. Pat each ball to flatten it slightly and set them aside. Cover the balls of dough with plastic wrap and allow them to rise until they have increased in size by about one fourth, about 15 minutes.

7. Once the balls have risen, cover them with a moist towel if you will be using them immediately. If you are reserving them for later use, place them, without letting them touch one another, in a container, seal it, and refrigerate it; use the dough within 2 days. To freeze the dough balls, arrange them, without touching, on a cookie sheet and freeze them until they are firm; then transfer them to a self-seal freezer bag or a heavy-duty plastic container and label it with the date; the frozen dough will keep for 3 months.

8. When you are ready to use the dough, let the refrigerated dough sit at room temperature for 30 minutes; let the frozen dough sit at room temperature for about 2 hours. Place the room-temperature dough on a lightly floured board (you can use semolina) and roll out each ball with a small-diameter rolling pin, rolling from the center just up to, but not over, the edges. Flip it over and roll the other side the same way until you have a 10-inch disk.

Red Chili
Quick Pizza

🌶️🌶️

Makes 1 individual pizza

If you have some thick chili—such as the Pecos River Bowl of Red (page 34) or the Navajo Green Chili (page 69)—on hand, it makes a wonderful quick sauce for a pizza. I frankly love chiles, so a chili sauce instead of the usual tomatoey one is a great change for me. If you have the chili on hand, the pizza is almost an immediate light meal or snack.

1 flour tortilla (10 to 12 inch), or 1 rolled-out
    disk Make-Ahead Pizza Dough (page 107)
1 cup thick chili, reheated (see page 97)
½ cup mixed grated Cheddar and
    Monterey Jack cheeses, or ½ cup
    grated mozzarella cheese
2 tablespoons finely minced onion
3 tablespoons sliced pickled jalapeño chiles

1. Preheat the oven to 425°F.

2. Place the tortilla or the dough on a baking sheet or pizza pan, and spread the chili over it. Then sprinkle on the cheese, onion, and jalapeños.

3. Place the pizza in the oven and bake until the crust is crisp and the cheeses have melted and are bubbling, 10 to 15 minutes if using a tortilla, 20 minutes if using pizza dough.

Chili-Chile
Farfalle Toss

🌶️🌶️

Serves 4

This recipe is really a concept for you to play with—you can take any leftover chili and use it as a pasta sauce. Most chilies toss well with pasta. I think farfalle, shaped like little butterflies or bows, is particularly good in this dish. Top it with some easy-melting cheese, onion, and a bit of jalapeño and you have a winner. The flavors are familiar—somewhat like chili topped with Fixin's and Mixin's. Here I suggest traditional pasta cheeses—Romano or Parmesan—but feel free to vary the cheese too! A Cheddar or Cheddar-Jack combination is great, as are Gouda, Jarlsberg, Muenster, and even chèvre.

Salt
1 tablespoon olive or vegetable oil
8 ounces farfalle or other short pasta
2 cups chili, preferably one of the thicker
    ones, such as Pecos River Bowl of Red
    (page 34), reheated (see box, page 97)
½ cup chopped onion
2 tablespoons chopped pickled jalapeño
    chiles, for garnish (optional)
2 tablespoons freshly grated Romano or
    Parmesan cheese, or to taste,
    for serving

1. Bring a large pot of salted water to a boil over high heat. Add the oil and the farfalle, and cook according to the package directions.

2. Drain the farfalle in a colander and return it to the cooking pot. Add the chili and toss to incorporate. If the mixture cools, place the pot over low heat and cook, stirring gently, until heated through.

3. Transfer the pasta-chili mixture to a large warmed platter, or divide it among warmed plates, and sprinkle with the jalapeño, if using, and the grated cheese.

Green Chili
Fettuccine

Serves 6

Perfect for a dinner party, this creamy fettuccine dish offers a healthier take on Alfredo sauce and is highlighted with luscious avocado and flavorful green chile–flecked chili. Even better, it's actually quite easy to prepare.

1½ teaspoons salt
1 pound white or green fettuccine
1½ cups Chickie Veggie Chili
  (page 74) or Navajo Green Chili
  (page 69), reheated (see box, page 97)

1½ cups half-and-half
4 ounces Monterey Jack cheese, grated
2 Hass avocados, pitted, peeled, and cubed
Freshly grated Romano or Parmesan
  cheese, to taste
2 teaspoons crushed caribe chile,
  for garnish

1. Bring a large pot of water to a boil over high heat. Add the salt and fettuccine, and cook according to the package directions until just tender.

2. Meanwhile, warm the chili in a medium saucepan over medium heat. Add the half-and-half to the chili and stir to combine well. Add the Jack cheese and stir until it is melted.

3. Drain the fettuccine in a colander and return it to the cooking pot. Add the warm chili-cheese mixture and the avocado chunks, and toss to combine. Divide the fettuccine among warmed plates, and top with the grated Romano cheese. Sprinkle with the crushed caribe chile, and serve immediately.

4

Chili Sidekicks

Surely you've heard the old saying "man cannot live on chili alone." Well, maybe he can, but it can't hurt to have a table loaded down with plenty of sides, salads, veggies, and other supporting players. Sometimes it's a matter of giving your taste buds a vacation from some searing chile-hotness, sometimes it's a matter of pleasing a finicky non-chili-eater (for shame!), and sometimes it's just a simple matter of getting extra vitamins from a source that has not been simmered over an open flame for an afternoon. I've never met a table that hasn't had room for a flavorful chili sidekick or two.

You could put together a picture-perfect summer picnic by flanking your spicy pot of chili with soothing Five Bean Salad, the tangy classic Maytag Blue Cheese Potato Salad, and Crispy Cilantro Coleslaw, with its sweet, peppery bite. Or fire up the grill and play off your chili's smoky undertones by serving Grilled Chile-Lime Corn on the Cob— a new take on the good ol' late summer standby. Of course there are salads galore— fresh veggies, sassy dressings, all spiked with surprising flourishes. Drive 'em wild with a big bowl of Guadalajara-Style Vegetable Salad, or with a flavor-packed presentation of Spinach Mango Salad with its bright Lemony Mustard Dressing. The Mexican Confetti Salad with Avocado Citrus Dressing makes any festive spread look cheerier and ready for a party. There's no way around the elegance of Chile Relleno Salad—a pretty, composed platter that holds its own against the heartiest chilies.

Speaking of salads, there's a special place at my table for nopalitos—the prepared pads of the prickly pear cactus. Sure, you need to wear gloves to de-needle them (if they haven't been prepared already at the grocer's), but Ensalada de Nopalitos San Miguel is one of those dishes you'll look for any excuse to eat.

And then there are rice dishes infused with a variety of flavors, two perfect recipes for the best beans you'll ever eat, potato preparations aplenty (no one, but no one, says no to Spicy Fries!), addictive spicy-crisp okra, and my favorite take on the old Southern staple, Fried Green Tomatoes with Blue Corn–Jalapeño Coating. You read that right: green tomatoes, blue corn, all mouthwatering.

SOME LIKE IT HOT . . .
These icons show how fiery each dish is.

🌶
MILD

🌶 🌶
A BIT OF BITE

🌶 🌶 🌶
HOT

🌶 🌶 🌶 🌶
HOT ENOUGH TO MAKE YOU . . .

Spinach Mango Salad
with Lemony Mustard Dressing

🌶

Serves 4

This is a refreshing salad, light enough to serve with even the heartiest chilies. The flavors and textures are very complementary to the spiciness of chili: cool-crisp baby spinach, sweet, juicy mango, and the mellow heat of red onion. The tart edge that the yummy dressing supplies is just perfect for taming an overheated palate.

4 cups fresh spinach, preferably baby spinach, well rinsed and dried
1 large ripe mango, peeled and cubed (see box, page 5)
Several thin slices red onion
1 recipe Lemony Mustard Dressing (page 125)

Place the spinach in a salad bowl, and scatter the mango and sliced onion over it. Cover the bowl with plastic wrap and place it in the refrigerator to chill, at least 30 minutes and up to 24 hours. Before serving, add the dressing and toss gently to coat.

Chile Relleno Salad

🌶 🌶 🌶

Serves 4

This composed salad offers a pretty
presentation and bright flavors: crescents of
cheese-stuffed chiles nestled in a piquant
salsa vinaigrette.

**4 fresh green chiles, such as Anaheim/
New Mexico chiles (4 to 6 inches long),
parched (see page 14) and peeled**
**Handful of baby salad greens, well rinsed
and dried**
**6 ounces sharp cheese, such as Cheddar,
queso blanco, or manchego, chopped**
**1 recipe Garden Salsa Vinaigrette
(page 124)**

1. Using a sharp knife, slice the tip end of each
chile halfway up, forming ¼-inch-wide strips.
Leave the top half of the chile intact—the bottom
half will look like a grass skirt.

2. Place the salad greens on a platter and
arrange the chiles on top. Nestle the cheese into
the top half of each chile, just under the stem,
arranging the strips of chile into a waving or
dancing arrangement.

3. Drizzle with the dressing and allow to
marinate at room temperature, uncovered,
for a few minutes before serving.

Black Bean Chipotle Salad

🌶

Serves 4

In this salad the strong smoky
overtones of chipotle chiles perfectly play
up the slight smokiness of black beans.
Add to that the salty tanginess of Mexican
queso or feta cheese and you've got a
great salad to serve with a spicy meal—
especially any of the heartier traditional
red chile–flavored dishes, such as Reno Red
(page 43).

**4 cups salad greens, well rinsed, dried,
and chilled**
**1 cup cooked black beans (canned is fine),
rinsed and drained**
1 medium-size tomato, coarsely chopped
½ cup finely chopped red onion
**½ cup crumbled queso blanco or feta
cheese**
½ teaspoon chipotle powder
**1 recipe Cilantro Vinaigrette (page 121) or
Chile Vinaigrette (page 124)**

Place the greens in a chilled salad bowl. Top with
the black beans, tomato, onion, and queso blanco.
Whisk the chipotle powder into the vinaigrette,
and drizzle over the salad. Toss well to coat.

Ensalada de Nopalitos San Miguel (Cactus Pad Salad)

Serves 6 to 8

While leading a group on a culinary tour of Mexico's colonial cities, we visited Mercedes Arteaga, the chef-owner of the Bugambilia restaurant in San Miguel de Allende (hence the name of this salad). She gladly showed us how to prepare one of her favorite salads. *Nopalitos* taste very much like green beans with an attitude—the somewhat slippery texture is akin to okra. This salad can be an accompaniment to a meal, or you can add some shredded meat to make it a light meal in its own right. I like to serve it with baked or fried Tortilla Chips (page 2).

HOT STUFF

One teaspoon of chile powder satisfies the recommended daily allowance (RDA) for vitamin A.

½ **teaspoon salt**
3 **large nopalitos (cactus pads), washed and scraped free of thorns (see box, facing page), or 1½ pounds fresh haricots verts**

2 **cloves garlic, minced**
4 **scallions, including tops, finely chopped**
3 **sprigs fresh cilantro**
1 **cup cooked black beans (canned is fine), rinsed and drained**
½ **cup crumbled farmer's cheese or feta**
¼ **cup chopped onion**
½ **cup coarsely chopped tomato**
2 **teaspoons chopped fresh oregano, or ½ teaspoon dried oregano, preferably Mexican**
2 **tablespoons extra-virgin olive oil**
½ **tablespoon pure ground hot red chile or caribe chile**

1. Bring a large pot of water to a boil, and add the salt. Then add the cactus pads, garlic, scallions, and cilantro. Reduce the heat to a simmer, cover the pot, and cook, skimming off the foam frequently, until the cactus is tender, about 20 minutes.

2. Drain the pads in a colander, then rinse in generous amounts of cool water, discarding the garlic, scallions, and cilantro.

3. Slice the cactus pads into long, thin strips. Place them in a large chilled salad bowl, or for composed salads, arrange them in spokes on six to eight chilled plates.

4. Sprinkle the black beans, cheese, chopped onion, and tomato over the cactus, and top with the oregano, olive oil, and ground red chile. Cover the salad with plastic wrap and chill for at least 2 hours in the refrigerator before serving.

Nopalitos

Nopalitos—or prickly pear cactus leaves—are popular in northern Mexico. They are used in salads, as a vegetable side dish, and as an ingredient in egg dishes.

To cook with the fresh leaves (or pads, as they are often called), the needles must be removed. This is often done before they are sold, but if it hasn't been, you'll have to do it yourself. While wearing heavy gloves, hold the cactus pad firmly and scrape with a large sharp knife at right angles to the surface, essentially shaving off the needles.

To prepare the nopalitos, bring a pot of salted water, to which you have added approximately 1 tablespoon coarsely diced onion per pad, to a boil. Add the pads and simmer over low heat for about 20 minutes, or until they are tender when pierced. While the pads are cooking, frequently skim the foam off the surface of the boiling water.

Most upscale and Hispanic markets carry fresh nopalitos in their produce section, but if you can't find any fresh ones, check to see if they are available canned (or see Sources). If neither canned nor fresh nopalitos can be found, a good substitute is green beans, particularly the French long string beans (haricots verts), which have a similar flavor.

Fall Medley Salad

Serves 4

This salad is delicious when made with the vegetables listed here, but you can mix and match the vegetables as you like. Just be sure that whatever you use is colorful, fresh, crisp, and hearty. The corn, onion, and bell peppers make the basic salad—but you could try using carrots, broccoli, or cauliflower.

3 large ears fresh corn, shucked
1 medium-size red onion, halved and peeled
1 recipe Lemony Mustard Vinaigrette (page 125), Cilantro Vinaigrette (page 121), or Chile Vinaigrette (page 124)
Olive oil (optional)
1 green bell pepper, stemmed, seeded, and very thinly sliced
1 red bell pepper, stemmed, seeded, and very thinly sliced
1 yellow bell pepper, stemmed, seeded, and very thinly sliced
2 cups arugula, well rinsed and dried
Freshly ground black pepper

1. Preheat a barbecue grill, grill pan, or broiler.

2. Brush the ears of corn and the onion halves with a bit of vinaigrette or with some olive oil. Grill or broil the corn and the onion halves, turning them occasionally, until the corn kernels just begin to blacken at the edges, 8 to 10 minutes, and the onions feel tender when pierced with a fork or squeezed with tongs, up to 15 minutes. Remove from the heat as each is done and let cool.

3. When the corn and onion have cooled, slice the corn kernels off each cob (for best results, hold the cob, stem end down, in a wide-mouthed bowl and cut down vertically, close to the cob). Chop the onion.

4. Place the corn kernels, onion, bell peppers, and arugula in a salad bowl, and add black pepper to taste. Add the remaining vinaigrette and toss to coat. Serve the salad at room temperature or chilled.

Guadalajara-Style
Vegetable Salad

Serves 4

This somewhat hearty, fresh-flavored salad is a great change from the predictable tossed salad and is not difficult to make. I like to grill fresh corn for this dish, but you can use ½ cup canned or cooked frozen corn kernels if the season isn't cooperating with you.

1 large ear fresh white or yellow corn
1 recipe Cilantro Vinaigrette (page 121)
Olive oil (optional)
1 ripe avocado, pitted, peeled, and diced
½ cup diced jicama (see box, facing page)
⅓ cup chopped red onion

1. Preheat a barbecue grill, grill pan, or broiler.

2. Brush the corn with a bit of the vinaigrette or with some olive oil. Grill or broil it, turning it occasionally, until the kernels just begin to blacken at the edges, 8 to 10 minutes. Remove from the heat and let cool.

3. When the corn is cool enough to handle, slice off the kernels (for best results, hold the cob, stem end down, in a wide-mouthed bowl and cut down vertically, close to the cob).

4. Combine the corn with the avocado, jicama, and onion, and drizzle with the remaining vinaigrette. Toss well to combine, and let marinate until the flavors blend, at least 30 minutes or up to 2 hours. Serve at room temperature or cover and chill for up to 1 hour.

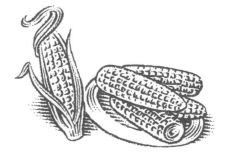

Mexican Confetti Salad
with Avocado Citrus Dressing

Serves 12

Crimson cabbage and beets are somewhat unusual partners in this colorful and flavorful salad. The crunchy texture makes it a pleasant contrast to numerous dishes, including any of the chilies or encores in this book. This salad originated in Mexico City and is sometimes called Rosaurio Salad.

1 tablespoon fresh lime juice
⅓ cup fresh orange juice
1 medium-size to large ripe Hass avocado, peeled, pitted, and cut into chunks
1 tablespoon honey
¼ teaspoon pequin quebrado
Salt
2 cups baby salad greens, baby spinach, or torn red-leaf lettuce, well rinsed and dried
3 cups finely shredded red cabbage
3 small beets, peeled and shredded (see Note)
1 jicama, peeled and shredded or cut into matchsticks (see box at right)

1 orange, peeled and sectioned
½ cup slivered blanched almonds

1. Place the lime juice, orange juice, avocado, honey, pequin quebrado, and salt to taste in a blender, and process until smooth. Pour the dressing into a small serving bowl or sauceboat.

2. Line a serving platter or chilled individual plates with the salad greens. Then compose the salad by arranging the shredded cabbage, beets, and jicama in sections or in rings on top of the greens. Top with the orange sections, and

Jicama

Jicama, often called the Mexican potato, is generally available in most food markets in the United States year-round. Good-quality jicamas are somewhat shiny and firm to the touch—they should not look shriveled. To prepare jicama, peel it as you would a peach. Then prepare the flesh as the recipe calls for: slice it, dice it, cut it in matchsticks, or shred it. Soak the jicama in cold water for at least 15 minutes to remove the excess starch before using it in a recipe.

If the jicama will be served raw, such as in an appetizer or salad, add a little lime juice or ascorbic acid mixture (such as Fruit-Fresh; see Sources) to the soaking water to prevent oxidation and discoloration.

sprinkle the almonds over all. Serve with the avocado dressing on the side.

Note: Peel raw beets with a vegetable peeler: hold the beets by the stem and peel them as you would a carrot to remove the outer skin. Then cut off and discard the stem end, and shred the beets with a box grater or in a food processor fitted with the shredding disk. I wear rubber gloves when peeling and grating beets—beet juice tends to stain hands.

Five Bean Salad

Serves 6 to 8

This hearty salad is a good traveler, ideal for picnics. The somewhat sweet-hot dressing is terrific on the combination of beans. It is filling, so you may want to pair it with a lighter dish, such as one of the seafood chilies. Or serve it as a satisfying and colorful entrée (one that will be especially welcomed by vegetarians), pairing it with Bear Paw Bread (page 144) or Caramelized-Onion Focaccia (page 146).

1 cup cooked pinto or kidney beans (canned is fine), rinsed and drained
1 cup cooked black beans (canned is fine), rinsed and drained
1 cup cooked garbanzo beans (chickpeas; canned is fine), rinsed and drained
1 cup cooked yellow wax beans
1 cup cooked green beans
1 small sweet onion, such as Vidalia, sliced into thin rings
2 red plum tomatoes, stemmed and diced
2 tablespoons chopped pickled jalapeño chiles
½ cup extra-virgin olive oil
¼ cup sherry vinegar
1 teaspoon Dijon mustard
2 teaspoons sugar
Freshly ground black pepper
Salt (optional)

Place all the beans in a large salad bowl, and add the onion, tomatoes, and jalapeños. In a small bowl, whisk together the oil, vinegar, mustard, and sugar. Grind pepper over the salad. Then drizzle the dressing over it, and toss. Taste, and add salt if you wish. Let marinate until the flavors blend, about 5 minutes. Serve at room temperature or cover and chill for up to 3 days.

Maytag Blue Cheese Potato Salad

Serves 4

The addition of high-quality blue cheese to potato salad really dresses it up and makes it more of a party dish to accompany almost any meal. Fred Maytag, the son of the inventor of the Maytag washer, worked long and hard to make Roquefort cheese in the United States. When he found that the bacteria that provide the particular Roquefort flavor just doesn't work the same in Iowa as it does in France, he committed to making the best blue cheese ever. Many connoisseurs agree that it is just that. Maytag Blue cheese is available at cheese shops and by mail order (see Sources).

Salt
4 russet potatoes, unpeeled, scrubbed and quartered
½ cup diced celery
2 tablespoons finely chopped scallions, including tops, or white onion
¼ cup mayonnaise, or to taste
¼ cup sour cream, or to taste
¼ cup crumbled Maytag Blue or other high-quality blue cheese
¼ teaspoon chipotle powder
1 teaspoon crushed caribe chile, for garnish

1. Bring 1 quart salted water to a boil in a large saucepan. Add the potatoes, cover the pan, and cook over low heat until tender, about 15 minutes. Remove the potatoes from the water, drain them in a colander, and let them cool. Then cut the potatoes into ½-inch dice and place them in a large bowl.

2. Add all the remaining ingredients (except the caribe chile) and about ½ teaspoon of salt. Toss gently to combine. Taste, and adjust the seasonings. Then transfer the salad to a serving bowl and garnish with the caribe chile.

Crispy Cilantro Coleslaw

Serves 4

The chopped cilantro that's folded into this "pickled" coleslaw contributes to its terrific variety of flavors. Its cool tanginess plays perfectly off almost any chili. I love it on tacos, too, where it's a bright counterpoint to rich savory fillings. The coleslaw is good both when freshly made and when it has been refrigerated for a day or two—in fact, it's best when prepared a day ahead. I have served it both chilled and at room temperature.

HOT STUFF

Chiles come in a rainbow of colors, including red, green, yellow—even purple!

¼ cup olive oil
¼ cup cider or white vinegar
2 tablespoons sugar
4 cups shredded cabbage
⅓ cup coarsely chopped fresh cilantro
2 tablespoons minced jalapeño chile
¼ cup chopped onion

1. Place the oil, vinegar, and sugar in a small saucepan over low heat. Bring to a simmer and cook, stirring, until the sugar dissolves, about 5 minutes. Remove from the heat.

2. Combine the cabbage, cilantro, jalapeño, and onion in a bowl. Drizzle the warm salad dressing over the mixture and toss well.

3. For the best flavor, prepare this 1 day ahead; cover and refrigerate. If you're short on time, allow it to sit for at least 1 hour at room temperature, and then serve.

Jicama Veggie Slaw

👀

Serves 4

Crisp and almost but not quite apple-like in flavor, jicama gives slaw a fresh taste and a nice crunch. A chile-lime vinaigrette really sets off the flavors of the vegetables and makes this a wonderful salad to serve with chili. Use a box grater or the grater blade of a food processor to prepare the jicama and carrot.

2 cups coarsely grated jicama (1 large or
    2 medium; see box, page 117)
1 cup grated carrots (3 large or 4 medium)
1 cup diced thin-skinned cucumber,
    such as English (hothouse) or Armenian
2 scallions, including tops, thinly sliced
1½ teaspoons salt, or to taste
¼ cup extra-virgin olive oil

2 tablespoons fresh lime juice
2 tablespoons cider vinegar
1 teaspoon pequin quebrado

1. Place the jicama, carrots, cucumber, and scallions in a large chilled bowl. Sprinkle with the salt and toss to combine.

2. In a small bowl, whisk the olive oil, lime juice, vinegar, and ½ teaspoon of the pequin quebrado together until combined. Drizzle this dressing over the vegetables and toss to mix well. Taste, and adjust the seasonings as needed. Then garnish with the remaining ½ teaspoon pequin quebrado.

Apple–Blue Cheese Slaw

👀

Serves 4

This salad is a breeze to put together and requires only a few minutes of marinating time. The sweet-and-savory combination of apples and blue cheese makes it a delicious complement for any chili made with pork or poultry, such as Santa Clara Chili (page 66) or Chili Talks Turkey (page 76).

½ cup coarsely chopped pecans
2½ cups thinly sliced or shredded cabbage

2 crisp apples, unpeeled, cored, and
    chopped
1 large stalk celery, chopped
¼ cup crumbled blue or Gorgonzola cheese
¼ cup cider vinegar
¼ cup buttermilk
1 tablespoon honey, or to taste
2 tablespoons mayonnaise

1. Preheat the oven to 350°F.

2. Spread the pecans on a rimmed baking sheet
and bake until they are just lightly toasted, about
5 minutes. Set them aside to cool.

3. Meanwhile, place the cabbage, apples, and
celery in a large bowl and sprinkle with the
cheese.

4. Combine the vinegar, buttermilk, honey, and
mayonnaise in a small bowl or liquid measuring
cup, and whisk until well blended. Drizzle this
dressing over the salad and toss to combine
well. Taste, and adjust the flavoring as needed.
Sprinkle the toasted pecans over the salad
before serving.

Cilantro Vinaigrette

😊 😊

Makes ½ cup (enough for a 4-serving salad)

The fresh, pungent flavor of cilantro
has always been a favorite of mine. I know
some do not like it, but I often find that those
who don't care for cilantro haven't had the
right introduction! In general cilantro should
be very coarsely chopped. If it is finely
chopped, its flavor dissipates quickly and
the herb dissolves into a brownish, smelly
liquid. For this vinaigrette I recommend
you chop the cilantro just before adding it
to the dressing. I like this dressing over any
greens or chopped vegetable assortment,
particularly a salad of tossed greens and
avocado.

3 tablespoons fresh lime juice (1 or 2 limes)
1 tablespoon honey
1 tablespoon coarsely chopped fresh
    cilantro
3 tablespoons extra-virgin olive oil
½ jalapeño chile (seeds removed, if you
    wish to reduce the heat), minced
Salt (optional)

Whisk the lime juice, honey, cilantro, olive oil,
and jalapeño together in a small bowl until
thoroughly combined. Taste and adjust the
seasonings as needed, adding a pinch of salt if
desired. Store, covered, in the refrigerator for
up to 1 month.

Dressing Up: Vinaigrette Basics

The basic recipe for vinaigrette is 3 parts oil to 1 part vinegar. My favorite oils to use are extra-virgin olive oil or, if I want a lighter flavor, best-quality vegetable oil. The vinegar can be any sort—balsamic, red wine, white wine— or even an acidic citrus like lemon or lime juice.

I like to add Dijon mustard: it serves as an emulsifier, which allows the oil and the vinegar (which is water-based) to stay mixed together. For every 3 tablespoons of oil, whisk ½ teaspoon Dijon mustard into the oil-vinegar mixture.

Some of my favorite combinations:

- Extra-virgin olive oil with balsamic vinegar and Dijon mustard: good over almost any vegetable combination, particularly grilled veggies.

- Extra-virgin olive oil with red wine vinegar, minced garlic, and basil: for a classic *caprese* salad of sliced tomatoes and mozzarella cheese.

- Vegetable or peanut oil with rice vinegar, Dijon mustard, and a little bit of honey: good for any Asian-inspired salad mixture such as cucumbers, lettuce, corn, and scallions.

- Walnut oil with sherry vinegar, minced garlic, and Dijon mustard: great on citrus wedges and on salads containing tart fruit.

- Sesame oil with cider vinegar and a teaspoon of sugar: an excellent base for a cucumber and onion relish.

Once mixed, homemade dressing can stay in an airtight container in the refrigerator for at least 1 month—often more, depending on whether perishable ingredients are used (for example, if you've made a Caesar dressing, which calls for a raw egg, use it immediately). To save time, I often make the dressing in the bottom of the bowl I am using to serve the salad, and then just toss the greens on top of it.

Gorgonzola Vinaigrette

Makes ¾ cup (enough for a 6-serving salad)

Gorgonzola, or any other blue-veined cheese, really dresses up a salad. The strong salty flavors and creaminess of the cheese also stand up very well to the bracing spiciness of chili, making this an ideal dressing for a side salad.

3 tablespoons white wine vinegar, or more to taste
2 cloves garlic, minced
1 teaspoon Dijon mustard
3 tablespoons crumbled Gorgonzola cheese, or more to taste
½ cup extra-virgin olive oil, or more to taste

1. Place the vinegar, garlic, mustard, and cheese in a blender or in a liquid measuring cup, and process or whisk until well combined (blending the ingredients will result in a smoother, creamier dressing). With the blender running on low speed, or while whisking, gradually add the oil and continue to blend or whisk until the dressing is smooth and thick.

2. Taste, and add more vinegar, oil, or cheese if desired. Store, covered, in the refrigerator for up to 1 month.

Guacamole Vinaigrette

Makes ½ cup (enough for a 4-serving salad)

This guacamole-based dressing adds a fiesta air to any veggie salad and is particularly flavorful if you add the crunch of corn chips, and perhaps sliced black or green olives, to the salad. It is a terrific way to give leftover guacamole a second life.

¼ cup extra-virgin olive
2 tablespoons red or white wine vinegar
¼ cup Guacamole (page 6)
1 tablespoon fresh lime juice, or to taste

Whisk the ingredients together in a small bowl until thoroughly combined. Store, covered, in the refrigerator for up to 1 month.

Garden Salsa Vinaigrette

🌶️ 🌶️

Makes ½ cup (enough for a 4-serving salad)

Never let any salsa go to waste! One great way to extend the life of a fresh salsa is to whisk it into a basic vinaigrette, as I've done here. I like this dressing on any vegetable or green salad, from a main-dish salad to a side salad. It is pretty much a staple at my house.

¼ cup extra-virgin olive oil
2 tablespoons Salsa Roja (page 4) or
     commercial salsa fresca
2 tablespoons red wine vinegar
1 teaspoon Dijon mustard

Whisk the ingredients together in a small bowl until thoroughly combined. Store, covered, in the refrigerator for up to 1 month.

Chile Vinaigrette

🌶️

Makes ½ cup (enough for a 4-serving salad)

Adding chiles to green salads is a good way to enhance the flavor and healthfulness of leafy greens. (Chiles are incredibly healthful, because of the capsaicin they contain, which is very healing and is the world's strongest antioxidant. One can truly never eat too many chiles!) There are many ways to add chiles to a salad: you can add fresh chiles, pickled or parched chiles, ground hot or mild chile, chile-infused vinegar or oil—the list goes on. Here I'm kicking up the chile factor by whisking pure ground chile into a simple vinaigrette.

⅓ cup extra-virgin olive oil
1 teaspoon pure ground hot or
     mild red chile, or to taste
2 tablespoons cider vinegar
1 teaspoon Dijon mustard

Whisk the ingredients together in a small bowl until thoroughly combined. Store, covered, in the refrigerator for up to 2 months.

Creamy Lime and Tomatillo Dressing

🌶️

Makes 1½ cups (enough for a 12-serving salad or a dip for 12)

This thick, creamy dressing is great on salads or as a dip for veggies. The lime juice and tomatillo both lend a tangy zest that also makes the dressing a cool, flavorful companion for crispy fried chicken or shrimp.

½ cup **Chipotle Verde Salsa,**
    Sonora Style (page 3)
    or commercial salsa verde
½ cup **mayonnaise**
½ cup **sour cream**
1 tablespoon **fresh lime juice,**
    plus more to taste
1 **jalapeño chile, stemmed, seeded**
    and minced
Crushed caribe chile, for garnish
    (optional)

Place the salsa, mayonnaise, sour cream, lime juice, and jalapeño in a small bowl and whisk together to combine. Taste, and adjust the flavoring as needed. Let sit at room temperature until the flavors blend, at least 15 minutes. If using as a dip, garnish with a sprinkling of caribe chile before serving. This dressing will keep for up to 2 weeks when stored in the refrigerator.

⅓ cup **extra-virgin olive oil**
3 tablespoons **fresh lemon juice**
1 tablespoon **honey**
2 teaspoons **Dijon mustard**

Whisk the ingredients together in a small bowl or liquid measuring cup until thoroughly combined. Cover and chill for about 30 minutes before using. Store, covered, in the refrigerator for up to 2 months.

Lemony Mustard Dressing

🌶

Makes ½ cup (enough for a 4-serving salad)

This is one of my favorite salad dressings, especially if fruit is used in the salad. The combination of fresh lemon and honey makes a wonderful complement to almost any fruit, no matter whether you use stone fruit or berries, or if the fruit is fresh or dried.

Hot Chile Oil

🌶 🌶 🌶 🌶

Makes 1 cup

Hot chile oil—great to have on hand for adding instant heat—is very popular in Asian cuisines and lends heat to many dishes. I love to use it in Southwestern cooking as well. It's easy to prepare, and when packaged in pretty bottles or jars, it makes a great gift. When the chiles soak in oil, their natural oils blend with it, creating a final product that's full of vibrant flavor and spice. I use this mostly for the oil in salad dressings. To keep it fresh, refrigerate it and then bring to room temperature before using.

1½ cups virgin olive oil, peanut oil, or vegetable oil
1 cup crushed caribe chile or pequin quebrado

Place the oil and chiles in a small saucepan over medium heat. Bring almost to a boil, watching closely. As soon as the first bubble appears, remove the pan from the heat so the chiles won't scorch. Cover the saucepan and set it aside for several hours. Then strain the oil through a colander into an absolutely clean glass container. The oil will keep indefinitely if stored, covered, in the refrigerator.

Hot Chile Vinegar

🌶 🌶 🌶 🌶

Makes 1½ cups

I use this hot chile vinegar in vegetable or tossed green salads. And when I'm watching calories, I sometimes use it

alone or with a bare drizzle of fabulously flavorful extra-virgin olive oil. You can use it in marinades or on cooked vegetables, or make a batch to give as a great gift. If you'd like to give the vinegar more complexity, add a few sprigs of fresh herbs. When fighting a cold, I like to add 2 tablespoons of the vinegar and honey to taste to a cup of hot water for a restorative drink.

1 quart cider vinegar or distilled white vinegar (at least 5% acidity)
1 cup small fresh red chiles, or a combination of red, yellow, and green chiles, such as serranos and yellow hots, washed and dried
Several sprigs (3 inches each) fresh rosemary and/or oregano

1. Place the vinegar in a small nonreactive saucepan over medium heat and bring it almost to a boil. When you see the first bubble, add the chiles and reduce the heat to a simmer. Add the herbs, if using. Cook gently, uncovered, until the chiles are tender when pierced with a fork, about 5 minutes.

2. Transfer the hot vinegar, chiles, and herbs, if using, to a sterilized quart-size jar or two sterilized pint-size jars (see Note) and seal with canning lid(s). Allow the vinegar to sit at room temperature for at least 1 week before using it. The vinegar will keep indefinitely if stored at a moderate room temperature (no higher than 75°F).

Note: Sterilize Mason-type canning jars and lids according to the manufacturer's instructions.

Asparagus with Gorgonzola

Serves 4 to 6

Asparagus being one of my favorite vegetables, I am always experimenting with different ways to prepare it. It is so mild tasting that I'm often wary of masking its delicious flavor. Yet I thought just maybe it would stand up to Gorgonzola cheese, and to my amazement, it held its own! This dish is truly terrific with almost any entrée.

1 pound fresh asparagus
2 tablespoons extra-virgin olive oil
3 tablespoons crumbled Gorgonzola
    cheese, or to taste
2 tablespoons balsamic vinegar
1 teaspoon crushed caribe chile

1. Wash and dry the asparagus well; then snap off and discard the tough ends. Place the asparagus in a microwave-safe dish with a lid, or cover it with plastic wrap. Microwave on high until the asparagus is just tender and bright green in color, about 6 minutes. (See box, at right.)

2. Remove the asparagus from the microwave and drizzle the olive oil over it; then sprinkle it with the cheese. Cover the dish and set it aside until the cheese has melted and the flavor of the cheese has "blossomed," 3 to 5 minutes.

Cooking Asparagus

I often microwave asparagus, as described in the recipe for Asparagus with Gorgonzola, at left. However, I sometimes cook asparagus using the same method that I am using to prepare the rest of the meal—if I'm grilling, I grill it, and if I'm roasting or broiling, then I roast or broil the asparagus.

- For grilling: Cook the asparagus over medium to medium-high heat for 3 to 5 minutes a side, or until the color deepens and a fork pierces it easily, about 10 minutes total.

- For roasting or broiling: Place the asparagus on a rimmed baking sheet and roast it in preheated 450°F oven, or broil it under a preheated broiler, turning it every 2 to 3 minutes, until the color deepens and a fork pierces it easily: 10 to 15 minutes for roasting, 5 to 10 minutes for broiling.

- For stovetop cooking: Preheat a stovetop grill or a heavy seasoned skillet over high heat. Place the asparagus on the hot surface and cook, turning it every 2 to 3 minutes, until the color deepens and a fork pierces it easily, about 10 minutes total.

3. Just before serving, sprinkle the balsamic vinegar and caribe chile on the asparagus. Enjoy at room temperature or chill before serving.

Grilled Chile-Lime Corn on the Cob

Serves 4

Grilling corn gives it so much more flavor than steaming or boiling it, and the addition of chile and lime really plays up corn's natural sweetness. If you don't feel like lighting up the grill (or heating a grill pan) and can live without the caramelized flavor that grilling lends, it's very easy to cook corn in a microwave: simply place the shucked ears in a microwave-safe plastic bag, seal it, and microwave them until tender, about 4 minutes per ear.

HOT STUFF

Beware of skinny, slope-shouldered chiles—the narrower the pod, the hotter it will be.

4 large ears fresh sweet corn, shucked
2 teaspoons vegetable oil or olive oil
4 teaspoons crushed caribe chile
1 lime, cut into 8 wedges

1. Preheat a barbecue grill, grill pan, or broiler.

2. Brush the ears of corn with the oil. When the cooking surface is hot, place the corn directly on the grill or on a rimmed baking sheet under the broiler. Cook, turning after about 4 minutes, until the corn is tender and the edges are slightly blackened, 8 to 10 minutes in all.

3. Transfer the corn to a serving platter, sprinkle with the caribe chile, and serve with the lime wedges alongside.

Fried Green Tomatoes with Blue Corn–Jalapeño Coating

Serves 4 to 6

Fried green tomatoes have been very popular since Fannie Flagg made them a signature dish in her *Original Whistle Stop Cafe Cookbook*. I have always loved the way my mother made them—simply dusted in flour and fried in bacon fat until they're soft inside and golden crisp on the outside. Here I've revamped the basic recipe, adding the crunch and strong corny flavor of blue corn and bits of spicy fresh jalapeño. I still like to fry them in bacon fat, but sometimes I use olive oil, butter, or vegetable oil.

4 to 6 medium-size green tomatoes
¼ cup bacon drippings, vegetable oil
   (not canola), olive oil, or butter,
   plus more as needed
½ cup blue, yellow, or white finely ground
   cornmeal, plus more as needed
1 jalapeño chile, stemmed, seeded,
   and minced
¾ teaspoon salt, plus more as needed

1. Slice the tomatoes into ½-inch-thick rounds. Place the bacon drippings in a large heavy skillet over high heat. Place the cornmeal on a plate, and stir in the jalapeño and salt.

2. Dredge the tomato slices in the cornmeal mixture, and set them aside.

3. Drop a bit of cornmeal into the fat to see if it is hot enough; when it is, the fat will bubble around the cornmeal. Working in batches, carefully lay the tomato slices into the fat in a single layer. Fry the tomatoes, carefully turning them once, until golden and crisp all over, 3 to 5 minutes in all. Transfer the fried tomatoes to

a paper-towel-lined plate, and repeat with the remaining tomatoes.

4. Serve immediately, or place the blotted tomatoes on an unlined plate and keep them in a low oven (150° to 250°F) until ready to serve.

Hot 'n' Spicy Okra

🌶 🌶 🌶 🌶
Serves 4

I love okra. My mother and her mother prepared it lots of different ways, and my favorite was always old-fashioned fried okra. It's messy to make, for sure, but so much fun to eat! We used to douse the crispy fried pieces with hot sauce just before eating them, but sometimes that made the crust soggy. So I thought, why not add spice to the coating instead? It works beautifully.

Vegetable oil (not canola)
1 pound okra, well washed and dried
2 eggs, beaten
2 tablespoons milk
5 dashes hot red pepper sauce,
   such as Tabasco, or more to taste
2 cups coarsely ground yellow cornmeal
1 teaspoon salt
2 teaspoons pequin quebrado

1. Pour the oil into a deep skillet, such as a chicken fryer, to a depth of ½ inch. Place it

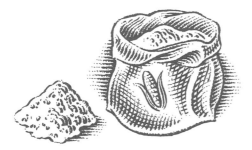

over high heat to warm. Line a plate with paper towels.

2. Meanwhile, slice the stems off the okra and cut it into ½-inch-thick rounds. Whisk the eggs, milk, and hot pepper sauce together in a shallow bowl. Stir the cornmeal, salt, and pequin quebrado together on a plate.

3. Submerge one third of the okra in the egg mixture. Using a slotted spoon, transfer the okra to the cornmeal mixture, and toss to coat it well.

4. When the oil is hot enough (test it by dropping in a single piece of okra—if the oil bubbles, it is ready), transfer the cornmeal-coated okra to the oil (the okra should fry in a single layer; cook it in batches if necessary).

5. Fry the okra, stirring it occasionally with a slotted spoon to prevent clumping, until it is golden brown, 3 to 4 minutes. Transfer the fried okra to the paper-towel-lined plate to drain. Repeat with the remaining okra (again, working in batches as necessary).

6. Serve hot.

Gordon's Fabulous Frijoles

Makes 2 quarts; serves 4 to 6 as a main course

These are the beans my husband,
Gordon, always makes. He prepares them with any kind of bean, from limas to black-eyed peas (to which he always adds sliced button mushrooms). Regardless of the type of beans Gordon uses, or the ways he tweaks the recipe, the beans are always highly flavorful, thanks to the use of chicken broth. Because these beans require a relatively long cooking time, I almost always make a large quantity, like the 2 pounds recommended here. I like to serve them as a side dish or layered under chili, or as a main course topped with chopped onions and pickled jalapeños (in which case cornbread on the side is a must).

2 pounds dried pinto beans, rinsed and
    picked over
2 ham hocks, or 1 meaty ham bone
1 teaspoon freshly ground black pepper
2 cloves garlic, minced
2 cups coarsely chopped Spanish onion
3 to 4 cups rich chicken broth
    (see Note, page 76), plus more
    as needed
Salt

1. Place the beans and the ham hocks in a heavy 5-quart pot. Add enough water to cover the beans and meat by 3 inches.

2. Add the pepper, garlic, and onion, and bring to a boil. Then reduce the heat to medium-low and simmer, uncovered, stirring occasionally, until a bean mashes easily when pressed against the side of the pot, about 2 hours. During this time, add the chicken broth as needed to maintain about 1 inch of liquid above the level of the bean mixture.

3. When the beans are cooked through, remove the ham hocks. Continue to simmer the beans, uncovered, until they have a slightly thick consistency, 2 to 3 hours. Taste, and add salt before serving.

Refritos

Serves 6 to 8

When made with home-cooked beans, such as Gordon's Fabulous Frijolos (facing page), these are sure to be the best-tasting refried beans you've ever had. The secret is in "tingeing" the garlic a bit (very, very lightly tanning the edges). You can serve these refritos plain, or topped with shredded cheese and pickled jalapeños. They also make a delicious filling for quesadillas, burritos, and enchiladas (see more suggestions in the box at right).

Refritos

Refritos—refried beans—are most often made with pintos, the most nutritious of all beans, although sometimes black beans are used. They're a must-have with anything spicy or cheesy—the flavors just seem to gravitate to each other.

Leftover refritos can be frozen for at least 6 months or can be called into action in any number of innovative uses:

- As a quick snack, top chips with a layer of beans, a thick chili such as Pecos River Bowl of Red (page 34), some chopped onion, some pickled jalapeño, and a sprinkle of Cheddar-Jack cheese.

- As an ingredient in quesadillas, along with Cheddar-Jack cheese, chorizo, chopped scallions or onion, chopped tomatoes, sliced fresh chiles, and cubes of avocado.

- As a filling for tacos, along with carnitas and salsa verde, served artfully decorated with Flavored Cremas (see page 25).

- As a component of tortilla-chili layered casseroles (such as Crazy Chili Casserole, page 91) that feature a ranchero sauce, sour cream, and queso blanco.

2 teaspoons butter, bacon drippings, or lard
1 clove garlic, minced
1 tablespoon finely chopped Spanish onion
2 cups cooked pinto beans, or 1 can
    (16 ounces) pinto beans with liquid
    (see Note)

1. Melt the butter in a large heavy skillet over medium heat. Add the garlic, and as soon as it starts to turn golden, add the onion. When the onion begins to soften, add the pinto beans with a little of their liquid. Mash them well, using a potato masher or heavy wooden spoon, stirring in more liquid as needed to achieve a smooth texture.

2. Cook the mashed beans over medium heat, stirring occasionally to prevent burning, until they reach a thick, pudding-like consistency, about 15 minutes. Serve piping hot.

Note: If you prefer, you can make these with home-cooked or canned black beans.

Spicy Fries

Serves 4 to 6

When I owned the Pecos River
Café in New York City, I served Spicy Curly Fries as a staple and was amazed at their popularity. One restaurant review called them the best French fries in New York City! To cut the fries into curls, you need a spiral cutter, which is an expensive tool, usually found only in professional kitchens. But you can use the spices on regular fries to make a delicious treat.

I've listed the spices for my favorite curly fry seasoning rub here, but you can purchase a commercial spice rub if you prefer (I also sell my spice rub through my Pecos Valley Spice Co., www.pecosvalley.com).

FOR THE FRIES:
2 teaspoons salt
4 medium-size or 3 large russet potatoes,
    unpeeled, well scrubbed
2 quarts vegetable oil (not canola)

FOR THE SEASONING RUB:
2½ tablespoons pure ground mild red chile
1 tablespoon sugar
2 teaspoons salt

1. Prepare the potatoes: Fill a bowl with warm water, add the salt, and stir until it has dissolved. Cut the potatoes in half lengthwise, then into ½-inch-wide slices. Slice each slice into ¼-inch-wide strips. Place the cut potatoes in the salted water, making sure they are covered. Let them soak until white starch appears in the bottom of the bowl, at least 30 minutes.

2. Heat the oil to 375°F in a deep 5-quart Dutch oven.

3. Combine the ingredients for the seasoning rub in a paper bag or salt shaker. Set aside.

4. When the oil is hot (375° to 400°F; use an instant-read deep-frying thermometer to check the temperature), lower about 1 cup of the potatoes into the oil, using a fry basket. Fry the potatoes until they are light gold and crisp on the outside and cooked in the center, 2 to 3 minutes. Transfer them to a paper-towel-lined plate, and repeat with the remaining potatoes.

5. Working in batches, gently shake the French fries in the paper bag containing the rub (or sprinkle the rub over them with the shaker). Serve hot.

Red-Hot Sweet Potato Lace

🐱 🐱

Serves 4 to 6

Sweet potatoes love spice! I often put ground red chile on them, or sometimes a sprinkling of cinnamon-sugar. Here I've dusted fried thin sweet potato rounds with a mixture of red chile, sugar, and salt. These are really fun—try them sometime soon!

2 quarts vegetable oil (not canola)
**2 large sweet potatoes (about 2 pounds),
     well scrubbed and dried**
**1½ tablespoons pure ground hot
     red chile**
1 tablespoon sugar
2 teaspoons salt

1. Pour the oil into a heavy pot that is at least 5 inches deep, such as a Dutch oven, and heat it over medium-high heat until it reads between 375° and 400°F on an instant-read deep-frying thermometer.

2. While the oil is heating, slice the sweet potatoes into very thin rounds, using a mandoline or a food processor fitted with the slicing attachment. Stir the chile, sugar, and salt together in a small bowl, pour the mixture into a paper bag, and set it aside.

3. When the oil is hot, lower about 1 cup of the sweet potatoes into the pot, using a fry basket. Fry the potatoes until crisp, about 30 seconds. Transfer them to a paper-towel-lined plate and repeat with the remaining potato slices.

4. Working in batches, coat the fried potatoes with a light dusting of the seasoning mixture by gently shaking them with the mixture in the paper bag. Serve warm.

Twice-Baked Potatoes
with Cheddar and Chiles

Serves 4 to 8

These hearty potatoes require a little more work than ordinary baked potatoes, but they're well worth the effort. The rich, creamy taste is a great complement to chili. If you wish to make the potatoes ahead of time, you can prepare them through step 4 up to 24 hours before serving; refrigerate them, covered, on a baking sheet, then heat them as directed in step 5, allowing about 30 minutes in the oven.

4 medium-size russet baking potatoes, well scrubbed and dried
4 tablespoons (½ stick) butter, or to taste
¼ cup sour cream, or to taste
2 tablespoons finely minced onion or chives
¼ cup grated sharp Cheddar cheese
2 teaspoons pure ground mild red chile, or ¼ cup chopped fresh green chiles, well drained

1. Preheat the oven to 400°F.

2. Place the potatoes on a baking sheet and bake until they are soft when pierced with a fork, about 45 minutes. Remove them from the oven and let them cool slightly.

3. When the potatoes are still warm but cool enough to handle, slice each one lengthwise down the center, making certain not to cut through the bottom. Carefully scoop out the baked potato flesh, leaving a ¼-inch margin of potato attached to the shell. Transfer the potato flesh to a medium-size bowl. Place the scooped-out shells on a baking sheet.

4. Add the butter to the potato flesh and toss gently until the butter melts. Then cover the bowl tightly with plastic wrap or a lid and allow the potatoes to fluff a bit, 3 to 4 minutes. Whip the potatoes with a handheld electric mixer on medium speed, or beat them with a potato masher, until smooth. Stir in all the remaining ingredients. Divide the potato mixture among the potato shells, spooning it roughly into the shells so the top has an uneven surface.

5. Place the filled potato shells in the oven and bake until the cheese melts and the potatoes are light gold on top, 15 to 20 minutes.

Cilantro-Chile Rice

◉ ◉

Serves 4 to 6

Green chile and cheese are totally meant for each other. This flavorful dish goes wonderfully with chilies and most any entrée. Any kind of cheese can be used, but if you're watching calories or fat grams, use less cheese and choose a flavorful variety, such as an extra-sharp Cheddar.

2½ cups chicken or vegetable broth
1¼ cups long-grain white rice
4 to 6 green chiles, parched
    (see box, page 14), peeled, stemmed,
    and chopped, or ¾ cup canned or
    thawed frozen chopped chiles
¾ cup grated Cheddar cheese, or a
    combination of Monterey Jack and
    Cheddar cheeses, or more to taste
½ cup sour cream or yogurt, or to taste
¼ cup coarsely chopped fresh cilantro

1. Bring the broth to a boil in a 3-quart saucepan with a close-fitting lid. Add the rice and reduce to a simmer. Cover the pan and cook, stirring occasionally, until the rice is tender and fluffy and all the liquid has been absorbed, about 15 minutes.

2. Remove the pan from the heat and stir in the chiles, cheese, and sour cream. Cover the pan to allow the cheese to melt and the flavors to blend, 3 to 5 minutes. Taste, and adjust the seasonings as needed. Fold in the cilantro, and serve.

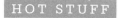

The chile pepper has been cultivated for centuries, not only as a food, but also for its medicinal properties.

Lime Rice

◉

Makes 2 cups; serves 4

This rice is refreshingly light and goes very well with any spicy entrée—especially chili.

2 teaspoons fresh lime juice
1 tablespoon powdered chicken bouillon,
    or 2 chicken bouillon cubes
1 tablespoon butter
1 cup long-grain white rice
¼ cup Chipotle Verde Salsa, Sonora Style
    (page 3) or commercial salsa verde
1 tablespoon coarsely chopped fresh
    cilantro

1. Place the lime juice, chicken bouillon, butter, and 1½ cups water in a large saucepan over high heat and bring to a boil. Stir in the rice, reduce the heat to a simmer, cover the pan, and cook, stirring occasionally, until the rice is tender and fluffy and all the liquid has been absorbed, 15 minutes.

2. When the rice is cooked, remove the pan from the heat and stir in the salsa and cilantro. Cover the pan for a few minutes; then fluff the rice with a fork before serving.

Cumin Rice

Serves 6 to 8

This is my all-time favorite
rice recipe. It goes very well with chili and other fiery entrées, but it's also delicious with dishes that are not so spicy—say, grilled salmon or chicken with a tomato or fruit salsa on the side.

2 tablespoons lard or butter
1 cup diced green bell pepper
1 cup diced red bell pepper
1 medium-size onion, finely chopped
1 clove garlic, minced
1 teaspoon ground cumin
1½ cups uncooked long-grain rice
1½ cups chicken broth, heated,
    or more as needed
Salt (optional)

1. Melt the lard in a 3-quart saucepan with a close-fitting lid over medium heat. Add the peppers and onion, and cook until the onion is translucent, about 5 minutes. Add the garlic, ½ teaspoon cumin, and rice, and stir until well combined.

2. Add the hot broth, and mix to distribute the rice evenly. Bring to a simmer, then reduce the heat to low, cover, and let cook for 15 minutes without lifting the lid. Then add the remaining cumin and stir. If the rice is not tender, cook it a few minutes more (if it is also dry at this point, add a bit more broth to moisten). Taste and add salt if you wish (the seasoning in the broth may preclude the need for it).

5

Breads & Sop-Ups

Corn and chili together go back about as far as chili itself does. Of course there's the age-old debate about using masa harina (corn flour) to thicken up the liquid: sacrilege or necessity? The world may never know. But the real heart of the corn-chili union tends to show up in a cast-iron skillet: cornbread.

Whether it's the sweetness, the crumbliness, or the indescribable magic that happens when brew meets bread, there's some-thing about cornbread that just makes it go hand in hand with chili of any type: green, red, or some-thing else entirely. So no matter what your pot contains, you'll find a cornbread recipe here to comple-ment it, from Jalapeño Corn Sticks (spicy but not too spicy) to the ineffable salty perfection of Bacon Crumble Cornbread. Tint the old yellow favorite blue by making Blue Corn Parfait Bread (practi-cally a meal in itself, with its cheesy layers) or Blue Corn Jalapeño Muffins.

If corn just gets to be too much (and that's okay—as great as it is, there can be welcome breaks from its richness), try Bear Paw Bread, a terrifically crusty white bread from the Pueblo Indians, or the dense buckwheat Beer Bread, so named for the dark beer that lends its flavor to the yeasty dough.

No matter what your choice of bread winds up being, the key is balance: dense breads to stand up to hearty chilies, lighter loaves so that you don't mask the flavors of delicate brews. And while making bread from scratch can be a daunting prospect if you haven't done it before, even on your first try you'll see how the homemade stuff leaves anything store-bought back in the dust. With just a little practice, you'll be churning out tins of cornbread, platters of Indian Fry Bread, and perfectly chewy loaves with almost no effort, ready to complement any type of chili that gets thrown at you. Have faith: follow the instructions, and don't be afraid to get your hands dirty— you'll have to, with all that kneading!

And when it's time for a quick weeknight chili meal and you want an easy sop-up to serve alongside, throw together the impossibly simple Cheesy Tortilla Wedges. You won't be disappointed.

SOME LIKE IT HOT . . .
These icons show how fiery each dish is.

🌶
MILD

🌶 🌶
A BIT OF BITE

🌶 🌶 🌶
HOT

🌶 🌶 🌶 🌶
HOT ENOUGH TO MAKE YOU . . .

Jalapeño Corn Sticks

🌶 🌶

Makes 18 large sticks or 24 small sticks

Corn sticks are small cornbreads baked in muffin tin–like pans that have cups shaped like little ears of corn. The petite cornbreads are cute as can be, and they also have a satisfyingly crispy, crusty exterior. I prefer blue corn flour for this recipe, as it yields a lighter, less crumbly texture than cornmeal. If you have trouble finding blue corn flour (see Sources), feel free to substitute yellow or white cornmeal.

Butter, for greasing the pans
2 eggs, beaten
¾ cup milk
8 tablespoons (1 stick) butter, melted,
    or ½ cup bacon drippings
1½ cups blue corn flour or cornmeal
    of any color
1½ teaspoons baking powder
½ teaspoon salt
1 tablespoon sugar
2 to 3 jalapeño chiles, stemmed, seeded
    (if you wish to reduce the heat),
    and minced

1. Preheat the oven to 350°F. Using a piece of slightly crumpled waxed paper, very generously butter the cups of the corn stick pans, making certain to coat every nook and cranny to prevent sticking.

2. Whisk the eggs, milk, and melted butter together in a medium bowl. In a larger bowl, stir the corn flour, baking powder, salt, and sugar together. Make a well in the center of the dry mixture, add the egg mixture and the jalapeños, and stir until just combined.

3. Spoon the batter into the buttered corn stick cups, filling each two thirds of the way. Bake until the corn sticks are lightly browned and the edges have pulled away from the pan, 15 to 20 minutes.

4. Remove the pans from the oven and place them on wire racks to cool for about 10 minutes. Then invert the pans and turn out the corn sticks onto the racks to finish cooling.

Note: The baked corn sticks can be frozen in a rigid container for up to 3 months. Reheat them, still frozen, wrapped in aluminum foil, in a preheated 350° to 375°F oven until warm, about 10 minutes.

Blue Corn
Jalapeño Muffins
🌶️ 🌶️
Makes 18 muffins

We used to serve these tempting muffins at the Saturday morning brunches at my cooking school, and they became very popular. They keep well and are less crumbly than some corn muffins. I like to warm them slightly before serving them.

½ **cup canned creamed corn**
¾ **cup milk**
⅓ **cup butter, melted, or vegetable oil**
2 **eggs, beaten**
1½ **cups blue cornmeal or blue corn flour**
1 **teaspoon baking powder**
½ **teaspoon baking soda**
1 **teaspoon salt**
1 **teaspoon sugar**
1 **cup grated Cheddar cheese, or**
    a combination of Cheddar and
    Monterey Jack, or more to taste
3 **fresh jalapeño chiles, stemmed and sliced**
    into thin rounds (seeds and all)

1. Preheat the oven to 400°F. Line 18 muffin cups with paper liners.

2. Place the corn, milk, butter, and eggs in a large bowl and mix to combine well. Combine the cornmeal, baking powder, baking soda, salt, and sugar in a separate large bowl, and make a well in the center. Add the wet mixture to the dry mixture, stirring until just combined.

3. Spoon some of the batter into the muffin cups, filling each slightly less than halfway. Top each with a small spoonful of cheese and 2 or 3 jalapeño rounds (you will have both left over). Divide the remaining batter among the half-filled muffin cups, and top each one with the remaining cheese and jalapeños, placing

1 jalapeño round on each muffin. Bake until the muffins are lightly browned and a toothpick inserted into the center of a muffin comes out mostly clean (it may have some cheese on it), 25 to 30 minutes.

4. Let the muffins cool in the pan for 10 minutes, then invert the pan and turn out the muffins onto a wire rack to finish cooling.

Blue Corn
Parfait Bread

Serves 9 to 12

I call this cornbread a "parfait" because, like the dessert of the same name, it is a layered dish. The sour cream–enriched blue cornbread has a layer of creamy Monterey Jack and spicy jalapeños in the center. The moist quality of this bread makes it a great keeper—it's a good choice to take camping or picnicking. And of course it tastes wonderful, too. Often when I serve it to houseguests, they ask, "Jane, if we get up earlier than you do, where can we find that cornbread?"

⅔ cup butter
1 cup blue corn flour or blue cornmeal
1½ teaspoons baking powder
¾ teaspoon salt
2 large eggs, at room temperature
1 cup sour cream
2 cups cooked or canned whole-kernel corn, drained (one 15-ounce can works well)
4 ounces Monterey Jack or Cheddar cheese, or a combination, sliced ¼ inch thick
¼ cup sliced pickled or fresh jalapeño chiles

1. Turn the oven on to 375°F.

2. Place the butter in a 9-inch cast-iron skillet, or in a 9-inch round or square cake pan, and place it in the preheating oven until the butter melts. Meanwhile, combine the corn flour, baking powder, and salt in a large bowl.

3. When the butter has melted, carefully remove the skillet from the oven, pour the butter into a separate large bowl, and set the skillet aside. Add the eggs and sour cream to the butter in the bowl, and whisk to combine thoroughly. Fold in the corn kernels. Make a well in the center of the flour mixture and pour the egg mixture into it. Mix until just combined.

4. Pour almost half of the batter into the skillet, and smooth it to the edges of the skillet with a spatula. Cover the batter evenly with the sliced cheese and chiles. Pour the remaining batter over the cheese and chiles, and carefully smooth it to cover the filling. Bake until the cornbread is lightly browned and a toothpick inserted in the center comes out mostly clean (it may have some cheese on it), 30 to 40 minutes. Cut the bread into wedges and serve warm, straight from the skillet.

Cornmeal's True Colors: White, Yellow, and Blue

White or yellow cornmeal is generally available in two types; stone-ground, which tends to be coarser, and steel-cut, which is finer. For white or yellow corn, these are pretty much interchangeable—with the coarser grind yielding somewhat denser baked goods.

But blue corn is different. Blue corn was developed by the Pueblo Indians of New Mexico, and it has a great deal of religious significance attached to it. Each of the nineteen Pueblos in New Mexico grows a slightly different variety; the varieties are diligently kept separate from one another, making large-scale farming of the blue corn difficult. The corn also has hard, flintlike kernels that are very difficult to grind, making it much easier to grind coarsely; however, this yields very dense textures in baked goods. Blue corn is much easier to cook with, and yields lighter results, when it is finely ground into corn flour.

The best blue cornmeal is smoked in adobe ovens and then lava-wheel-ground to a fine flourlike consistency. But with the popularity of blue corn these days, a lot of the blue cornmeal on the market is "filled," or blended with white or yellow corn. For the best flavor and texture, be sure to buy pure blue corn flour (see Sources).

Bacon Crumble
Cornbread

Serves 4 to 8

There is something about cornbread that really complements chili, and there's something about bacon that really complements cornbread. This cornbread combines the smoky, rich flavor of bacon with the gritty, satisfying texture and pleasing earthiness of cornmeal—and it's delicious alongside any number of chilis. You can use fine or coarsely ground cornmeal—the finer the grind, the lighter the bread.

4 strips thick-cut (or 8 strips thin-cut) good-quality bacon
1 cup yellow, white, or blue cornmeal
1 cup unbleached all-purpose flour
2 tablespoons sugar
2 teaspoons baking powder
1 teaspoon kosher salt
1 egg
1 cup milk

1. Preheat the oven to 400°F.

2. Using kitchen scissors or a sharp knife, cut the bacon crosswise into ¼-inch-wide strips. Place them in a 9-inch cast-iron or other heavy ovenproof skillet over medium-low heat and cook, turning occasionally, until crisp, 6 to 8 minutes. Transfer the bacon to a paper-towel-lined plate to drain. Reserve 3 tablespoons of the bacon drippings in the skillet and pour off the rest.

3. Combine the cornmeal, flour, sugar, baking powder, and salt in a large bowl. In a separate bowl, whisk the egg and milk together. Add the egg mixture to the dry mixture, and stir to combine.

4. Pour the bacon drippings into the batter and stir until just combined. Pour the batter into the unwashed skillet, top with the bacon, and bake until a toothpick inserted in the center of the cornbread comes out clean, 20 minutes.

5. Let the cornbread cool in the skillet. Then cut it into wedges and serve it straight from the pan.

For Good Measure

When measuring wheat flour, don't use the measuring cup to scoop up the flour you need—you'll end up with too much flour, which will make your bread heavy or tough. Instead, use a spoon to carefully fluff the flour in its container. Then spoon the flour into a dry measuring cup and level it with the flat edge of a spatula. This will give you a more accurate measurement and better baking results.

Multi-Grain
Cornbread

Serves 6

My husband, Gordon, and I often eat this cornbread with chili, and many times we've polished off the entire loaf! I love the combination of whole wheat and cornmeal, especially when it is flavored with aromatic honey and savory bacon drippings. Of course, if you find bacon drippings objectionable, feel free to substitute butter, which works just fine.

2 tablespoons bacon drippings or
    unsalted butter
1 cup white, yellow, or blue cornmeal,
    either fine or coarsely ground
½ cup whole-wheat flour
2 teaspoons baking powder
¾ teaspoon kosher salt
1 egg
1 cup milk
3 tablespoons honey

1. Turn the oven on to 375°F.

2. Place the bacon drippings in an 8-inch cast-iron or other heavy ovenproof skillet, and transfer it to the preheating oven to melt the fat.

3. Combine the cornmeal, flour, baking powder,

and salt in large bowl. In a separate bowl, whisk the egg, milk, and honey together. Add the egg mixture to the cornmeal mixture, and stir to combine.

4. Carefully remove the hot skillet from the oven and pour the melted drippings into the batter, stirring until just combined. Pour the batter into the skillet and bake until the cornbread is lightly browned on top and the edges have pulled away from the pan, or a toothpick inserted in the center comes out clean, 30 minutes.

5. Cut the cornbread into wedges and serve it hot, right from the skillet.

Indian Fry Bread

Makes 6 portions

Although not a traditional food, fry bread became a staple in American Indian communities after the U.S. government relocated tribes from their native lands to reservations in the 19th century. Though born of hard times and necessity, fry bread has become quite popular throughout the West. Rich, satisfying, and wonderfully flavorful, fry bread is similar to doughnuts, beignets, and sopaipillas—it's a simple dough that's shaped into rounds and fried. Delicious on its own, with just some sugar or honey, it's also the basis for savory dishes such as the Navajo Tacos on page 96.

3 cups unbleached all-purpose flour
¾ teaspoon salt
1 tablespoon baking powder
About 1 cup warm water (100° to 115°F)
2 quarts vegetable oil (not canola)

1. Combine the flour, salt, and baking powder in a large bowl. Make a well in the center of the flour mixture, add 1 cup warm water, and stir to combine thoroughly. The dough should be soft and pliable; if it is dry, gradually add more warm water until it has reached the desired texture.

2. Knead the dough by hand on a lightly floured board until it is smooth, 3 to 5 minutes. (When it is sufficiently kneaded, a pinch of dough will stretch and yield thin threads when pulled between your fingers.) Cover the dough by inverting the bowl over it, and let it rise in a warm place until it retains an indentation when pressed with a finger, 15 to 30 minutes.

3. Meanwhile, pour the oil into a deep fryer and heat it to 375° to 400°F. Line a baking sheet with paper towels and set it aside.

4. Separate the dough into 6 equal pieces and form each piece into a round ball by tucking the dough underneath itself. Work with 1 ball of dough at a time, keeping the rest covered so they will not dry out. Using a lightly floured board and rolling pin, roll each piece of dough from the center, pressing down as you roll, to create a uniformly thin ⅛-inch-thick disk of dough.

5. Carefully place a disk of dough in the hot oil, and fry, turning it with tongs as it cooks, until it is golden, 1 to 2 minutes. Use tongs to transfer the fry bread to the prepared baking sheet and repeat with the remaining dough. Serve warm.

Bear Paw Bread

Serves 6 to 8

The Pueblo Indians make
a wonderful crusty bread that is very reminiscent of good French bread, but instead of being shaped like a baguette, the dough is folded and cut to resemble a bear's paw. It is wonderful with chili, because the yeasty, crusty bread has a personality all its own—strong enough to be noticed when eating chili. And kids love it for both its flavor and its name.

1 scant tablespoon (1 packet)
active dry yeast
¼ cup warm water (110° to 115°F)
½ teaspoon honey
¾ teaspoon salt
1½ teaspoons lard or butter
About 4½ cups unbleached all-purpose flour

1. In the bowl of an electric mixer fitted with the dough hook, dissolve the yeast in the warm water.

2. Heat 1 cup water in a microwave oven at full power for 45 seconds, or heat it in a small saucepan over high heat until hot. Combine the honey, salt, ½ teaspoon of the lard, and the hot water in a small bowl, and whisk until combined. Let the mixture cool to room temperature. Then add it to the yeast mixture.

3. Add 2 cups of the flour to the yeast mixture and mix at the lowest speed until the flour is moistened. Increase the speed to medium and beat for about 30 seconds to activate the gluten in the flour. (If a stand mixer is not available, a handheld mixer or food processor can be used. Switch to beating by hand if the machine is bogging down.) Add another cup of flour, again beginning at low speed and increasing to medium until the flour is incorporated, about 30 seconds. Add a fourth cup of flour, and mix at medium speed until the dough is very thick and climbing up the dough hook, 1 to 2 minutes. If the dough is not quite thick enough, add another ½ cup of flour and mix at medium speed until the desired consistency is reached.

4. Turn the dough out onto a lightly floured board and knead it by hand until it is very smooth and the gluten is well developed, about 5 minutes. (When the dough is sufficiently kneaded, a pinch of dough will stretch and yield long threads when

pulled between your fingers.) Invert the mixing bowl over the dough and let the dough rise in a warm place until doubled in bulk, about 1 hour.

5. Grease two baking sheets with the remaining 1 teaspoon lard. Punch the dough down and divide it in half. Form each half into a smooth round ball by tucking the dough under itself. Using a lightly floured rolling pin on a lightly floured board, roll out each ball to form an oval about 1 inch thick and 8 inches wide. Fold about a third of the dough over the oval, so the lower layer extends about 1 inch beyond the upper layer, stollen fashion. Then pull the two long ends of the dough together and pinch firmly. Place each bear paw on a prepared baking sheet.

6. Using a sharp knife, make two ½-inch-deep slashes about 1 inch from the outside folded edge of the dough, cutting the dough to resemble a paw. Cover each bear paw with a moist cloth and let it rise until doubled, about 30 minutes.

7. Toward the end of the rising time, preheat the oven to 350°F.

8. Place a shallow pan of water in the oven (the water will give the bread a thicker crust). Bake the bear paws, checking periodically to make sure they're browning evenly, until the crusts are lightly browned and the loaves sound hollow when thumped with a finger, about 40 minutes. If the breads are browning unevenly, reverse the position of the baking sheets.

9. Transfer the bear paws to wire racks to cool slightly. Serve warm or at room temperature.

Beer Bread

Serves 6 to 8

I have always loved dense, dark breads like the kinds you get in Germany and Denmark. Here is my version: a yeasty, highly flavored bread that is very dense—great with chili or layered with an assortment of cheeses and flavored butters. The beer combined with the dark honey and buckwheat flour yields a rich, hearty loaf.

2½ cups dark beer
¼ cup dark honey, such as buckwheat honey
4 tablespoons (½ stick) butter, melted, or ½ cup vegetable oil, at room temperature
½ cup warm water (110° to 115°F)
2 scant tablespoons (2 packets) active dry yeast
About 5 cups whole-wheat flour
1 cup buckwheat flour
1½ teaspoon salt
2 cups gluten flour (see Note)
1½ teaspoons dried dill weed (optional)
Butter, for greasing the baking sheets

1. Combine the beer, honey, and melted butter in a small bowl.

2. Warm the bowl of a heavy-duty mixer under warm water. Return the warmed bowl to the mixer, and in it combine the ½ cup warm water and the yeast; let stand until foamy, 3 to 5 minutes.

3. Fit the heavy-duty mixer with the dough hook attachment. Add the honey mixture to the yeast mixture, and using the dough hook, beat to combine, starting at the lowest speed and increasing to medium speed until well mixed, about 1 minute. Add 2½ cups of the whole-wheat flour, and the buckwheat flour, gluten flour, salt, and dill if using. Beat, again starting at the lowest speed, then increasing to medium speed, until smooth, about 2 minutes. Add more whole-wheat flour, a cup at a time, as needed to make a stiff dough.

4. Turn the dough out onto a lightly floured board and knead until smooth, about 8 minutes. (When the dough is sufficiently kneaded, a pinch of dough will stretch and yield long threads when pulled between your fingers.) Invert the mixing bowl over the dough and let the dough rise in a warm place until it retains an indentation when pressed with a finger, about 1 hour.

5. Grease two baking sheets with butter. Punch the dough down and form it into 2 round loaves by tucking it underneath itself. Place each loaf on a prepared baking sheet, cover them with a damp towel, and let them rise until doubled in size, about 45 minutes.

6. Toward the end of the rising time, preheat the oven to 350°F.

7. Bake the loaves until they sound hollow when thumped with a finger, about 40 minutes. Let the bread cool slightly on a wire rack, and serve warm.

Note: Gluten flour is sold at natural food stores. If it's unavailable, reduce the amount of whole-wheat flour to 3½ cups and use 3½ cups bread flour or unbleached all-purpose flour.

Caramelized-Onion Focaccia

Serves 6 to 8

This is my all-time favorite recipe for focaccia. The generous onion topping is laced with the herbal flavor of rosemary and pairs perfectly with the tangy white cheese that melts atop the bread. Of course it is great with any type of chili, but it's also a delicious appetizer.

4 cups unbleached all-purpose flour

1 teaspoon salt

1 scant tablespoon (1 packet) active
    dry yeast

1¼ cups warm water (110° to 115°F),
    plus extra as needed

¼ cup olive oil

8 tablespoons (1 stick) unsalted butter, plus
    extra for greasing the baking sheet

3 medium-size red onions, sliced into thin
    rounds

2 teaspoons sugar

4 cloves garlic, minced

2 tablespoons coarsely chopped fresh
    rosemary leaves, or 1 tablespoon dried
    rosemary, crushed

¼ cup red wine vinegar

¾ cup crumbled white cheese such as
    asadero, feta, or goat cheese

1. Place the flour and salt in the bowl of a heavy-duty mixer fitted with the dough hook, or in another large bowl.

2. In a small bowl, dissolve the yeast in the warm water.

3. When the yeast is foamy, add the oil. Pour this mixture into the bowl containing the flour. If you're using a mixer, beat at the lowest speed until the flour is moistened; then use a higher speed to develop the gluten, about 1 minute. The dough should be smooth and should spring back when firmly tossed on the counter. If you're not using a mixer, stir the yeast mixture into the flour and mix well. Then beat the dough by hand until it is springy, 2 to 3 minutes. Beat quickly

to develop the gluten, using a wooden or large metal spoon. If the dough becomes quite stiff, knead in a bit of warm water until it is smooth and springy.

4. Turn the dough out onto a lightly floured board and knead until it is smooth and soft and the gluten is well developed, about 3 minutes. (You can tell when the gluten is well developed by stretching a small pinch of dough between your fingers: springy threads should form. If there are no threads, more kneading is required.) Invert

Focaccia Free-for-All

Have fun with your focaccia. Besides the toppings recommended here, you can use almost anything you have on hand. Think of a focaccia like a pizza— take inspiration from your fridge and your pantry. In need of a jumping-off point? Try one of these combinations:

• grilled vegetables, such as mushrooms, zucchini, and bell peppers

• basil pesto, sautéed chopped onion, chopped tomato, mozzarella, and Parmesan

• fresh rosemary, pitted and halved Mediterranean olives, and Romano cheese

• grilled or steamed asparagus spears, tomato slices, sliced scallions, shredded Jarlsberg, and grated Romano cheese

the bowl over the dough and set it aside in a warm place until it doubles in bulk, about 30 minutes.

5. Prepare the topping: Melt the butter in a large shallow skillet over medium-low heat. Add the onions, sprinkle them with the sugar, and cook, stirring, until the onions are lightly browned, 5 to 8 minutes. Stir in the garlic, rosemary, and vinegar and set aside.

6. Preheat the oven to 400°F. Lightly butter a large baking sheet.

7. Using a rolling pin or your fingers, spread the dough out onto the baking sheet to form a large disk about ¼ inch thick and as wide as the pan you are using, allowing a bit of dough to form a rim around the edges (it should be slightly thicker at the edge in order to hold the topping). Poke your fingers into the dough all over the top to create 2- to 3-inch-wide indentations to hold the filling. Spread the onion topping evenly over the dough, and sprinkle with the cheese. Bake until the focaccia is lightly browned and the cheese is soft, about 20 minutes. Cool on a wire rack for about 10 minutes, and serve warm.

Garlic Sticks

Makes about 48 sticks

When I think of garlic sticks, I think of two kinds: the soft type, served at some chain restaurants such as Olive Garden, and the crispy-crusted variety. I have always preferred the crisp, chewy ones, which are what this recipe yields. I hope you like them as much as I do.

I recommend using a heavy-duty stand mixer for this recipe, if you have one. It will save you a lot of time.

1 scant tablespoon (1 packet) active
    dry yeast
2 teaspoons sugar
1¾ cups warm water (110° to 115°F)
1 teaspoon salt
About 6 cups unbleached all-purpose flour
4 tablespoons (½ stick) butter, plus extra
    for greasing the pans
6 cloves garlic, finely minced

1. In the bowl of a heavy-duty mixer fitted with the dough hook, stir the yeast and sugar together. Whisk in the warm water, and let sit until the yeast and sugar are dissolved and the mixture is foamy, 3 to 5 minutes. Add the salt and mix on low speed.

2. Add 2 cups of the flour and mix on low speed until well combined. Then mix on medium speed until the dough is smooth and springy, 2 to 3 minutes. Add 2 more cups of the flour, again mixing on low and then increasing the speed to medium. Add 1 cup flour and mix on low speed, switching to medium to create a very stiff, smooth dough. If the dough is not very stiff, add more flour, a tablespoon at a time, and mix on medium speed until the desired consistency is reached.

3. Turn the dough out onto a lightly floured board and knead until it is smooth and forms long threads when a pinch is pulled apart between your fingers, 3 to 5 minutes. Invert the mixing bowl over the dough and let it rise in a warm place until doubled in size, about 30 minutes.

4. Punch the dough down and allow it to double in size again, about 30 minutes.

5. Melt the butter in a small pan over low heat. Add the garlic and cook, stirring, until the garlic is lightly colored, 2 to 3 minutes. Set aside.

6. Preheat the oven to 400°F. Lightly butter two large baking sheets.

7. Roll the dough out on a lightly floured board to form 4 long, thin ropes, each just under 1 inch in diameter. Cut the ropes into the desired lengths, 4 to 6 inches. Place the dough sticks on the prepared baking sheets, about 2 inches apart. Holding one end of the stick against the baking sheet, twist each stick tightly. Brush with the butter-garlic mixture, and bake until the twists are golden and sound hollow when thumped with a finger, 20 to 30 minutes. Serve warm.

Active Dry Yeast

Active dry yeast, in granular form, is sold in scant-tablespoon-size packets and in larger jars or bags. They are always stamped with a use-by date, but if kept refrigerated, the yeast will be good long past the date on the container. If frozen, it will keep even longer.

To activate the yeast, measure the amount needed into a small bowl or cup. Then, using a liquid measuring cup, measure the appropriate amount of warm water (it should be in the range of 110° to 115°F—check it with an instant-read thermometer). Add the yeast to the warm water, and whisk or quickly mix with a fork until the yeast granules have dissolved. Let the mixture sit until it becomes foamy. (This is called "proofing" the yeast, because it "proves" that the yeast is functioning properly and ready to use.) If you like, you can add a bit of sugar or honey to speed things along.

If you wish to make bread and only have instant or bread machine yeast, the conversion is simple: use 25 percent less than the recipe requires (so if the recipe calls for 1 tablespoon, use ¾ tablespoon instant yeast). Because yeast multiplies very rapidly, it's not necessary to be a stickler about extremely precise measurements.

Cheesy Tortilla Wedges

Makes 24 pieces

These wedges are a wonderful accompaniment to chili or a great stand-alone snack with salsa. The cheese makes them much richer and more interesting than traditional tortilla crisps.

6 corn tortillas (6 inches each), quartered
¾ cup mixed grated Monterey Jack and
 Cheddar cheeses
1 tablespoon crushed caribe chile

1. Preheat the oven to 425°F.

2. Place the tortilla wedges on a baking sheet and bake until they are slightly crisp, about 5 minutes.

3. Sprinkle the cheese over the tortillas and return them to the oven. Bake until the tortillas are completely crisp and the cheese is melted, 4 to 5 minutes.

4. Place the wedges on a warmed platter, sprinkle with the caribe chile, and serve immediately.

6

Sweet Endings

There comes a time in the life of every chilihead when he or she realizes that chili makes the ideal breakfast, lunch, snack, and dinner. But while chocolate makes an appearance in plenty of main-dish chili recipes, I haven't yet had a bowl of chili that I would characterize as dessert.

It goes without saying that chili's a tough act to follow. Depending on the contents of the pot, you might want something intense and flavorful to keep the train going, or something light and airy to fill in what little space remains. These recipes, all tried-and-true follow-ups to hearty chili-filled meals, will do the right thing for your sweet tooth.

For the chocolate-lovers, there are Hot Fudge Soufflés, Double-Chocolate Farmer's Cakes, Hot Devil's Food Cake, Quick & Light Brownies . . . the list goes on. Or for something on the more refreshing side, the salty-limey-sweet Creamy Margarita Pie (complete with tequila) will have you convinced that you're sipping on drinks, beach-side; and Lemon Bars, with their shortbread crust and puckery-sour lemon curd topping, will transport you immediately to the middle of summer.

Of course chile has to make an appearance: Cinnamon-Chocolate-Chile Ice Cream is one of those

SOME LIKE IT HOT . . .
These icons show how fiery each dish is.

MILD

A BIT OF BITE

HOT

HOT ENOUGH TO MAKE YOU . . .

eye-openers that will change the way you think about dessert—especially if you pair it with Spicy Chocolate Chile Cupcakes. Who says a sweet ending can't also be a hot and spicy one?

Applesauce Cake
with Creamy Frosting and Spiced Walnuts

Serves 12

This is a fabulous cake, which I have enjoyed for special occasions forever. In fact, it is the one I wanted for my fortieth birthday. A wonderful ending to any dinner, this cake is dressy enough for even the most regal occasions. It will certainly impress and please any crowd, and it's festive party fare, whether at a bridal shower or at a family potluck. If you're preparing a big meal and are pressed for time, an option would be to bake the cake layers ahead of time, freeze them, and then assemble and frost the cake just before serving (see box, facing page).

FOR THE SPICED WALNUTS:
¾ cup walnut halves or large pieces
1 egg white
2 tablespoons sugar
1 teaspoon ground cinnamon
Several gratings of fresh nutmeg

FOR THE CAKE:
1 cup walnuts
12 tablespoons (1½ sticks) butter, plus
    1 teaspoon for buttering the pans
1 cup plus 2 tablespoons sugar
1 large egg
1¾ cups unbleached all-purpose flour
1 teaspoon ground cinnamon
½ teaspoon ground cloves
½ teaspoon ground allspice
¼ teaspoon salt
1 teaspoon baking soda
1 cup unsweetened organic applesauce
½ cup dried currants, plus 1 teaspoon
    for garnish
Creamy Frosting (recipe follows)

1. Prepare the Spiced Walnuts: Preheat the oven to 375°F.

2. Place the walnut halves in a shallow bowl. Beat the egg white in a small bowl until foamy; then add the remaining ingredients and mix until the sugar is dissolved. Pour this over the walnut halves and stir carefully so as not to break the walnuts.

3. Place the spiced walnut halves on an aluminum-foil-lined baking sheet, separating them so they do not touch each other. Place the walnuts for the cake in a single layer in a shallow ovenproof pan. Bake both walnuts until toasted, 10 minutes. Set aside the spiced walnuts until needed (see Note). Chop the toasted walnuts for the cake, and set them aside. Turn the oven down to 350°F.

4. Prepare the cake: Butter the sides of two 9-inch round cake pans. Cut a piece of waxed paper to fit the bottom of each pan, and line the pans. Set them aside.

5. Place the 12 tablespoons butter in the large bowl of an electric mixer and beat on medium speed until fluffy, about 2 minutes. Add the sugar and beat until completely incorporated. Add the egg and beat until fluffy again, about 1 minute.

6. Combine the flour, spices, salt, and baking soda in a bowl and stir to mix well. Add half of the flour mixture to the butter mixture. Then add ½ cup of the applesauce, and mix on low speed until well mixed, about 1 minute. Add the remaining flour mixture, then the remaining ½ cup applesauce, and mix again until completely incorporated, about 1 minute. Add the reserved chopped walnuts and the currants, and mix in.

7. Divide the batter between the prepared cake pans, and smooth the tops. Bake until a tester inserted in the center comes out clean, about 35 minutes.

8. Place the cake pans on wire racks to cool for 10 minutes. Then run a knife around the edge of each cake to loosen it from the pan, and invert them onto the wire racks to cool for an additional 15 minutes. Meanwhile, prepare the frosting.

Make the Cake—In Advance

Ever have cake crumbs ruin a perfectly good frosting job? It's practically inevitable if you try to frost a freshly baked cake, especially a rich, moist one with lots of crumbs on the top and sides or when you are using a contrasting colored frosting, such as a white buttercream on a dark spice cake.

For the best results, bake the cake in advance, cool the layers on wire racks for about 10 minutes, and then remove them from the baking pans. If there are obvious loose crumbs, brush them off with your fingers or a soft brush. Then  place the cake layers on a flat sheet pan and—here's the trick— freeze them.

When the cake is frozen firm, cover it with plastic wrap until you're ready to use it. You can prepare the cake up to 4 months before you wish to frost it! When your frosting is prepared and it's time to frost the cake, take the cake from the freezer, immediately remove the plastic wrapping, and place the bottom layer on the plate or cake stand you plan to use. Then frost as desired, let it thaw, and enjoy!

9. To assemble the cake, place one cake layer on a cake plate and spread one third of the frosting on top. Place the second layer on the first, and spread the remaining frosting over the top and sides of the cake.

10. Sprinkle the spiced walnuts in a ring about 1 inch in from the edge of the cake. Scatter the teaspoon of currants over the walnuts.

Note: The spiced walnuts will keep in a sealed plastic container for 1 month at room temperature, 3 months in the refrigerator, or 6 months in the freezer.

Creamy Frosting

Makes 4 to 5 cups

This classic cream cheese frosting is especially good on moist cakes, such as carrot, zucchini, or the applesauce cake on page 152. It's also good on cinnamon rolls. It can be made several days ahead and kept sealed in a plastic container in the refrigerator, or for up to 6 months in the freezer.

8 tablespoons (1 stick) butter,
    at room temperature
1 package (8 ounces) cream cheese,
    at room temperature
5 cups confectioners' sugar
1 teaspoon vanilla extract,
    preferably Mexican

1. Place the butter and cream cheese in a mixer bowl and mix on medium speed until fluffy, about 1 minute.

2. Add 2 cups of the confectioners' sugar and combine on low speed until well mixed. Add the vanilla. Continue to add the confectioners' sugar, 1 cup at a time, beating after each addition, until all the sugar is completely incorporated and the frosting is stiff.

Hot Devil's Food Cake

🌶️ 🌶️

Serves 12

This is the ultimate devil's food cake: rich, dark, velvety, flavored with both chocolate and chile, and enrobed with a caramel-flavored fudge frosting (recipe follows).

8 tablespoons (1 stick) butter,
    plus extra for buttering the pans
¼ cup crushed caribe chile
6 tablespoons unsweetened cocoa powder
1 teaspoon baking soda
1 teaspoon pure vanilla extract,
    preferably Mexican
2 cups sugar
3 large eggs
2 cups unbleached all-purpose flour
½ teaspoon salt

½ cup buttermilk
Chopped pecans and/or crushed caribe
   chile, for garnish (optional)

1. Preheat the oven to 350°F. Butter the sides
of the cake pans (either three 8-inch or two
9-inch pans). Cut out waxed paper rounds to
fit the bottoms of the pans. Line the pans, and
flour them.

2. Bring 1 cup water to a boil in a small saucepan.
Add the chile and cook for 10 minutes. Remove the
pan from the heat and let it stand for a few minutes.
(This can be done a few hours ahead of time.)

3. Strain the chile and water through a fine-
mesh strainer into a bowl, rubbing with a wooden
spoon or rubber spatula to press as much pulp
through the strainer as possible. Pour the chile

High-Altitude Baking

Baking poses a challenge when your
oven is at an altitude of 5,000 feet or
more. Having lived a great deal of my life
at high altitude (and having written about
and taught high-altitude cooking and
baking for years), here are my best
hints for success:

- Always use all-purpose flour
  instead of cake flour.

- Decrease the baking powder. At
  5,000 feet, use only ¾ teaspoon
  for each 1 teaspoon called for,
  and at 7,000 feet, cut the amount
  in half.

- Bake the cake in an oven that's 25 degrees
  hotter than the recipe calls for.

If your cake is not satisfactory after
making these adjustments, then each
ingredient needs to be reviewed and
tinkered with. The more a cake varies from
the standard formula of 1 part shortening

to 2 parts sugar to 4 parts flour, the more
adjustments are required. It is best to
adjust just one element at a time.

- *Liquid:* If the cake is dry or the batter
  is thick, add up to 4 tablespoons liquid,
  1 tablespoon at a time.

- *Flour:* If you have a thin batter,
  add flour in 1-tablespoon
  increments, plus ½ tablespoon
  liquid for each tablespoon of
  flour added.

- *Sugar:* If more sugar than the
  standard formula is called for,
  often the cake will fall or be
  coarse-textured. At 5,000 feet reduce
  the sugar by 1 tablespoon for each
  1 cup sugar; at 7,000 feet, reduce it
  by 2 tablespoons.

- *Eggs:* Always use large eggs. For a rich
  cake, such as German chocolate, adding
  an extra egg can help adjust the cake to
  the altitude.

water into a measuring cup. Add enough hot water to make 1 cup liquid. Stir the cocoa powder into the chile water to make a smooth paste. Add the baking soda and vanilla, stir, and set aside.

4. In a large bowl, beat the 8 tablespoons butter with an electric mixer on medium speed until it is light and fluffy. Then gradually add the sugar, beating until very fluffy. Add the eggs, one at a time, beating vigorously after each addition.

5. Sift the flour and salt into a small bowl. Beat this into the egg mixture, alternating with the buttermilk, on low speed. Raise the speed to medium and beat until smooth. Then add the cocoa mixture and mix well for about 1 minute.

6. Divide the batter among the prepared pans, smoothing it to the edges. Bake until the cake springs back when lightly pressed, 20 to 25 minutes.

7. Let the cake cool in the pans for 10 minutes. Then turn the layers out onto wire racks to cool completely.

8. Prepare the Fudge Frosting. While the frosting is still warm, assemble the cake. Place one cake layer on a cake plate, and spread one third of the frosting over the top (or one fourth if you made 3 layers). Place the second cake layer on the first, and spread the remaining frosting over the top and sides (or, if you made 3 layers, spread one fourth of the frosting over it and then top with the third layer and the remaining frosting). Sprinkle with the nuts and/or crushed chile, if desired.

Fudge Frosting

Makes about 3 cups

2 cups granulated sugar
1 cup packed light brown sugar
3 tablespoons unsweetened cocoa powder
3 tablespoons light corn syrup
1½ cups half-and-half, plus more as needed

1. Mix the sugars and cocoa powder together in a medium heavy saucepan. Add the corn syrup and half-and-half. Cook over medium heat, stirring occasionally, until the mixture comes to a boil. Then cook without stirring until the mixture reaches 236°F on an instant-read thermometer, or until a soft ball forms when a teaspoon of the mixture is dropped into cold water. Remove from the heat.

2. Beat the mixture vigorously until it becomes less glossy, adding more half-and-half if needed to make a creamy fudge. Use it to frost the cake while the frosting is still warm.

Double-Chocolate Farmer's Cakes

Makes 18 individual cakes

These fudgy desserts are just wonderful! They are like chocolate cupcakes with a creamy center—and they're always a big hit. They were most likely named after Fannie Farmer, one of the first famous American cookbook authors. Although they keep well in the refrigerator and even in the freezer, they're best served warm: cover with aluminum foil and heat at 350°F for 5 to 8 minutes.

FOR THE FILLING:
8 ounces cream cheese,
    at room temperature
1 large egg
⅓ cup sugar
6 ounces semisweet chocolate chips

FOR THE CAKES:
3 cups unbleached all-purpose flour
2 cups sugar
½ cup unsweetened cocoa powder
2 teaspoons baking soda
⅔ cup vegetable oil
2 teaspoons pure vanilla extract
2 tablespoons cider vinegar

1. Preheat the oven to 350°F. Line 18 muffin cups with paper liners.

2. Prepare the filling: Mix the cream cheese, egg, sugar, and chocolate chips together in a large bowl until thoroughly combined. Set the filling aside.

3. Prepare the cake batter: Mix the flour, sugar, cocoa powder, and baking soda together in a large mixing bowl. In a separate bowl, combine the oil, vanilla, vinegar, and 2 cups water. Pour the liquid ingredients into the dry ingredients and mix on low speed until combined, about 1 minute. Increase the speed by one level and mix until the batter is lump-free, about 3 minutes.

4. Scoop the batter into the lined muffin cups, filling them approximately three-fourths full. Drop a small spoonful of filling on top of the batter in each cup.

5. Bake until the tops of the cakes are firm when pressed, 18 to 20 minutes. Let them cool slightly, and serve warm.

Hot Fudge Soufflés
with Dulce de Leche Ice Cream

Makes 8 individual soufflés

These are devilishly good and rich and best made with very high quality bittersweet chocolate. *Do not substitute an inferior chocolate!* Valhrona is my favorite— if it's not available, Ghirardelli or Hershey's is a good alternative.

12 tablespoons (1½ sticks) unsalted butter,
    plus 2 teaspoons for the baking dishes
8 ounces high-quality bittersweet chocolate
3 large whole eggs
3 large egg yolks
⅓ cup sugar
2 tablespoons unbleached all-purpose flour
Dulce de leche ice cream, for serving

1. Butter eight individual baking dishes or soufflé cups with the 2 teaspoons butter.

2. Combine the 12 tablespoons butter and the chocolate in a small saucepan over low heat and stir constantly until melted. Set the pan aside, off the heat.

3. Place the whole eggs, the yolks, and the sugar in the bowl of an electric mixer and beat on medium speed, scraping down the bowl with a rubber spatula to be sure the sugar is mixed in well, until lemon-colored, about 1 minute.

4. Add about one fourth of the chocolate mixture to the egg mixture, and mix on medium speed until well blended. Continue adding the chocolate mixture in batches, mixing well after each addition, until the two mixtures have been blended well. Then slowly stir in the flour, mixing well and scraping down the sides of the bowl. Spoon the mixture into the prepared baking dishes until about half full. Set them aside until just ready to serve. (The baking dishes can be covered and refrigerated a day or two ahead; bring to room temperature before baking.)

5. About 20 minutes before serving, preheat the oven to 425°F. Position a rack in the center of the oven.

6. Place the baking dishes in a rimmed baking pan and pour hot water around them to a depth of ½ inch. Bake until the edges are puffed up and a bit dry or cracked around the edges, 12 to 14 minutes. The center should be indented and soft and move a bit when shaken.

7. Serve warm, with a scoop of dulce de leche ice cream alongside.

Spicy Chocolate Chile Cupcakes

Makes 12 cupcakes

These doubly chocolate cupcakes, heated up with some spicy red chile, are extraordinarily special. The mellowness of the milk chocolate contrasted with the richness of the semisweet chocolate is a taste treat you won't forget. These are perfect for everything from a birthday party to an afternoon tea—a great snack when you feel the urge for chocolate, and an ideal dessert for a chili meal. Frost them with your favorite chocolate buttercream frosting, or make the Creamy Frosting on page 154, stirring 2 ounces melted bittersweet chocolate into the prepared frosting.

2 cups semisweet chocolate chips
14 tablespoons (1¾ sticks)
    unsalted butter
4 large eggs
¾ cup sugar
1 teaspoon pure vanilla extract,
    preferably Mexican

Pinch of salt
2 tablespoons pure ground hot red chile
1 cup unbleached all-purpose flour
¾ cup milk chocolate chips
½ cup coarsely chopped pecans

1. Position a rack in the center of the oven and preheat the oven to 375°F. Place paper liners in 12 muffin cups.

2. Place the semisweet chocolate chips and all the butter in a medium microwave-safe mixing bowl. Cover it with plastic wrap and microwave on full power for 1 minute. Stir, and repeat until the chocolate and butter are just melted—do not overheat, as it will ruin the chocolate. (If you prefer, you can melt the butter and chocolate together in a heavy saucepan. Start over medium heat and then switch to low for the best results, 6 to 8 minutes total.)

3. Place the eggs in a small bowl and lightly whisk them. Then add the sugar, vanilla, salt, and chile, and mix until well blended.

4. Add the flour to the egg mixture and stir only until just blended. Add the chocolate-butter mixture, the chocolate chips, and the pecans, and mix only until just blended. Spoon the batter into the lined muffin cups, and bake until just barely done, 30 to 35 minutes. A toothpick inserted in the center should come out almost clean, with perhaps a crumb or two.

5. Set the muffin tin on a wire rack, and let it cool for 10 minutes. Then remove the cupcakes from the tin and let them cool completely.

Creamy Margarita Pie

Serves 8 to 12

I created this recipe for the Pecos River Café, my New York City restaurant, when I wanted an unusual dessert. I came up with a pretzel crust to replicate the taste of a salted margarita glass, then made a creamy, flavorful filling using lime juice, sweetened condensed milk, whipped cream, tequila, and triple sec. I have since used this recipe in some of my cooking classes and have discovered that the cliché "more is better" does not work with the quantity of liquor here! If you use any more than is called for, the filling will not set up. Any leftover slices can be wrapped carefully in freezer-proof plastic wrap and frozen.

⅓ **cup butter, melted**
1¼ **cups finely crushed salted pretzels**
¼ **cup sugar**
1 **cup heavy (whipping) cream**
1 **can (14 ounces) sweetened condensed milk**
⅓ **cup fresh lime juice, plus 1 whole lime**
2 **tablespoons tequila**
2 **tablespoons triple sec**

1. Pour the melted butter into a 9-inch pie plate.

Add the crushed pretzels and sugar, and mix well in the pie plate. Then press the mixture firmly onto the bottom and up the sides to the rim of the plate. Refrigerate the crust while you make the filling.

2. Whip the cream in a mixing bowl until soft peaks form.

3. Combine the sweetened condensed milk, lime juice, tequila, and triple sec in a large bowl, and mix well. Fold in the whipped cream, and pour the filling into the prepared crust.

4. Slice the lime into thin rounds. Using a sharp knife, slice through the center of each slice up to the inside of the peel on the opposite side. Twist the slice in opposite directions to create a ruffle effect, and place it on the pie in a decorative manner. Repeat with the remaining lime slices.

5. Freeze the pie, uncovered, until firm, at least 4 hours. You may freeze the pie for up to 24 hours; when it is frozen solid, cover it. If the pie is frozen solid, let it soften in the refrigerator for about 30 minutes before serving.

Variation: Frozen Strawberry Margarita Pie

Margarita pie is delicious when made with strawberries. In fact, just like its namesake drink, it can be made with a variety of fruits.

In step 3, substitute 1 tablespoon lime juice for the ⅓ cup lime juice, and add ⅓ cup thawed frozen sweetened strawberries. Decorate the top of the pie with fresh whole strawberries and twisted lime slices.

Fresh Lemon Custard Pie, Shaker Style

Serves 6 to 8

In the late 1960s, my husband and I visited the Shaker Village of Pleasant Hill in Harrodsburg, Kentucky, and had a delightfully delicious lunch topped off by this amazingly good pie. I liked it so much that I asked for the recipe. I am so happy to share it with you. It is a very easy pie to make, especially good in the winter. I like it with the White Lobster Chili (see page 80)—or any of the seafood or veggie chilis. The tart, sweet flavor is a fabulous counterpoint to the spiciness of chili.

1 store-bought single-crust pie crust
    (or homemade if you like)
2 organic lemons, rind and all,
    sliced very thin, seeds removed
2 cups sugar
4 large eggs, beaten

1. Preheat the oven to 425°F (400°F if using a glass pie plate). Line a pie plate with the crust, and create your favorite edging on the pie crust.

2. Place the lemon slices in a large mixing bowl.

Sweets and Heat: Perfect Pairs

For the most delightful chilicentric meals, team your brew with a flattering dessert. I've found that lighter, subtler chili flavors work well when followed by a heavier, richer dessert—and vice versa.

Here are some particularly delicious pairings:

- Pecos River Bowl of Red (page 34) with Cinnamon-Chocolate-Chile Ice Cream (page 164)
- Vegetarian Chili (page 82) with Applesauce Cake with Creamy Frosting and Spiced Walnuts (page 152)
- Navajo Green Chili (page 69) with Double-Chocolate Farmer's Cakes (page 157)
- Chipotle Chili (page 45) with Creamy Margarita Pie (page 160)
- White Lobster Chili (page 80) with Lemon Bars (page 170)
- A Red Chili Nightmare (page 66) with vanilla ice cream and Cajeta Sauce (page 171)

Add the sugar and stir gently. Then add the eggs, and mix together. Pour the mixture into the pie crust.

3. Bake for 15 minutes. Then reduce the heat to 350°F (325°F for a glass pan) and continue baking until the custard is set, about 30 minutes. The pie is done when it is set solid and does not shake, or when a toothpick inserted in the center comes out clean.

4. Serve immediately, or if holding for later, refrigerate, covered, and then allow the pie to come to room temperature before serving. (It will keep in the refrigerator for up to 5 days— it does not freeze well.)

French Silk Pie
with a Toasted Nut Crust

Serves 8

This somewhat retro recipe is a difficult one to come by, as some pastry chefs will not share it if they have been lucky enough to obtain it. The pie has the appearance and texture of a chocolate cheesecake, but of course it does not contain any cream cheese. My version is made even more special with the nut crust. The flavors are fabulous, but it is very rich and is best served with a light meal, such as one of the simpler, lighter chilis like Chickie Veggie Chili (page 74), Mexican Tortilla Chili (page 81), or Pecos River Bowl of Red (page 34). I think that after the spiciness of a good bowl of chili, a sweet dessert tastes even more delicious. And with a lighter chili, one can afford to eat a decadent dessert like this one.

FOR THE CRUST:
1 cup walnuts, toasted (see box at right)
1½ cups pecans, toasted (see box at right)
¾ cup packed light brown sugar
4 tablespoons (½ stick) butter, melted
½ teaspoon ground cinnamon

FOR THE FILLING:
12 ounces bittersweet chocolate
6 tablespoons (¾ stick) butter
1½ cups granulated sugar
6 large eggs
2 tablespoons heavy (whipping) cream
¼ teaspoon pure vanilla extract

1. Prepare the crust: Place all the crust ingredients in the bowl of a food processor, and pulse until some of the nuts are so fine that you can press them momentarily together in your hand. Do not overprocess—there should still be some larger pieces of nuts visible.

2. Press the crust mixture firmly into the bottom of a 9-inch pie plate or springform pan.

3. Prepare the filling: Melt the chocolate slowly in a double boiler, or in a heavy saucepan over low heat, being careful not to let it burn. Set it aside to cool to room temperature.

4. Using an electric mixer, cream the butter and sugar together until smooth, about 1 minute. Add the eggs, one at a time, beating well after each addition and scraping the sides of the bowl often.

5. In a small bowl, use a small whisk to whip the cream to soft peaks. Mix in the vanilla, and set the bowl aside.

6. Add one third of the melted chocolate to the egg mixture, starting on the lowest speed and then switching to high and mixing for about 30 seconds. Repeat with the remaining chocolate, in two additions. Gently fold the whipped cream into the mixture. Pour the filling into the prepared pan. Refrigerate until completely set, about 2 hours.

7. If you used a springform pan, remove the side before serving. Cut the pie into small wedges, and serve.

Toasting Nuts

Nuts can be toasted on the stove or in the oven. I prefer to toast them in a heavy pan over medium heat, stirring frequently until they are browned. (Keep an eye on them—the nuts burn easily.)

When using the oven, place the nuts on a baking sheet and toast them at a lower heat, such as 250°F, so as to slowly brown them. Toast for 5 minutes, then check on—and stir—the nuts every 2 minutes until they are done.

Kahlúa Mocha Fudge Pie

Serves 6 to 8

Chocolate and coffee have long been a flavorful and popular combination. In this quick-to-make refrigerator pie, the chocolate crust supplies a great texture contrast with the silky-smooth filling.

FOR THE CRUST:
1½ cups chocolate cookie crumbs
4 tablespoons (½ stick) butter, melted
¼ cup granulated sugar

FOR THE FILLING:
1 envelope (1 tablespoon) unflavored gelatin
½ cup packed light brown sugar
3 large eggs, separated
2 ounces bittersweet chocolate
½ cup Kahlúa or other coffee-flavored liqueur
1½ cups heavy (whipping) cream

FOR THE GARNISH:
1 ounce bittersweet chocolate, at room temperature

1. Preheat the oven to 350°F (325°F if using a glass pie plate).

2. Prepare the cookie crumb crust: Combine the crumbs, butter, and sugar in a bowl, and mix well. Press the mixture onto the bottom and up the sides of the pie plate. Place it in the oven and bake just until firm, about 10 minutes. Set aside.

3. Prepare the filling: Pour ½ cup cold water into a small saucepan. Sprinkle the gelatin over it, and stir to dissolve. Add ¼ cup of the brown sugar and stir until the sugar dissolves.

4. Beat the 3 egg yolks with a whisk or fork, and add them to the gelatin mixture, along with the chocolate. Cook over low heat, stirring constantly, until the mixture thickens, 2 to 3 minutes.

5. Transfer the mixture to a bowl and add the Kahlúa. Refrigerate, stirring occasionally, until the mixture is thick enough to mound on a spoon, about 4 hours.

6. Whip the cream in a large bowl until stiff peaks form. Then, using a clean bowl and the whisk beater of an electric mixer, beat the egg whites at the highest speed. When they are foamy, sprinkle the remaining ¼ cup brown sugar over the egg whites. Continue beating until a stiff meringue results.

7. Carefully fold the meringue into the gelatin mixture. Then fold in two thirds of the whipped cream, being careful not to beat—just gently combine. Spread the mixture in the cookie crumb crust. Refrigerate until firm, about 2 hours. Cover the remaining whipped cream with plastic wrap and refrigerate it.

8. When ready to serve, place decorative dollops of the remaining whipped cream over the top of the pie, and using a vegetable peeler, shave curls of chocolate over them.

Cinnamon-Chocolate-Chile Ice Cream

Makes 1½ quarts

Chile and chocolate were made for each other. They both release our endorphins and seem to produce an inner glow. This chocolate ice cream, which is finished in an ice cream machine, incorporates both chile and cinnamon for a double treat.

¼ cup crushed caribe chile
⅔ cup sugar
2 cinnamon sticks, preferably canela (3 inches each)
12 ounces bittersweet chocolate, broken into chunks
3 cups heavy (whipping) cream
3 large eggs

1. Place the chile and ¾ cup water in a small saucepan and bring to a boil. Reduce the heat and simmer until the skin slips off the chile, about 20 minutes. Strain the water into a bowl through a fine-mesh strainer, rubbing the chile with a spoon to push as much pulp as possible through the strainer.

2. Place the strained chile water in the same saucepan, and add ⅓ cup of the sugar and the cinnamon sticks. Boil for 1 minute. Then remove the pan from the heat and allow it to sit for 5 minutes.

3. Discard the cinnamon sticks and add the chocolate chunks. Stir until the chocolate melts. (If necessary, return the saucepan to low heat to melt the chocolate.)

4. In another saucepan, warm the cream over low heat. Combine the eggs with the remaining ⅓ cup sugar in a medium bowl just until the sugar is dissolved. Beat in a little warm cream, and then some more. Pour the entire egg mixture over the cream, and whisk well to combine. Cook over low heat, stirring, until the mixture is warm and thickened, about 5 minutes. Add the chocolate mixture, whisking to combine well. Transfer the mixture to a bowl, and refrigerate it until chilled, at least 1 hour and up to 2 days.

5. Stir or whisk the mixture to mix it well, and place it in the canister of an ice cream maker. Freeze according to the manufacturer's instructions.

Fresh Peach Ice Cream

Approximately 1 gallon

This recipe harkens back to
my days as the Home Service Director for an electric utility company. I had a staff of seven home economists and one year we decided to publish a special brochure for our customers on the very best homemade ice cream recipes—all to be prepared in an electric ice cream maker, of course.

The very fresh peachy flavor results from using juicy, ripe peaches. This recipe is smooth and rich tasting, yet has a minimum of heavy cream, making it quite a bit less rich than most homemade ice creams. It is very easy to make—no cooking and fussing around with extra steps to ready the ice cream mixture . . . all you do is place the ingredients in the freezer can, check the sugar as noted below, and proceed.

4 cups milk
1 can (15 ounces) sweetened condensed milk
1 can (14 ounces) evaporated milk
½ pint heavy (whipping) cream
About 1 cup sugar
1 tablespoon vanilla extract
3 cups mashed fresh or frozen peaches

1. Place the milk, condensed milk, evaporated milk, heavy cream, ½ cup sugar, vanilla, and peaches in the freezing can of an electric ice cream maker. Stir to combine.

2. Taste the mixture for sweetness (fresh peaches tend to be less sweet than frozen, so they usually require more sugar). If it is not sweet enough, add more sugar.

3. Cover the can and place it in the ice cream maker. Freeze according to the manufacturer's instructions. Serve the ice cream immediately or transfer it to plastic containers for storage in the freezer.

Swirled Raspberry-Chocolate Parfaits

Makes 4 parfaits

This simple yet luscious do-ahead dessert is just right after a lighter chili, such as the Chickie Veggie Chili (page 74) or the Clam and Green Chile Chili (page 79). The layers of chocolate ice cream and whipped cream, infused with sweet-tart raspberry jam, cool the palate and round out a good meal. You can make the parfaits ahead of time and keep them in the freezer. Place them in the refrigerator just before you sit down to eat.

1 pint rich chocolate fudge ice cream, softened
4 tablespoons seedless red raspberry jam
½ cup heavy (whipping) cream
2 tablespoons vanilla sugar, or
    2 tablespoons granulated sugar and
    ¼ teaspoon vanilla extract

1. Divide one third of the chocolate ice cream into four parfait glasses. Top each portion with about 1 teaspoon of the jam, swirling the jam down into the ice cream. Repeat twice more, to create layered parfaits.

2. Place the cream in a small bowl and whip it to soft peaks, adding the vanilla sugar toward the end of the whipping. Spoon a dollop of whipped cream on top of the ice cream in each glass, and place them in the freezer until ready to serve. (Cover them only after they are frozen solid.) If the parfaits are frozen solid, let them soften in the refrigerator for 30 minutes before serving.

Banana Capriotada

Makes 8 pastries

This is a takeoff on capriotada, which is a rich bread pudding. Here we reinvent the dish, replacing the bready pudding with flaky pastry and adding sweet caramelized bananas to boot. This recipe is fun and fast to make—it just takes some cooling time. The flavors are reminiscent of Bananas Foster, a famous New Orleans dish that combines bananas, butter, sugar, and rum to luxurious effect.

2 tablespoons unsalted butter
¼ cup pine nuts
8 ripe bananas, sliced
3 tablespoons light brown sugar
¼ cup spiced rum, such as Captain Morgan's
Butter or nonstick cooking spray,
    for greasing the cookie sheet
1 sheet puff pastry, defrosted if frozen
    (see Note)
1 large egg
¼ cup milk
1 quart rich French-style vanilla ice cream
8 fresh mint sprigs, for garnish
24 fresh red raspberries, for garnish

1. Preheat the oven to 350°F.

2. Place the butter in a sauté pan with a close-fitting lid, and melt it over low heat. Add the pine nuts and sauté until the nuts are brown, about 4 minutes. Add the bananas and sauté until they are very soft, about 2 minutes. Sprinkle the brown sugar over the bananas, and then deglaze the pan with the spiced rum. The mixture in the sauté pan should be hot and bubbling slightly. Stand back, light a match, and carefully ignite the mixture, letting the alcohol in the rum burn off. Set the pan aside.

3. Butter a cookie sheet or spray it with nonstick cooking spray. Place the puff pastry on a work surface, and cut it into 8 squares. Transfer the pastry squares to the prepared cookie sheet, making sure they do not touch each other. Using a fork, mix the egg and milk together in a small bowl to create an egg wash. Spoon some banana mixture onto the center of each pastry, arranging it diagonally across the square. Fold the open corners together, making a triangle, and pinch the edges to seal. Brush each pastry with the egg wash, and use a sharp knife to make three shallow slices across the top of each one. Bake until they are golden brown and flaky, about 10 minutes.

4. Remove the pastries from the oven and let them cool on a wire rack for 45 minutes to 1 hour.

5. Serve with the ice cream alongside, and garnish with the mint sprigs and raspberries.

Note: Frozen puff pastry is available in the frozen food section of most supermarkets.

Maple-Teased Apple Cranberry Crisp

Serves 4

There's something yummy

about apple and maple combinations—whether in pancakes or desserts. Here the tart tinge of cranberries balances the natural sweetness of the apples and the syrup. This crisp is especially great served with a scoop of rich vanilla or butter pecan ice cream or frozen yogurt.

6 tablespoons (¾ stick) unsalted butter,
    plus extra for greasing the baking dish
5 medium-size or 4 large tart apples,
    peeled, cored, and cut into thin wedges
    or slices (about 4½ cups)
½ cup fresh cranberries (see Note)
¼ cup maple syrup
¾ cup sugar
1 tablespoon unsulphured molasses
½ cup oatmeal (rolled oats)
½ cup whole-wheat flour
1 teaspoon ground cinnamon
½ teaspoon ground nutmeg

1. Preheat the oven to 375°F. Butter a 3-quart casserole.

2. Spread the apples over the bottom of the casserole, and scatter the cranberries over them. Drizzle the syrup and sprinkle ¼ cup of the sugar evenly over the fruit.

3. Combine the remaining ½ cup sugar with the molasses, oatmeal, flour, cinnamon, and nutmeg in a medium-size bowl. Cut in the 6 tablespoons butter with a knife, and mix with your fingers or with a pastry blender until the mixture resembles coarse crumbs. Scatter this mixture over the fruit. Bake until a knife inserted in the center comes out clean, about 45 minutes.

Note: You can substitute dried cranberries, but use only a scant ½ cup.

Butterscotch Chocolate Marshmallow Bars

Makes 36 bars

These are like butterscotch brownies

with chocolate bits and marshmallows thrown in. They are very moist when first baked, but will stay that way only if they are stored in an airtight container.

8 tablespoons (1 stick) unsalted butter, at room temperature, plus extra for buttering the pan
1 cup granulated sugar
1 whole large egg
2 large eggs, separated
1 cup unbleached all-purpose flour
1 teaspoon baking powder
¼ teaspoon salt
1 cup chopped pecans
¾ cup semisweet chocolate morsels
1 cup miniature marshmallows
1 cup packed light brown sugar

1. Preheat the oven to 350°F. Butter a 9-inch square baking pan.

2. Cut the butter into a large bowl and beat it with an electric mixer on low speed until it softens. Then raise the speed to high and beat until the butter becomes fluffy. Add the granulated sugar, whole egg, and egg yolks, beating constantly.

3. Beat in ½ cup of the flour. Then add the remaining ½ cup flour, along with the baking powder and salt, beating on low speed until the dry ingredients are incorporated, and then on medium speed to combine well.

4. Pour the batter into the prepared pan and smooth the top with a spatula. Sprinkle the pecans, chocolate pieces, and marshmallows over the batter.

5. Beat the egg whites in a small bowl until they form stiff peaks. Then sprinkle the brown sugar over the whites, a small amount at a time, carefully folding in each addition until well combined. Be sure not to break down the egg whites. Spread the egg whites evenly over the pecan-chocolate-marshmallow topping. Bake until a toothpick inserted in the center comes out clean, 15 to 20 minutes.

6. Let cool in the pan for about 30 minutes, and then carefully cut into rectangular bars. Store until serving time, for up to 1 week, in a vapor-proof rigid food storage container, with a double layer of waxed paper separating the layers. These can be served cool or slightly warmed.

Quick & Light
Brownies

Makes 16 brownies

These brownies are so quick to prepare and are so low in calories (just 80 calories per serving), it is truly amazing that they taste so good. They are best when freshly baked.

Butter or nonstick cooking spray,
   for greasing the pan
½ cup unbleached all-purpose flour
½ cup unsweetened cocoa powder
Pinch of salt
2 egg whites
1 whole large egg
¾ cup sugar
⅓ cup unsweetened applesauce
2 tablespoons vegetable oil
2 teaspoons pure vanilla extract
¼ cup chopped walnuts or pecans
   (optional)

1. Preheat the oven to 375°F. Butter or spray an 8-inch square baking pan, or grease the sides and cut a piece of waxed paper to fit the bottom.

2. In a small bowl, combine the flour, cocoa powder, and salt. In a large bowl, combine the egg whites, whole egg, sugar, applesauce, oil, and vanilla; mix well. Mix the flour mixture into the egg mixture, and then pour the batter into the prepared pan. Sprinkle the top with the nuts, if desired. Bake until the brownies spring back when pressed with a finger, or until a toothpick inserted in the center comes out clean, about 20 minutes.

3. Let the pan cool on a wire rack for 10 minutes. Then invert the pan and let the brownies slip out. Let the brownies cool on the rack until cool to the touch. Then cut into 16 squares.

Variations:

For additional flavor, spread this simple chocolate glaze over the brownies: In a small pan, melt 2 squares semisweet chocolate and 1 tablespoon unsalted butter over low heat. Remove from the heat and whisk in ½ cup confectioners' sugar. Mix in 2 to 3 tablespoons milk, enough to reach the desired glazing consistency. Glaze the brownies after they cool. Scatter 2 tablespoons chopped nuts over the top, if desired. Or for a spicy variation, sprinkle 1 or more tablespoons crushed caribe chile over the glaze.

Lemon Bars

Makes 24 bars

This has long been one of my favorite desserts. The refreshing lemon complements the rich, sweet shortbread crust, making for a decadent bar cookie that is very good any time you can get one!

FOR THE COOKIE BASE:
1 cup (2 sticks) unsalted butter,
   melted
½ cup confectioners' sugar
2 cups unbleached all-purpose flour

FOR THE LEMON TOPPING:
2 cups granulated sugar
¼ cup unbleached all-purpose flour
½ teaspoon baking powder
4 large eggs
6 tablespoons fresh lemon juice
½ teaspoon grated lemon zest,
    preferably from an organic lemon

FOR THE GARNISH:
Confectioners' sugar, for dusting

1. Preheat the oven to 350°F.

2. Prepare the cookie base: Mix the melted butter, confectioners' sugar, and flour together in a large bowl. Press the mixture over the bottom of a 9 × 13-inch glass baking dish. Bake until it is firm to the finger when pressed and is a very pale golden-white color, about 20 minutes. Remove from the oven and set aside. Leave the oven on.

3. Make the lemon topping: Sift the granulated sugar, flour, and baking powder together into a large bowl. Add the eggs, lemon juice, and lemon zest. Beat by hand, or with an electric mixer, starting on the lowest speed and switching to medium speed when the dry ingredients are incorporated into the wet ingredients, until well blended, about 2 minutes.

4. Pour the lemon mixture over the prepared crust, and smooth it with a spatula to cover the crust completely. Bake until the topping is firm and a toothpick inserted in the center comes out clean, about 25 minutes.

5. Let cool in the pan on a wire rack. Then dust the top with confectioners' sugar and cut into 24 squares.

Cajeta Sauce

Makes 1¼ cups

This Mexican caramel sauce is very popular on or in several desserts. It can be used as a topping for ice cream and crêpes, or as a plating sauce for a small cake or confection. If you like caramel, you are sure to love it. I make lots and keep it in sealed glass or plastic containers in the freezer, ready for thawing, warming, and serving (see Note).

Feel free to vary the thickness of the sauce by playing with the cooking time in step 2: thick sauces are good over ice cream, while a thinner sauce is good over crêpes.

¾ cup sugar
1 can (12 ounces) evaporated goat's milk
    (see Note)

1. Place the sugar and 2 tablespoons water in a heavy skillet. Place over medium-high heat and cook, stirring constantly, until the sugar becomes liquid and then turns a medium-brown color, about 5 minutes.

2. Remove the skillet from the heat and gradually pour in the evaporated milk, stirring continuously. Return the skillet to medium-high heat and cook, stirring frequently, until the sauce thickens, about 1 hour for a thick sauce, 40 minutes for a thinner sauce.

Notes: Store the sauce in a glass jar. It will keep for up to 1 month in the refrigerator and 6 months in the freezer. If using it for plate decoration, place it in a squirt bottle.

Evaporated goat's milk can be found at specialty food stores or in the Hispanic foods aisle of some supermarkets. If you can't find it, substitute whole evaporated milk. The cajeta will still be delicious, however it's not quite the real thing when made without goat's milk.

7

Good Libations

It's no surprise that a big boiling pot of chili is going to draw a crowd, and it's no surprise that a crowd is going to want something to drink. When you serve chili, be ready to serve plenty of beverages: they'll disappear as fast as the food. Wine's always a popular choice: Champagne, sangria (using red or white wine and plenty of orange, lemon, and lime slices), or a vigorous red (maybe a Zinfandel or a Shiraz)—all are good accompaniments to the muscular zing of your main dish.

While wine and beer are excellent with chili, it's a nice nod to chili's Southwestern and Mexican heritage to pair a bowl of the hot stuff with a refreshing margarita, made with freshly squeezed lime juice, a good tequila, and orange liqueur. It's a perfect partner to your zesty meal. While the iconic margarita is iconic for a reason (try the Crawl Home Margarita, if you need a refresher course), there's fruit to be had (literally!) in branching out. Whether it's the watermelon-infused Special Sandia Margarita, the summery Berry Berry Margarita, the unusual flavor of the Prickly Pear Margarita, or the grapefruit-tinged Frosty Virgin Margarita, the sour sweetness goes a long way in holding its own against even the fieriest, smokiest chili. No wonder the margarita is famous as a chili drink!

And so, for that matter, is beer. Bridging the gap between one classic chili drink and the other, don't shy away from the Poor Man's Margarita, Guadalajara style: a can of beer, a wedge of lime, a pinch of salt . . . and thou. Or take the beer one step further: Chile Beer is exactly what it sounds like. For a more conventional libation, serve Mexican beer the south-of-the-border way: with lime.

Whether you're mixing up a pitcher of Sangria or one of Zingy Tea, be sure to make plenty: the hotter your chili, the more you're going to need these refreshers to help cool the whole thing down.

Crawl Home
Margaritas

🌶

Makes 4 drinks

The national drink of Mexico, margaritas are definitely best when made with freshly squeezed lime juice, good-quality tequila, and an orange liqueur such as triple sec or Cointreau. I think this recipe yields perfect margaritas—but they are strong, so be careful! I started calling them "Crawl Home Margaritas" after a dear friend and neighbor literally crawled home, ages ago, after having a few too many on a beautiful starry night in Albuquerque.

Wedge of lime and coarse salt, for salting the glasses (optional; see box, opposite)
2 ounces fresh lime juice (4 or 5 limes), plus more as needed
6 ounces high-quality tequila (see box, page 177)
2 ounces triple sec or Cointreau, plus more as needed
3 to 4 ice cubes, plus more for serving

Salt the rims of four margarita glasses, if desired. Place the glasses or goblets in the freezer to chill. When the glasses are frosted, combine the lime juice, tequila, triple sec, and 3 to 4 ice cubes in a blender, and puree. When the ice has been liquefied, taste, and add more lime juice or triple sec, if desired. Pour into the frosted glasses, over ice, and serve.

Variations:

Lemon-Lime Perfect Margaritas: Use a combination of fresh lemon juice and lime juice for a delicious, if unconventional, margarita.

"Walk Home" Margaritas: For less potent margaritas, reduce the tequila to 3 ounces.

Shaker Margaritas: In Mexico, people frequently shake the margarita and strain out the ice. This makes for a stronger drink.

Margaritas, As You Like 'Em

Want to salt your margarita glasses the way they do in restaurants? It's easy! Simply pour a layer of coarse salt into a saucer or a shallow bowl. Run a cut lime around the rim of each glass, and then dip the moistened rim into the salt to lightly coat it. Place the salted goblets in the freezer to frost them; remove them just before serving.

If you like a frothy head on your margaritas, use a blender to combine the liquid elements. If you wish, add 1 teaspoon slightly beaten egg white to the drink mixture before blending it—it will actually make the margarita mellower, and it will help it hold a frothy head for longer.

For frozen margaritas, mix up the drinks in a blender, continually adding ice and blending until the mixture is slushy and firm.

Berry Berry Margaritas

Makes 4 drinks

This is but one of the zillion variations on margaritas you can make. One valuable tip is that frozen sweetened fruit makes better fruit margaritas than does fresh fruit, which needs sweetening. If you use fresh fruit, it is often hard to get just the right flavor because the drink requires more doctoring.

Wedge of lime and coarse salt, for salting
    the glasses (optional; see box, at left)
4 ounces high-quality tequila
2 ounces triple sec or Cointreau,
    plus more as needed
1 ounce fresh lime juice, plus more as
    needed
¼ cup sweetened frozen berries, preferably
    strawberries, a blend of strawberries
    and raspberries, or mixed berries
About 6 ice cubes

Salt the rims of four margarita glasses, if desired. Place the glasses in the freezer to chill. When the glasses are frosted, combine the tequila, triple sec, lime juice, frozen berries, and ice cubes in a blender. Blend until pureed. Taste, and add more lime juice or triple sec, if desired. Pour into the frosted glasses, and serve.

Prickly Pear
Margaritas

Makes 4 drinks

Prickly pear margaritas, which have a beautiful color, have become quite fashionable in resort dining rooms across the United States and Mexico. The prickly pears turn red when cooked. To make the juice, the pears can be stewed until soft, about 30 minutes over medium heat, and then the juice strained out. However, it is easier to buy prickly pear juice or nectar in a specialty store. The flavor of the juice is not very strong, so it is often enhanced with citrus, such as orange juice, or with frozen red raspberries.

Wedge of lime and coarse salt, for salting the glasses (optional; see box, page 175)
4 ounces high-quality tequila
2 ounces triple sec or Cointreau, plus more as needed
1 ounce fresh lime juice, plus more if needed
2 ounces prickly pear juice (see Note)
About 6 ice cubes

Salt the rims of four glasses, if desired. Place the glasses in the freezer to chill. When the glasses are frosted, combine the tequila, triple sec, lime juice, prickly pear juice, and ice cubes in a blender. Blend until pureed. Taste, and add more lime juice or triple sec, if desired. Pour into the frosted glasses, and serve.

Note: Prickly pear juice is available in Mexican specialty food stores and in supermarkets with an extensive line of Mexican ingredients.

Special Sandia
Margaritas

Makes 4 drinks

The mountains that form the backdrop for Albuquerque, New Mexico, are called the Sandias because for just a few moments every day they reflect the sunset and become a beautiful watermelon color (*sandia* is the Spanish word for "watermelon"). These margaritas are rather mellow, not as strongly flavored as the other fruit varieties in this book.

Wedge of lime and coarse salt, for salting the glasses (optional; see box, page 175)
4 ounces high-quality tequila
2 ounces triple sec or Cointreau, plus more as needed
1 ounce fresh lime juice, or more as needed
2/3 cup cubed seeded watermelon
About 6 ice cubes

Salt the rims of four glasses, if desired. Place the glasses in the freezer to chill. When the glasses are frosted, combine the tequila, triple sec, lime juice, watermelon, and ice cubes in a blender. Blend until the mixture is pureed. Taste, and add more lime juice or triple sec, if desired. Pour into the frosted glasses, and serve.

Frosty Virgin
Margaritas

Makes 24 drinks

Though the alcoholic kick is gone, this drink still has a fresh, cooling "zap." It can be served either frozen, as indicated, or over ice cubes in a pitcher (in which case you should omit the ice cubes from the blender). This recipe makes enough drinks for a crowd, so you'll need to make it in two batches.

3 cans (12 ounces each) frozen limeade
1 can (6 ounces) frozen orange juice
    concentrate (pulpy variety)
1 can (6 ounces) frozen grapefruit juice
32 ounces ginger ale
Ice cubes
2 limes, cut into 24 thin rounds, for garnish

1. Put half of the frozen juice concentrates and half of the ginger ale in a blender. Add some ice cubes and process on low speed for a few seconds. Gradually work up to high speed,

Top-notch Tequilas

Tequila, by definition, has to hail from either the Mexican village of Tequila or from specific designated regions that are allowed to grow the blue agave plant. (If agave liquor is made in other regions of Mexico, the liquor is called mescal.)

Really terrific tequilas are made with 100 percent blue agave *pinas* (the center of the agave plant). Clear tequila is the least aged, the highest in alcohol content, and the usual choice for margaritas.

If aged a few months to 2 years or more, the tequila takes on a light amber color and is called *reposado*. These tequilas are mellower and usually contain less alcohol. Some very good brands are Don Eduardo, Herradura, Chinaco, and Patrón. Watch out, though! Many "aged" gold tequilas sold in the United States have been colored with dark corn syrup.

The *añejo* and extra-*añejo* varieties of tequila have been aged 3 years or more, often in oak barrels. These extra-premium tequilas are often compared to single-malt scotches or brandies, and are best savored straight up or on the rocks. They are pure, pricey, and have a rich, robust flavor that varies from brand to brand (or often cask to cask). Some labels to remember are Gran Centenario Leyenda, Partida Elegante, Sauza Tres Generaciones, 1800 Colección, and José Cuervo Reserva de la Familia.

adding more ice until you have your desired slushy consistency. Pour the mixture into a pitcher or directly into large goblets.

2. Make a second batch, using the remaining concentrates and ginger ale.

3. Cut a slit halfway into each lime slice, position a slice on the rim of each goblet, and serve.

Poor Man's Margarita

Makes 1 drink

The first place I ever tasted this drink was in Guadalajara, and it was so delicious! It is truly amazing what a difference the salt and lime make to the beer. They create a more complex flavor, definitely different from the taste that results from adding just lime. You do have to be careful to first add the lime, and then the salt—otherwise, you will have a mini Mount Vesuvius in your hands.

1 small lime
1 teaspoon coarse or kosher salt
1 can or bottle (12 ounces) beer,
    preferably a Mexican beer

Cut the lime in half, and place the salt in a shallow saucer. Open the can of beer and rub the lime half around the rim of the can, generously squeezing out some juice. Then, taking a pinch at a time, place some salt near the opening of the beer can. While you drink the beer, keep adding pinches of salt near the opening of the can to prevent the beer from spewing.

Variation:

Squeeze some lime juice onto the rim of a glass and dip the rim in salt. Then serve the beer in the glass. This a fancier way to serve it, but the drink loses some of its authenticity.

Chile Beer

Makes 1 drink

Many people like the taste of hot stuff so much that they like to heat up cold beer. I know of one company in Arizona that makes chile beer. You can make your own if you plan ahead a bit. It's best to use bottled beer here, because the chile could bring out a metallic taste in canned beer. Chile beer can be served with anything you would serve regular beer with.

1 bottle or can (12 ounces) beer
1 small serrano chile, washed

At least 2 hours before serving it, open the bottle of beer and place the chile in the bottle. Close the bottle with a beverage sealer. Place the beer in the refrigerator and chill until serving time.

Bloody Maria

🌶️ 🌶️

Makes 4 drinks

Bloody Marias are almost the same as Bloody Marys, except they are made with tequila. They are particularly fitting with a southwestern brunch of quesadillas (pages 24 and 102), Migas (page 89), Chili Scramble (page 88), and the like. I often use a cucumber curl as a garnish, but you can use celery stalks if you wish.

Juice of 1 lime
1 cup tomato-vegetable juice,
such as V8 juice
1 tablespoon Worcestershire sauce

Several drops of hot pepper sauce,
such as Tabasco
½ teaspoon celery salt, or to taste
1 large cucumber (dark-green-skinned
variety), unpeeled
Ice cubes
4 ounces tequila

1. Place four glasses in the freezer to chill.

2. Mix the lime juice, tomato-vegetable juice, Worcestershire sauce, hot pepper sauce, and celery salt together in a pitcher. Refrigerate for at least 1 hour and up to 24 hours.

3. Prepare cucumber curls: Slice the cucumber in half lengthwise. Then cut one half into 4 narrow lengthwise wedges (you may have some cucumber left over depending on the diameter of the cucumber). Place the wedges on a cutting board, and using a sharp knife, slice each wedge just inside the peel in one continuous cut, leaving the peel attached to the cucumber wedge at one end. Wrap the peel into a curl around your finger, secure it with a toothpick, and place the cucumber wedges in a bowl of ice water in the refrigerator. Reserve the remaining cucumber half for another use.

4. When you are ready to serve the drinks, fill the frosted glasses with ice cubes. Pour 1 ounce of tequila into each glass. Top with the chilled Bloody Maria mix and stir well. Garnish each drink with a cucumber wedge (remove the toothpick), sticking it in so that the curl rests on the rim of the glass. Enjoy.

Sangria

Makes 6 drinks

Originally from Spain, sangria has crossed all boundaries. Though it is great with Tex-Mex food, it's an excellent accompaniment for almost any kind of cooking. Sangria is a wonderful punch to serve at large parties and outdoor events.

½ cup sugar
1 cinnamon stick, preferably canela
    (Mexican cinnamon)
1 lemon, preferably organic
1 lime, preferably organic
1 orange, preferably organic
1 quart red wine, such as Zinfandel,
    Rioja, Cabernet, or Merlot

1. Place the sugar and cinnamon stick in a small saucepan, add ½ cup water, and bring to a boil over medium-high heat. Boil for 5 minutes. Then remove the pan from the heat and let the syrup cool. Remove the cinnamon stick.

2. Using a very sharp knife, peel the lemon, starting at one end and making one long continuous spiral. Do the same with the lime and orange. Cut the lemon, lime, and orange into thick rounds. Place the rounds and the zests in a bowl, and pour the cooled syrup over them. Chill in the refrigerator for several hours.

3. Place six glasses in the freezer to chill.

4. Fill a glass pitcher less than halfway with ice cubes, and add the sliced fruit, half of the cinnamon syrup (see Note), and the wine. Stir the mixture thoroughly, mashing the fruit slightly.

5. Serve the Sangria in the chilled glasses, garnishing each glass with some of the sliced fruit.

Note: The remaining syrup can be either used to make a second batch or mixed with more fruit and served later. The syrup will keep in the refrigerator, covered, for at least 1 month.

Variation: Blond Sangria

Substitute California chablis or white Spanish Rioja for the red wine. Blond sangria often includes summer fruits, such as peaches and raspberries, along with the citrus.

Wine Coolers

Makes 1 drink

Wine coolers are a wonderful accompaniment to chili—they're the perfect drink when you're eating a fiery brew and want something crisp and refreshing but not overly alcoholic. You can make them out of any favorite wine, and even wines of moderate quality work just fine. They're also a great way to use leftover wine. The flavorings and garnishes can depend on your mood, the type of chili you are serving, and what's available in your kitchen. For example, with a traditional red chili, serve a robust red wine cooler like a Zinfandel with a garnish of red berries, such as strawberries. With a lighter chili, such as ones with a green chile base, serve the wine cooler described here.

4 to 6 ice cubes
2 ounces white wine,
    such as Sauvignon Blanc

3 thin slices lemon, preferably organic
3 thin slices lime, preferably organic
2 ounces club soda or seltzer
1 medium-size sprig fresh mint

1. Place the ice cubes in a tall, slender glass, pour in the wine, and then muddle 2 lemon slices and 2 lime slices in the glass, pressing them with the back of a spoon.

2. Add the club soda. Then cut the remaining lemon and lime slices almost in half through the center, just to the inside of the peel on the opposite side. Place the lemon and lime slices over the rim of the glass, add the sprig of mint, and serve.

Choosing Chili-Friendly Wine

While my personal feeling is that any wine that you like with any particular food is just fine, here are some tried-and-true pairing suggestions.

For traditional red chile–based chilies, try uncorking a good Zinfandel, which has enough spiciness and fruitiness to make it a really great complement for the deep flavors of the bowl of red. Also a great counterpoint: the deep berry notes of a good Shiraz or Shiraz blend, a Malbec, or any wine made with Sangiovese grapes (including Chiantis and other Tuscan blends). These are excellent accompaniments to just about any full-flavored red chile

chili, whether meat- or vegetable-based.

For a green-chile dish, try sipping a Sauvignon Blanc, a dry Riesling, a rich Viognier, or another white possessing some spiciness and a hint of fruitiness. I love how the sweet notes in a fruity white wine help bring out the natural flavors of green chiles.

With chili of virtually any variety, you can't go wrong with Champagne— its bubbly texture and celebratory mood take chili into another dimension.

Experiment with pairing different wines with your favorite chilies until you find a combination you enjoy. Have fun with it!

Zingy Tea

Makes 4 drinks

Teas made with hibiscus buds or calyxes, such as Celestial Seasonings' Red Zinger, are quite refreshing—and healthy, too: the hibiscus buds contain a generous amount of vitamin C. In Mexico the tea is known as jamaica (pronounced *ha*-my-*ka*); it is popular as a refreshing drink when there is too much heat—either from the weather or from chiles. Here is my version. It is delicious either hot or cold.

¼ cup dried hibiscus buds (see Note)
1 quart boiling water (see Note)
1 orange, thinly sliced
2 tablespoons honey

1. Place the hibiscus buds in a tea ball and place it in a large teapot or heat-resistant pitcher. Add the boiling water and allow to steep for about 15 minutes.

2. Remove the tea ball, and add the orange slices and honey. Stir to blend. Serve hot, in mugs, or chill and serve over ice cubes in tall glasses.

Notes: Dried hibiscus buds are available in Mexican groceries and in health food stores. If you'd like to make sun tea instead of boiled tea, place the hibiscus-filled tea ball in a quart of water in a clear glass jar or pitcher, and let it sit in a sunny place for several hours, until the water is infused with the tea. Remove the tea ball before adding the orange slices and honey.

Sources

Ingredients

A great bowl of brew—and the dishes that accompany it—requires the best ingredients. You'll find sources for spices, herbs, seasoning mixes, chiles, and more directly below, and after that, a list of individual ingredients and where to procure them.

For blue corn flour, chipotle powder, a wide variety of dried chiles, frozen green chiles, Southwestern and Mexican herbs and spices, masa, seasoning rubs, and more:
Pecos Valley Spice Co.
2655 Pan American NE, Suite F
Albuquerque, NM 87107
(800) 473-8226
www.pecosvalley.com
info@pecosvalley.com

For a variety of spices, seasoning mixes, and herbs:
Penzeys Spices
12001 W. Capitol Drive
Wauwatosa, WI 53222
(800) 741-7787
www.penzeys.com
answers@penzeys.com

For frozen chiles, dried chile powders, salsas, chile sauces, and tortillas:
Bueno Foods
P. O. Box 293
Albuquerque, NM 87103
(800) 952-4453
www.buenofoods.com
mailorder@buenofoods.com

For organic cornmeal, flours, and other products made from grains, nuts, and seeds:
Arrowhead Mills
The Hain Celestial Group
4600 Sleepytime Drive
Boulder, CO 80301
(800) 434-4246
www.arrowheadmills.com

Blue corn flour:
Available at Pecos Valley Spice Co.

Blue cornmeal (and other organic cornmeals and flours):
Available at Arrowhead Mills

Coonridge goat cheese:
Go to www.coonridge.com/catalog

Dried chiles:
Available at Pecos Valley Spice Co.

Dried chile powders:
Available at Pecos Valley Spice Co. and Bueno Foods

Frozen green chiles:
Available at Pecos Valley Spice Co. and Bueno Foods

Fruit-Fresh:
Available at most supermarkets; for more information, visit www.fruit-fresh.com

Masa:
Available at Pecos Valley Spice Co. and Arrowhead Mills

Posole:
Available at Pecos Valley Spice Co.

Maytag Blue cheese:
For a catalog or to order, visit www.maytagdairyfarms.com or call (800) 247-2458 (toll free) or (641) 792-1133 (direct)

Nopalitos:
Fresh nopalitos are available at many Latin specialty stores. If you can't find them fresh, you can use jarred nopalitos instead.
They are available at LatinMerchant .com: visit www.latinmerchant.com or call (206) 223-9374

Traditional chipotles:
These are sold whole, in bulk, at The Spice House: visit www.thespicehouse.com or call (847) 328-3711

Chili Societies

The following societies list local and regional cookoffs and provide participation guidelines:

Chili Appreciation Society International, Inc. (CASI)
112 Leaning Oak Circle
Johnson City, TX 78636
(512) 567-2835
www.chili.org

International Chili Society (ICS)
32244 Paseo Adelanto, Suite D3
San Juan Capistrano, CA 92675
(877) 777-4427
www.chilicookoff.com
ics@chilicookoff.com

Chili and Chile Publications

Goat Gap Gazette:
"The clarion of the chili and BBQ world."
Goat Gap Gazette
P. O. Box "J"
Waxahachie, TX 75168-0356
(972) 351-0022
www.goatgap.com
goatgapgazette@sbcglobal.net

Chile Pepper Magazine:
"The hottest magazine around for those who love bold, flavorful food."
Chile Pepper Magazine
250 W. 57th Sreet, Suite 728
New York, NY 10107
(212) 262-2247
www.chilepepper.com

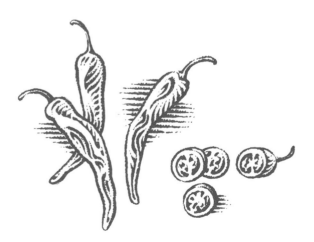

Educational Information

Research-based information on chile growing, processing, and more, provided by New Mexico State University's College of Agriculture and Home Economics:

The Chile Pepper Institute
P. O. Box 30003 MSC 3Q
Las Cruces, NM 88003-8003
(575) 646-3028
www.chilepepperinstitute.org
hotchile@nmsu.edu

Jane Butel's Online Chile Education Course, "All About Chiles":
Offered through the Learning Center, University of British Columbia. To register, go to www.janebutel.com
For questions, e-mail info@janebutel.com

Growing chiles and additional chile information:
www.gardenweb.com or
www.chilepepperinstitute.org
(click on CPI Shop)

Chile heat and technical facts:
www.ushotstuff.com

General information about chiles and related topics, Fiery Foods & BBQ *magazine subscriptions, and the* National Fiery Foods & Barbecue Show:
www.fiery-foods.com

Conversion Tables

Tablespoons and Ounces to Grams

U.S. Customary System	Metric System
1 pinch = less than ⅛ teaspoon (dry)	0.50 grams
1 dash = 3 drops to ¼ teaspoon (liquid)	1.25 grams
1 teaspoon (liquid)	5.00 grams
3 teaspoons = 1 tablespoon = ½ ounce	14.30 grams
2 tablespoons = 1 ounce	28.35 grams
4 tablespoons = 2 ounces = ¼ cup	56.70 grams
8 tablespoons = 4 ounces = ¼ cup (1 stick of butter)	113.40 grams
8 tablespoons (flour) = about 2 ounces	72.00 grams
16 tablespoons = 8 ounces = 1 cup = ½ pound	226.80 grams
32 tablespoons = 16 ounces = 2 cups = 1 pound	453.60 grams or 0.4536 kilogram
64 tablespoons = 32 ounces = 1 quart = 2 pounds	907.00 grams or 0.9070 kilogram
1 quart = (roughly 1 liter)	

Temperatures: °Fahrenheit (F) to °Celsius (C)

-10°F = -23.3°C (freezer storage)
0°F = -17.7°C
32°F = 0°C (water freezes)
50°F = 10°C
68°F = 20°C (room temperature)
100°F = 37.7°C
150°F = 65.5°C
205°F = 96.1°C (water simmers)
212°F = 100°C (water boils)
300°F = 148.8°C
325°F = 162.8°C
350°F = 177°C (baking)
375°F = 190.5°C
400°F = 204.4°C (hot oven)
425°F = 218.3°C
450°F = 232°C (very hot oven)
475°F = 246.1°C
500°F = 260°C (broiling)

Conversion Factors

ounces to grams: multiply ounce figure by 28.3 to get number of grams
grams to ounces: multiply gram figure by 0.0353 to get number of ounces
pounds to grams: multiply pound figure by 453.59 to get number of grams
pounds to kilograms: multiply pound figure by 0.45 to get number of kilograms
ounces to milliliters: multiply ounce figure by 30 to get number of milliliters
cups to liters: multiply cup figure by 0.24 to get number of liters
Fahrenheit to Celsius: subtract 32 from the Fahrenheit figure, multiply by 5, then divide by 9 to get Celsius figure
Celsius to Fahrenheit: multiply Celsius figure by 9, divide by 5, then add 32 to get Fahrenheit figure
inches to centimeters: multiply inch figure by 2.54 to get number of centimeters
centimeters to inches: multiply centimeter figure by 0.39 to get number of inches

Acknowledgments

I wish to thank my current staff — Farrah Yazzie, Peggy McCormick, and Frances Harsany—who assisted me with the research, cooking, testing, and finally the word processing to get this book off to my editor, Kylie Foxx McDonald.

Also, I would be remiss in not thanking my former staff—Gwynne MacManus, Lark Wittens, Ann Weninger, and Vivian Batts—as well as my daughter, Amy, and my mother. All were always enthusiastic and ready to assist with the tasting and development of the recipes in the original edition of the book.

My heartfelt thanks are extended to Kylie Foxx McDonald for the perfect and patient review she gave to all my words and thoughts, to Francesca Messina for her beautiful and thoughtful design, and to Helen Rosner for her diligence and attention to detail. Finally, to Suzanne Rafer, Executive Editor/Director of Cookbook Publishing at Workman, who was the spirit behind this expanded edition, as well as the originator of the idea for the first book back in 1979.

Photo Credits

Index